COMPARATIVE TH

KEITH WARD

COMPARATIVE THEOLOGY

Essays for Keith Ward

Edited by

T. W. BARTEL

First published in Great Britain in 2003 by
Society for Promoting Christian Knowledge
Holy Trinity Church
Marylebone Road
London NW1 4DU

British Library Cataloguing-in-Publication Data
A catalogue record for this book is available from the British Library

ISBN 0-281-05474-6

1 3 5 7 9 10 8 6 4 2

Typeset by Kenneth Burnley, Wirral, Cheshire
Printed in Great Britain by MPG Books, Bodmin, Cornwall

Contents

Contributors

WILLIAM J. ABRAHAM works as a philosophical and systematic theologian at Perkins School of Theology, Southern Methodist University, Dallas, where he holds the Albert Cook Outler Chair of Wesley Studies. His publications include *The Divine Inspiration of Holy Scripture* (Oxford University Press, 1981), *Divine Revelation and the Limits of Historical Criticism* (Oxford University Press, 1982), *An Introduction to the Philosophy of Religion* (Prentice–Hall, 1985), *The Logic of Evangelism* (Eerdmans, 1989), *Waking from Doctrinal Amnesia* (Abingdon Press, 1995) and *Canon and Criterion in Christian Theology* (Oxford University Press, 1998).

PAUL AVIS is General Secretary of the Church of England's Council for Christian Unity and Sub-Dean of Exeter Cathedral. He is also a Fellow of the University of Exeter in the Department of Theology and Director of the Centre for the Study of the Christian Church. His recent publications include *God and the Creative Imagination* (Routledge, 1999), *The Anglican Understanding of the Church: An Introduction* (SPCK, 2000), *Church, State and Establishment* (SPCK, 2001), *Anglicanism and the Christian Church: Theological Resources in Historical Perspective* (T&T Clark, 2nd edn 2002) and *The Christian Church: An Introduction to the Major Traditions* (editor; SPCK, 2002). He is an editor of the *International Journal for the Study of the Christian Church*.

T[IMOTHY] W. BARTEL was a Lecturer in the Philosophy of Religion at King's College London, where he was a colleague of Keith Ward. He has published an extensive range of articles on the philosophical problems of the doctrines of the Trinity and the Incarnation. His piece for this volume is a foretaste of his current main research project, a book on divine providence, human freedom and the problem of evil. He lives in Oxford.

DAVID BROWN is Van Mildert Professor of Divinity in the University of Durham, and a Residentiary Canon of the city's cathedral. He has written seven books and edited a further four (mostly jointly). His most recent work is two related volumes: *Tradition and Imagination: Revelation and Change* (Oxford University Press, 1999) and *Discipleship and Imagination: Christian Tradition and Truth* (Oxford University Press, 2000). His current major project is on sacramentality and culture. He was elected a Fellow of the British Academy in 2002.

VINCENT BRÜMMER is Emeritus Professor in the Philosophy of Religion at Utrecht University and former Director of the Dutch National School of Advanced Studies in Theology and Religion (NOSTER). He is also a former President of the British Society for the Study of Theology and of the European Society for Philosophy of Religion. His writings include: *Theology and Philosophical Enquiry* (Macmillan, 1981), *What Are We Doing When We Pray?* (SCM Press, 1984), *Speaking of a Personal God* (Cambridge University Press, 1992) and *The Model of Love* (Cambridge University Press, 1993).

PETER BYRNE is Professor of Ethics and the Philosophy of Religion at King's College London and editor of *Religious Studies*. His most recent books are: *The Moral Interpretation of Religion* (Edinburgh University Press, 1998), *The Philosophical and Theological Foundations of Ethics* (Macmillan, 2nd edn 1999) and *Philosophical and Ethical Problems in Mental Handicap* (Macmillan, 2000).

GAVIN D'COSTA is an Indian Roman Catholic and Reader in Christian Theology at the University of Bristol. He has authored four books: *Theology and Religious Pluralism* (Blackwell, 1986), *John Hick's Theology of Religions* (University Press of America, 1987), *The Meeting of Religions and the Trinity* (T&T Clark, 2000) and *Sexing the Trinity* (SCM Press, 2000). He has also edited *Christian Uniqueness Reconsidered* (Orbis Books, 1990) and *Resurrection Reconsidered* (Oneworld Publications, 1996). He is a consultant to the Vatican, the Roman Catholic Bishops in England and Wales, and the Church of England Board of Mission on matters related to other religions.

RICHARD HARRIES has been Bishop of Oxford since 1987. Before that he was Dean of King's College London. He has been Chairman of the Church of England's Board for Social Responsibility and also chaired the House of Lords Select Committee on Stem Cell Research. He is the author of more than twenty books, including *Christianity and War in a Nuclear Age* (Mowbray, 1986), *Art and the Beauty of God* (Mowbray, 2nd edn 2000), *God Outside the Box: Why Spiritual People Object to Christianity* (SPCK, 2002) and *After the Evil: Theological Reflections on Christianity and Judaism in the Light of the Holocaust* (Oxford University Press, 2003). He was elected a Fellow of the Royal Society of Literature in 1996. He is currently a member of the Nuffield Council on Bioethics.

PAUL HELM was Professor of the History and Philosophy of Religion at King's College London (1993–2000). Prior to that he was Reader in Philosophy at the University of Liverpool. Among his books are *Eternal God* (Clarendon Press, 1988), *The Providence of God* (Inter-Varsity Press, 1993), *Faith and Understanding* (Edinburgh University Press, 1997) and *Faith With Reason* (Oxford University Press, 2000). He currently holds the J. I. Packer Chair of Philosophical Theology at Regent College, Vancouver, and is finishing a book on *John Calvin's Ideas* (forthcoming from Oxford University Press).

JOHN HICK has taught the philosophy of religion in both the USA and the UK and is the author of a number of books, including *Death and Eternal Life* and *Evil and the God of Love* (both Macmillan, 2nd edns 1985). His Gifford lectures, *An Interpretation of Religion* (Macmillan, 1989), was awarded the Grawemeyer Prize for significant new thinking in religion. He is currently a Fellow of the Institute for Advanced Research in Arts and Social Sciences at the University of Birmingham.

URSULA KING is Professor Emerita and Senior Research Fellow at the University of Bristol, where she held the Chair in Theology and Religious Studies from 1989 to 2001, after teaching for many years at the University of Leeds, in London and in India. She has also been Visiting Professor in Feminist Theology at the University of Oslo (1998–2001) and held the Charles Brueggeman Chair in Ecumenical Theology and Interreligious Dialogue at Xavier University, Cincinnati (autumn 1999). She has published numerous books and articles and contributed to many broadcasts and TV programmes. Among her recent publications are *Spirit of Fire: The Life and Vision of Teilhard de Chardin* (Orbis Books, 1996), the 1996 Bampton Lectures, *Christ in All Things: Exploring Spirituality with Teilhard de Chardin* (SCM Press and Orbis Books, 1997), *Faith and Praxis in a Postmodern Age* (editor; Cassell, 1998), *Christian Mystics* (Paulist Press, 2001) and *Spirituality and Society in the New Millennium* (editor; Sussex Academic Press, 2001). Her current research is concerned with aspects of contemporary spirituality, and with comparative gender perspectives in different world religions.

ROBERT CUMMINGS NEVILLE is Professor of Philosophy, Religion and Theology at Boston University, where he is also Dean of the School of Theology. He is a past president of the American Academy of Religion, the Metaphysical Society of America and the International Society for Chinese Philosophy. He is the author of a trilogy called 'Axiology of Thinking' (SUNY Press), which consists of *Reconstruction of Thinking* (1981), *Recovery of the Measure* (1989) and *Normative Cultures* (1995). Recently he has published *The Truth of Broken Symbols* (SUNY Press, 1996), *Boston Confucianism* (SUNY Press, 2000), *Symbols of Jesus* (Cambridge University Press, 2001) and *Religion in Late Modernity* (SUNY Press, 2002). He also directed the Comparative Religious Ideas Project at Boston University, and edited the resulting three volumes: *The Human Condition*, *Ultimate Realities* and *Religious Truth* (all SUNY Press, 2001).

JOHN POLKINGHORNE was Professor of Mathematical Physics (1968–79) and President of Queens' College at the University of Cambridge (1989–96). He is an Anglican priest and a Fellow of the Royal Society, and was knighted in 1977. The author of many books on science and religion, including *Science and Christian Belief* (SPCK, 1994), *Belief in God in an Age of Science* (Yale University Press, 1998) and *The God of Hope and the End of the World* (SPCK, 2002), he was awarded the Templeton Prize in 2002.

RICHARD SWINBURNE was Nolloth Professor of the Philosophy of the Christian Religion at the University of Oxford (1985–2002). Previously he was Professor of Philosophy at the University of Keele (1972–84). He has written many books on the philosophy of religion and other philosophical topics. He is the author of a trilogy on the philosophy of theism (Clarendon Press): *The Coherence of Theism* (rev. edn 1993), *The Existence of God* (rev. edn 1991) and *Faith and Reason* (1981). He has also written a tetralogy on the philosophical issues involved in Christian doctrine (Clarendon Press): *Responsibility and Atonement* (1989), *Revelation* (1992), *The Christian God* (1994) and *Providence and the Problem of Evil* (1998). His most recent book, *The Resurrection of God Incarnate* (Oxford University Press, 2003), is about the historical evidence for the resurrection of Jesus.

HENK VROOM is Professor of the Philosophy of Religion at the Vrije Universiteit in Amsterdam and President of the European Society of Religion. He has published widely on hermeneutics, interfaith relations, cultural pluralism and comparative theology, including *Religions and the Truth* (Eerdmans, 1989) and *No Other Gods* (Eerdmans, 1996). He is co-editor of *Studies in Interreligious Dialogue* and of the series 'Religieus Pluralisme en Multiculturaliteit', and has also co-edited a dozen books, most recently *Religion, Conflict, and Reconciliation* (Rodopi, 2002) and *Theology between Church, University, and Society* (Van Gorcum, 2003).

VERNON WHITE is currently Director of the Southern Theological Education and Training Scheme in Salisbury. He was previously Canon Chancellor of Lincoln Cathedral and Special Lecturer in Theology in the University of Nottingham. His publications include: *The Fall of a Sparrow: A Concept of Special Divine Action* (Paternoster, 1985), *Atonement and Incarnation* (Cambridge University Press, 1991), *Paying Attention to People: An Essay on Individualism and Christian Belief* (SPCK, 1996) and *Identity* (SCM Press, 2002).

MARK WYNN has held teaching appointments at King's College London and the Australian Catholic University, and in 1997 was the Gifford Research Fellow at the University of Glasgow. He is currently a Lecturer in Philosophy of Religion and Christian Ethics at the University of Exeter. His publications include *God and Goodness: A Natural Theological Perspective* (Routledge, 1999). His contribution to this volume forms part of a larger research project concerned with the importance of the emotions for religious understanding and practice.

Preface

Nearly a decade ago, Keith Ward published a book titled *Religion and Revelation*, which he introduced to his readers as 'an essay in comparative theology'.[1] At many points in the book, when explaining what he means by 'comparative theology', Ward emphasises one highly significant respect in which it marks a radical departure from systematic Christian theology as traditionally pursued: it pays exceedingly close attention to the beliefs and practices of a broad variety of religions other than one's own. To be sure, Ward does not believe that comparative theology can be conducted from an Archimedean standpoint – while the comparative theologian need not participate in a religious community, no one can honestly claim to float free of all prejudices. And he makes it clear at the beginning of *Religion and Revelation* that he intends his own explorations in comparative theology to remain within the purview of orthodox Christianity. But he also insists that careful, sympathetic comparison of one's own views with those of other religions is a necessary corrective to theological myopia, whatever one's views may be.

At a more general level, however, Ward's notion of comparative theology proves to be thoroughly traditional. In *Religion and Revelation* the very first theologian Ward chooses as a foil for his own opinions on the nature of theology is Thomas Aquinas. I think this a most felicitous choice – but not, for the most part, because Aquinas serves as a foil. He certainly does, on a good many fundamental matters of theological methodology: for example, Ward denies that the canonical Christian scriptures are inerrant; and, though he argues that mainstream Christian orthodoxy is rationally defensible, he denies that any of the articles of the Christian faith can be established beyond reasonable doubt. But Ward also frequently acknowledges, in passages such as the following, that from a broader perspective the method of comparative theology is precisely the same as Aquinas's:

> [In theological thinking] there is an essential element of contextualization, as new knowledge from other areas – in the sciences, in philosophy, or in social and political relationships – changes the relationship of religion to those areas. (34)[2]

That is, comparative theology pays heed, not just to the full range of religious phenomena, but to the full range of human knowledge – indeed, as Ward notes elsewhere, to the full range of human experience. How could it be otherwise, since, as he observes, theology is not only an objective discipline, but a perfectly global one: it aims at understanding the truth as a whole (31).

This is an observation of the greatest importance – but of course it is nothing more than the prolegomenon to comparative theology. All the hard work remains to be done, and Ward's beautifully lucid exposition of the nature of comparative theology in part I of *Religion and Revelation* simply makes it all too obvious how much hard work there is to do. Fortunately, Ward was not intimidated. In the rest of the book he provided a magisterial lesson in comparative theology, unfolding a rich, subtle, comprehensive and distinctively Christian conception of divine revelation that takes with the utmost seriousness the problems posed for Christian claims to revealed knowledge by the wealth of conflicting claims to religious revelation, the development of historical criticism, the Enlightenment attack on religious authority in the name of individual autonomy, and the root-and-branch revision of traditional conceptions of the physical cosmos which the modern natural sciences have forced upon us. And that, combined with his twenty years of extremely productive reflections in comparative theology prior to *Religion and Revelation*, already entitled him to a place among the most eminent theologians of this generation. (One may gain a fair idea from the present volume of the esteem in which *Religion and Revelation* is held – the first four chapters amount to a lengthy symposium on the book by leading thinkers on the topic of divine revelation.) Ward could thus have been excused for spending the rest of his academic career merely in elaborating, or for that matter merely in refining, the theory of revelation presented in that book. Instead, over the next six years he wrote three further volumes which applied the methods and tools of comparative theology, on an equally ambitious scale, to three further vast and highly controversial theological themes, and with equal success: *Religion and Creation*, *Religion and Human Nature* and *Religion and Community*.[3] When the final volume was published, crowning thirty years of outstanding contributions to comparative theology, it was evident that Keith Ward has demonstrated, more clearly and in greater depth than anyone else, how systematic theology ought to be done at the beginning of the twenty-first century. On the occasion of his retirement this year from the Regius Professorship of Divinity at Oxford University and its associated canonry of Christ Church cathedral, this collection of essays is an expression of the admiration and gratitude of all concerned for that magnificent achievement.

I should like to express a small measure of my own admiration and gratitude here by drawing attention to one important part of Ward's magisterial lesson in systematic theology that is not, I think, usually given the prominence it deserves. In the passage from *Religion and Revelation* quoted above, Ward points out, in effect, that the systematic theologian has a duty to reinterpret religious belief in the light of new developments in philosophy. For philosophical commitments are part and parcel of all religions having any theology worthy of the name – and, although the central philosophical concepts, categories, positions and arguments embodied in earlier forms of a religion can prove remarkably durable, not all can reasonably be expected to survive centuries of philosophical advances. So the continuing plausibility and intellectual vitality of a religious form of life depends upon its ability to come to terms with progress in philosophy. Or, to put it more succinctly, philosophical reconstruction of doctrine lies at the very heart of systematic theology.

And one crucial fact can be manifest even to one who knows nothing more about Ward's tetralogy than the main themes of each of its volumes: he has embarked on a task that one cannot possibly hope to accomplish without being thoroughly conversant with just about every main subject area of philosophy. As my rather potted summary of *Religion and Revelation* suggests, one had better be conversant, for a start, with epistemology and the philosophy of science. In *Religion and Creation*, not only does Ward consider the nature of God and of divine creation, which plunges one instantly into the thickets of metaphysics; he also confronts the logically prior matter of whether it is even possible to speak of God as an objective reality, and if so, whether it is possible to speak of God non-metaphorically – which demands a firm grasp of the philosophy of language. *Religion and Human Nature* concentrates on issues of human nature and destiny – how human selves are related to the material world, and what will ultimately become of them – so we must add philosophy of mind and moral philosophy to the list. And *Religion and Community* considers the notion of a religious community – in particular, what the ideal religious community consists in, and how a religious community should be related to the wider cultures in which it is embedded – topics obviously also within the ambit of moral philosophy, but just as obviously within the ambit of social and political philosophy. Not to mention that, as Ward repeatedly reminds us, comparative theology aims to study religions in their widest possible historical context – for which a thorough grounding in the history of philosophy is essential, including the history of eastern philosophy. Nor, of course, may we forget the philosophy of religion. Nor may we forget that philosophy is a rapidly changing discipline: anyone, for instance, who had a sound knowledge of philosophy of religion thirty years ago, but who has been out of touch with the subject since then, would have to start again practically from scratch in order to regain contact – just like anyone who has been out of touch with particle physics for the past thirty years. Again, since systematic theology ought to be systematic, Ward's project requires, not only an encyclopaedic knowledge of philosophical detail, but an intimate knowledge of the extensive network of connections between those details – and, last but not least, it requires a prodigious amount of philosophical creativity.

It is therefore high praise indeed to affirm that, throughout virtually the whole tetralogy, Keith Ward's philosophical expertise is equal to the task. And it is somewhat invidious to single out just a handful of places where that expertise yields especially rewarding results for theology. If we bear that in mind, however, it is worth mentioning, as a small sample, his meticulous defence in *Religion and Revelation* of the reasonableness of grounding revealed faith in historical claims (232–58); in *Religion and Creation*, the finely nuanced account of metaphor and analogy in religious language (ch. 6) and his articulation of the doctrine of the Trinity in the final chapter, which is expertly woven from a great many strands of argument developed earlier in the book; in *Religion and Human Nature*, the learned and thoughtful, but remarkably accessible, examination of the intricate Buddhist doctrine of the self (ch. 5) and his sophisticated treatment of the philosophical problems of the doctrine of the bodily resurrection (300–7); and, in *Religion and Community*, the critical but sensitive consideration of the paramount Muslim social ideal, the universal *umma*, and of how the historical reality of Islam measures up to that ideal (ch. 2) – a model for anyone who wishes to comment on present relations between Islam and the West – and the wide-ranging but tightly knit discussion of Christian morality (ch. 9).[4]

The overall plan of the first four parts of this collection mirrors the overall plan of the tetralogy: each of these parts is devoted to the main theme of a volume of the tetralogy, the order of the themes in the collection following their order in the tetralogy. Part V is an essay by Keith Ward looking back on the twists and turns of his theological pilgrimage; and the book concludes with a comprehensive bibliography of his publications. Given the enormous scope of his own contribution to the project of comparative theology, it is inevitable that some of his major accomplishments are not fully reflected in this volume. In particular, given the splendid example that Ward has set for us in theological ecumenism, it would have been especially satisfying to have had at least one essay from a representative of a non-Christian religion, or at least more discussion of living non-Christian religions. On the other hand, the greater part of Ward's tetralogy, and of the rest of his published work, consists of conversation with the two traditions which are represented here – fellow-Christians and those of no religious faith – and the reader will find in these pages an impressive diversity of theological viewpoints. Furthermore, though not all of the essays directly discuss Ward's own work, they do all consider central theological topics to which he has made indispensable contributions. And essays in one part of the festschrift often take up the main theme of at least one other part, shedding fresh light on the latter – as befits a volume in honour of a theologian who notes, in the first sentence of his master work, that 'There is no one proper starting-point in theology, since every question leads on to every other.'[5]

Since Keith has shown himself so skilful at setting theology in a global context, I feel I ought to conclude by trying to do the same for all the tributes in this volume. Keith is justly admired for his delightfully mercurial sense of humour – who else could have written, in the midst of a serious discussion of free will and determinism, 'The opposite of compatibilism is libertarianism. This is not, as some of my American colleagues think, the right to own a sub-machine gun or to live on Venice Beach with a preferred other of your choice'?[6] But on many occasions he displays an uncompromising sense of the depths to which those who supposedly bear the *imago Dei* have fallen – as in this portrait of original sin:

> Deprived of empowering relationship with God, the natural drive to sexuality, freed from the restraints of instinct, will devalue personality by regarding others as means to pleasure, and so lead to a lack of respect for personhood. The drive to territorial possession, freed from the limits of tribal life, will lead to unlimited acquisitiveness. The drive to aggression, extended by the invention of weapons, will lead to the subjugation of possible competitors. Falling from unity with the love, wisdom, and

creativity of God, humans come to exhibit a grossly distorted perception and vitriolic hatred of others, together with a seemingly boundless personal greed. Greed, hatred, and delusion become the passions which control the lives of human beings, driving them to cause pain and suffering to countless sentient creatures, and to destroy their own environment and ultimately themselves.[7]

Here, in unadorned modern diction, is a vision of human nature as dark as any to be found in Pascal.

As that vision can scarcely be said to exaggerate the state of our world at the beginning of the third Christian millennium, the one tribute above all others that we owe to Keith Ward is to strive with all our heart – and all our mind – to find 'ways in which [we] can be positive and constructive forces in the contemporary project of constructing a consciously global society whose members can live in mutual understanding and co-operative action'.[8]

Further thanks are due to all the contributors, for graciously meeting every deadline; to John Polkinghorne, for especially timely assistance; to Alison Barr, the commissioning editor, for her unfailing enthusiasm and level-headedness; to Kathryn Wolfendale, the project editor, not least for patiently unscrambling my e-mailed version of the text; to Richard Jeffery, the copy-editor, for reading the manuscript with such an assiduous, expert eye; and particularly to Mark Wynn, for indispensable advice and encouragement at every stage of the project.

T. W. B.

NOTES

1   Keith Ward, *Religion and Revelation* (Oxford: Clarendon Press, 1994), 2.
2   In fact, Ward mentions that Aquinas himself rethought Christian doctrine by drawing on new knowledge in other areas, especially Aristotelian philosophy (37).
3   Keith Ward, *Religion and Creation* (Oxford: Clarendon Press, 1996), *Religion and Human Nature* (Oxford: Clarendon Press, 1998) and *Religion and Community* (Oxford: Clarendon Press, 2000).
4   There are occasional lapses. For instance, although the Molinist theory of divine providence is a reputable alternative to his own view, it goes entirely unmentioned, not only in the tetralogy but also in the rest of his work. But even taken collectively, these lapses do not cast much of a shadow over the brilliance of his achievement.
     Ward, incidentally, provides an excellent summary of the whole of his tetralogy in the final chapter of its final volume: *Religion and Community*, 338–61. Also well worth consulting is a substantial review article on the first three volumes of the tetralogy by Paul Avis, 'An Anglican *Magnum Opus*: The Comparative Theology of Keith Ward', *Anglican Theological Review*, 82 (2000), 181–9.
5   Ward, *Religion and Revelation*, 1.
6   Keith Ward, *God: A Guide for the Perplexed* (Oxford: Oneworld Publications, 2002), 132.
7   Ward, *Religion and Human Nature*, 168; this portrait continues, its bleakness unabated, for five more paragraphs.
8   Ward, *Religion and Community*, 6.

For Jennifer

What are heavy? sea-sand and sorrow:
What are brief? to-day and to-morrow:
What are frail? Spring blossoms and youth:
What are deep? the ocean and truth.

Christina Rossetti,
Sing-Song: A Nursery Rhyme Book

Part I

REVELATION

1

Keith Ward on
Religion and Revelation

WILLIAM J. ABRAHAM

As Matthew Arnold noted many years ago, Oxford is the home of lost causes. The most recent lost cause to be retrieved and pursued is the articulation and defence of a substantial vision of divine revelation as essential to the intellectual health of the Christian tradition. Within the space of two years two splendidly argued proposals emanated from the Oxford faculty of theology. In 1992, Richard Swinburne's *Revelation: From Metaphor to Analogy*[1] appeared; in 1994 Keith Ward's *Religion and Revelation: A Theology of Revelation in the World's Religions*.[2] Alongside George Mavrodes' neglected but fascinating treatment of revelation in his *Revelation in Religious Belief*,[3] these two texts represent a major revisiting of a topic long ignored in theological and philosophical circles.

Both texts are part of much longer projects in the understanding of the Christian faith. Both reflect prolonged earlier work in the analytical philosophy of religion. Moreover, both Swinburne and Ward in their own ways seek to make room for and rehabilitate a robustly orthodox vision of the Christian tradition. Both authors see significant analogies between religious and scientific forms of thinking. Both develop substantial accounts of Scripture as essential to a comprehensive vision of revelation. Both are entirely happy to articulate a vision of propositional revelation, a theme which has virtually gone off the radar screen of mainstream theology since the 1950s.

Yet it is hard to imagine two texts more different in their basic orientation. Where Swinburne can deal with revelation in non-Christian religions in the space of two pages,[4] Ward's whole project is driven by the desire to take into account the nature and content of revelation outside the Christian tradition. Where Swinburne comes across as hopelessly brief and even dismissive of other faiths,[5] Ward is determined to make encounter with other religions a central feature of a whole new vision of theology that he aptly names comparative theology.

Ward's project is ambitious to say the least. He offers in *Religion and Revelation* a prolegomenon to systematic theology, a conceptual analysis of 'religion' and 'revelation', a theory of 'primal religion', an explication of four major religious traditions, a material account of divine revelation in the Christian religion, and an analysis of the place of revelation and religion in a post-Enlightenment world. Even this list of items does not do justice to Ward, for his book is full of densely packed argument, comment and description, sometimes developed at breakneck speed. This is a volume to be pondered and mulled over at leisure. It is the product of a very versatile, nimble, learned and incisive mind. It is the work of a theologian who believes in truth as a description of objective reality, and who believes in getting at truth in the old-fashioned way, that is, by engaging with texts, developing appropriate conceptual tools, constructing arguments, marshalling evidence, and refuting objections.

In this chapter, I am particularly interested in examining Ward's claims about revelation, as this constitutes a crucial component of Ward's work as a whole. I shall explore some of its nooks and crannies for conceptual consistency and for explanatory adequacy. I shall argue overall that Ward, in trying to resolve a deep dilemma at the core of his project, exposes serious difficulties below the surface. I shall begin by noting why Ward thinks it essential to theology to explore the whole gamut of religion.

Central to Ward's work is the aim of doing justice to the history and content of religious traditions outside Christianity. For many this might be a burden; after all, coming to terms with the length and breadth of the great religious traditions of the world is a daunting task. For Ward it is a methodological necessity. For him Christian theology must now move beyond its own narrow confessional confines and take into account the whole religious history of humankind. It must shift from a narrowly confessional stance to a truly comparative stance.

In part this methodological shift is a hermeneutical necessity: to understand religious phenomena requires that we understand them in their widest possible religious context. In part it is derived from an epistemic claim: given the diversity of claims about revelation, it is not possible to claim with certainty that one's own scriptural tradition is the one and only revelation. Hence there is a duty to explore other claims to divine revelation. More importantly, it is derived from a basic theological conviction that can be expressed in at least two ways. First, given that God is good, God could not ignore millions of human beings and fail to reveal anything of the Divine to them.[6] This is either an a priori argument or an argument based on specifically Christian premises.[7] Second, theology is 'a body of disciplined reasoning about Divine things based on revealed truths' (6). Given that revelation is not confined to Christianity, theology must now attend to every significant manifestation of revelation. In short, attending to revelation in the world's religions is materially required by Ward's beliefs about the manifestation of the Divine and formally required by his conception of theology.

The immediate challenge facing Ward's thesis is this. Given that divine revelation is an epistemic concept, that is, that divine revelation constitutes knowledge, how can Ward maintain the following two propositions at once: first, theology is essentially disciplined reasoning based on revealed truths (a claim he derives from Aquinas), and second, there is radical diversity in, if not contradictions between, the revelatory claims of the great religious traditions of the world? On the surface the tensions between these two claims threaten to bring down Ward's whole project. Indeed to resolve the problems that lie below the surface, Ward has to commit himself to a series of highly disputable proposals.

The core of Ward's resolution of this dilemma takes us to the heart of both his conception and his vision of divine revelation. It involves an ambitious effort to hold together the following three theses.

First, God essentially guides or inspires human agents as they think about the Divine and related matters in their particular historical and religious context. Revelation is essentially a form of divine luring or guidance. The material content of that revelation, in its human embodiment, generally takes the form of varied canonical scriptures. It follows from this general thesis that there is some element of truth at the core of the great religious traditions of the world. Religions disclose a suprasensory reality of power and value that gives meaning and structure to human existence. Competing religious visions should be considered prima facie as complementary accounts of the one suprasensory reality. Quite different insights from other religious traditions can be incorporated into a wider or richer articulation of the theologian's original starting point without abandoning the insights already gained from one's own tradition.

Second, human agents in their fallibility and sin fail to grasp fully all that has been revealed to them. They mix the truth about ultimate reality with prejudice, bias, error, false turns, bad theorising and the like. Hence it is not surprising that radically different and even contradictory visions of ultimate reality emerge and develop. The comparative theologian is under an obligation to sift through all claims to divine revelation, holding on to those insights that are valid, and rejecting those that are false or inadequately conceptualised.

Third, exposure to and critical examination of other religious traditions leaves intact the fundamental theological proposals of the Christian tradition. Thus, while such exposure and examination may enrich the Christian tradition, it does not radically undercut the central theological claims of this tradition as found in the central intentions of Scripture and such grand doctrines as the Incarnation, the Trinity, the resurrection of Jesus and so on. In short, such exposure and examination calls not for the abandoning of orthodoxy but for the development of an open and generous orthodoxy.

It will be obvious at first glance that there will be no ready-made refutation of Ward's project. It is much too complex and subtle for this kind of treatment. Of course, virtually every move can be contested. Ward is fully aware of this and does all he can to make his case and to fend off objections. What he offers is the first instalment of a full-scale systematic theology. The great value of a work like this is precisely its soaring contours and its detailed architecture. To change metaphors, it is the first dish of a five- or six-course meal whose final assessment can only be completed after all the courses have been savoured and consumed. In the mean time there are plenty of preliminary questions to be raised.

First, it is worth asking this: what is the relation between revelation and reason? I detect an interesting ambivalence. On the one hand, Ward excoriates Barth and Brunner for failing to provide any reasons for holding that Scripture is a valid revelation. Barth and Brunner are essentially guilty of pride and self-interest. Over against this, says Ward, it is the task of the theologian to spell out the 'factors which make it reasonable to accept something as a revelation at all' (18). On the other hand, this evidentialist claim comes on the heels of a discussion of certainty where Ward commits himself to a broadly Wittgensteinian analysis of forms of life, conceptual schemes and framework beliefs. These phenomena are not amenable to evidence but provide the context within which evidence functions as evidence. Furthermore, 'Theology can be seen as the articulation of tacit framework beliefs. Since there are many justifiable religious forms of life, each will have an appropriate theology' (15). Presumably such theologies will have their own account of revelation. If then each theology has its own justifiable religious form of life, and if a form of life is constituted by its own conceptual scheme or its framework beliefs, it is hard to see how any reason could be given for these, in that reasons would function within these rather than providing some 'external' justification for them. How are these two components of Ward's programme to be reconciled? On the one hand he seems to say that the enterprise is such that reasons cannot be available, and on the other he insists in his criticisms of Barth that they are essential.

I am struck, moreover, by the brevity and vehemence of Ward's treatment of Barth. Barth is committed to a very complex and sophisticated form of particularism that is sufficiently rich to be developed in a variety of directions.[8] It is this epistemological particularism that undergirds his account of the relation between revelation and reason. Surely Barth's position cannot be disposed of so easily without looking deeply into the epistemology of his theology? Yet in fact Ward does not explore this epistemology in any detail.[9] Moreover, for Barth belief is a matter of grace; given this view it makes no sense within his Reformed account of faith to take any credit whatsoever for his Christian commitments. In so far as pride or self-interest is the root of belief then such belief cannot be a matter of grace. This is required by his doctrine of the Christian life. Is Ward's treatment of Barth an instance where an Anglican who is calling for a sensitive openness to other religions has failed to take the measure of his next-door neighbours in the Reformed tradition in Europe?[10]

While I am on this topic let me add that I am equally struck by the lack of attention given to modern Roman Catholic treatments of divine revelation that insist on a pivotal place for the bishop of Rome in arriving at the true content of divine revelation. Given Ward's initial interest in Aquinas, and given his suggestion that human agents clearly can misunderstand what God has sought to reveal, it is odd to see him ignore the careful way in which the Roman Catholic tradition has sought to argue the case that God, through the bishop of Rome, really has gotten through to the Church and hence to the world. Indeed the whole point of appealing to the bishop of Rome as an infallible epistemic mechanism is to resolve doubts and worries about the content of divine revelation, an issue of great importance to Ward. I do not myself hold to the Roman Catholic position, but I do not see how a contemporary analysis of divine revelation can ignore the relevance of the claim to papal infallibility.[11] I think that it is very easy to be distracted at this point by changing the subject to the topic of confessional theology, by hinting at the dangers of propaganda, and by dragging in worries about inerrancy and infallibility. Is this a case where Christian sensitivity to outsiders is correlated with Protestant insensitivity to Roman Catholicism?

Second, it is not clear to me that Ward has made the case for the existence of revelation in general or for the existence of the Christian revelation in particular. Ward
has certainly fended off a host of objections against the existence of divine revelation,
but it is not clear that from within his own perspective fending off objections will do
the job. Moreover, there are times when Ward provides various cumulative-case
arguments for this or that claim about divine speaking to the prophets or for the
presence of the divine life in Jesus. Yet the general drift of his programme is to
provide a phenomenological analysis of revelation across the great religious traditions of the world. When he does make the shift from the descriptive to the
normative we surely need a lot more by way of argument. Thus after his account of
the content of primal religions he makes this comment:

> From these examples, taken from a vast source of materials which are
> now available, one might draw some general conclusions. If one is not
> going to regard all these phenomena as based on illusion, it is possible to
> discern a certain structure which seems to be expressed in them. For
> primal religions, the world of sensory experience manifests a deeper
> reality of very varied character, which can be apprehended at a precon-
> ceptual level by minds which have been prepared for it. (68)

What Ward has in mind here is a form of 'perception' which helps to define what
is truly good. He continues:

> One might say, from the theologian's viewpoint, that whatever the
> ultimate reality is, if it reveals itself in primal religions it does so in a
> myriad names and forms which are accommodated to the histories,
> beliefs, environments, and practices of different tribal societies. Such
> societies are not bereft of access to the spiritual realm, and may even have
> much to teach more economically advanced societies about the interior
> character and value of natural powers. (69)

Surely this is a very weak case. Illusion is ruled out *ab initio*; it is simply asserted
rather than argued that we have here a case of perception; the theologian appears to be
given a free licence to operate with the theologian's viewpoint; and the hint seems to be
that somehow morally enriching beliefs are to be given a free ride from an epistemic
point of view.[12] Once we add the staggering Christian claim to incarnation then it is
imperative, given Ward's own strictures about reasons, to provide a really compelling
case for the existence of such revelation. There are times when Ward's exposition of the
Christian claim to revelation is exquisite in its subtlety, rhetorical skill and density (see
esp. 232). He is also exceptionally adept at providing rigorous and compelling rebuttals
to various objections to the Christian claim based, say, on the nature of historical criticism or on the requirements of freedom and autonomy. Yet it is far from clear how he
wants to develop a really compelling case for the actual existence of divine revelation, as
he understands it. Such a case is required by his own objections to Barth and Brunner.

Mention of Ward's understanding of revelation takes me to the third topic I want to explore. The question I want to pursue is this: does Ward provide us with a consistent conception of revelation that will stand up to scrutiny? More particularly, can we develop a conception of revelation that will fit the varied religious traditions of the world in the way envisaged by Ward? The dilemma that is worth pursuing at this point revolves around the way Ward shifts from revelation as communication to revelation as insight and to revelation as manifestation. These are dramatic shifts indeed, so much so that in the case of the shift to insight one wonders if the concept of revelation has not collapsed under pressure from below.

Ward begins in a bold manner by expounding Aquinas's vision of revelation. He begins, that is, with a broadly propositional conception of revelation. Almost immediately, however, he begins to whittle away the very idea of propositional revelation even in Aquinas himself. Drawing back from complete rejection of this idea he says that revelation 'can, however, still be usefully defined as a communication of knowledge by God or by a suprahuman spiritual source' (15). More precisely, 'revelation in the full theistic sense occurs when God directly intends someone to know something beyond normal human cognitive capacity, and brings it about that they do know it, and they know that God has so intentionally caused it' (16). The knowledge granted by God in the case of revelation is salvific in content.

This is relatively familiar territory. Characteristically such claims are accompanied by the additional claim that such revelation is sufficiently clear for its recipients. After all, if God is the agent involved, if the knowledge at issue is beyond human cognitive capacity, and if what is at stake is salvation, it would be very strange not to have a revelation that was relatively clear. The Reformed and Roman Catholic churches have traditionally agreed to this, even though they differ on how the appropriate clarity is to be secured. The Reformers have rested their case on the perspicuity of Scripture; the Roman Catholic Church has insisted on the hermeneutical assistance of tradition and the Pope.

Ward proceeds to reject the whole idea of a clear revelation on what we might call inductive grounds. No such revelation exists, for God has not given us a clear and uncontested revelation. Indeed to make such a claim is 'to utter a dangerous misunderstanding of what God actually is and wants of us' (22). What we really have when we go looking for revelation is argument and perplexity. This calls for a radical change of perspective: 'What must be done is to locate claims to revelation in human history, so that one may see in what way one might actually discern Divine revelation taking form amidst all the ambiguities and conflicts of human belief and practice' (23). In practice this means setting aside exclusivist claims to revelation and exploring the whole range of religion and culture:

> Instead of thinking of God (assuming for the moment that there is one) as breaking into a human framework, ignoring it completely, and giving direct Divine knowledge, it seems more plausible, and more in keeping with the actual history of religions, to think of God as communicating within the framework that societies have themselves developed. To the

English, one might say, using a rather crude analogy, God speaks English; to the Arab God speaks Arabic; and to the Hebrew God speaks Hebrew. Not only does God use the natural language of a people; God uses their thought-forms, their characteristic modes of expression, and their penumbra of tacit connotations and resonances. If one thinks of revelation as a communication from God to humans, then this communication might be expected to take shape in forms the humans can comprehend. One might therefore expect God to set about revealing the ultimate Divine purpose in terms of the interests and goals of particular societies. (24)

Clearly Ward has a deep problem here. On the one side, he is still claiming that divine speaking or divine communication is the heart of divine revelation. On the other side, he does not really know what divine revelation looks like until he examines the major religious traditions of the world to see what God has actually done in revelation. On the one hand, he has already put in place a conception of divine revelation: it takes the form of divine speaking or communication. On the other hand, he has already identified a body of revealed materials: the great religious traditions of the world.[13] Until we carefully examine what they say, we have no idea that the claim to revelation represented by the great religious traditions takes the form of divine speaking or communication. And even if they do conceive of revelation as divine speaking, this does not in itself mean that we should accept this designation of their scripture or tradition and give this or that religion a free ride to truth. The great danger here is that Ward is importing his own prior conception into his understanding of other religions, even though he then turns around and abandons this conception in the name of inductive investigation.

There is an interesting parallel here to what has happened to the study of revelation and inspiration in the Christian tradition over the last century. Much of that study has been conducted on the methodological principle that the Christian Scriptures are divinely inspired or that they constitute canonical revelation. The task thereafter is essentially inductive. Let us go and see, it is proposed, what God has actually done in producing the Scriptures. Thereby we will know what divine revelation and divine inspiration are really like. In my judgement the results of this kind of work have not been altogether happy. On the one side it has led to a neglect of the grammar of such concepts as 'speaking', 'inspire' and 'reveal' as predicated of God. On the other it has led to visions of Scripture that invariably place Scripture on a Procrustean bed of divine revelation. Canon is reduced to Scripture and then interpreted in epistemological categories that warp its proper function in the Church.[14]

Ward falls prey to precisely these intellectual forces. Thus on the conceptual side he effectively abandons the idea of divine speaking and replaces it with the notion of either divine manifestation or divine luring, shaping and guiding of ideas and insights. The reason for this is obvious. When he gets down to examining other religious traditions, he rightly observes that in some cases the best he can find is not some divine agent but a suprasensory realm of value and power. In this case he has to modify the idea of divine revelation in the direction of a general disclosure or manifestation. In other cases he rightly finds all sorts of material that is constituted by human reflection. In this case he has to modify the concept of divine revelation away from any idea of divine speaking or definite communication and in the direction of guiding, luring and directing the human agent's thoughts in this way or that. Of course, if need be he will deploy the idea of revelation as propositional revelation, as happens in his reading of some of the Christian material (225–6).

At crucial points Ward stops to provide a review of his account of divine revelation by laying out various models of revelation (e.g. 224–7, 324–9). As Ward himself acknowledges (226–7, 327–9), there is plenty of precedent for this, most recently in Avery Dulles's book *Models of Revelation*.[15] However, this kind of analysis is misleading in the extreme. The models are entirely parasitic on the ideas that have been brought to the research in the first place. They assume that the canonical Scriptures constitute canonical revelation. Not surprisingly the models simply catalogue what has already been found; they add no new light to the topic in hand. The models are a kind of feast that has been cooked in the kitchen of the researcher using ingredients from his own larder. They have no independent status or significance.

On the material side of the ledger, Ward's strategy perpetuates the line that Scripture and canon are to be seen first and foremost in terms of revelation. Thus 'a canon of Scripture is defined by the communal authorities, marking a significant completion of a matrix of *revelation* for this community' (218, emphasis added), and 'The selection of the canon is the definitive decision by the community on what the founding events are which define the form of its relationship to the Divine. It is not that God once gave a *revelation* and then stopped. God continues to inspire, guide, and prompt human thoughts and lives. But a *canonical revelation* presents a particular view of the nature of the Supreme Reality and Value' (278, emphasis added).[16] So canon and revelation are constantly conflated or interchanged. Not surprisingly Ward reverses this and virtually substitutes revelation for canon when he proposes that 'the Koran can be taken by Christians as the Word of God somewhat as the Old Testament is' (190).

Ward is wrestling with two quite different but closely related enterprises here.[17] On the one hand, he is in search of a viable conception of divine revelation. This search, however, needs far more conceptual labour on the notion of revelation. We need careful work on how revelation is to be understood when it is predicated of God, a suprasensory realm of value, Nirvana and the like. Nor can we assume that either the agent or subject matter of revelation makes no difference to how we think about divine revelation. We can only go so far with formal analysis; we also need material analysis of the specific content of claims to divine revelation. On the other hand, Ward is in search of a critically informed vision of Scripture as we actually find it within and without Christianity. We do indeed need critically informed, accurate accounts of the nature of the scriptures of the world religions. Moreover, Ward is right to argue that this work cannot be carried out in a vacuum when scriptures are read either in the academy or in our religious communities. At some level of our research we will become methodological theists, atheists, agnostics, Buddhists,

Hindus and so on. However, this historical work must always be conducted with a systematic sensitivity to the conceptual options available. Our historical work needs to be permeated by an awareness of a full array of pertinent ideas of revelation. What is crucial is that we find a way to engage in both the conceptual and the historical work required in all their fullness and complexity.

The unavoidability of substantive methodological commitments reveals something very significant about the role of framework beliefs in our research, including framework beliefs that involve divine revelation. For too long we have been captive to various forms of intellectual imperialism in this domain. One of the great merits of Ward's work is that it makes us aware of these conceptual frameworks and breaks open space to pursue the study of other religions from various theological perspectives. Unfortunately I find Ward's work too infected by long-standing problems, not only with the concept of revelation, but also with the concept and content of canon as these apply to the Christian tradition. Given the difficulties engendered by our understanding and appropriation of the Christian tradition, I cannot applaud the extension of those conceptual and material problems to the study and appropriation of other religious traditions. One of the great merits of Ward's work, however, is that it should provoke us to more incisive conceptual analysis in this arena. Happily, this is one of the least of the benefits that awaits the reader of his many volumes of constructive theology.

NOTES

1 Richard Swinburne, *Revelation: From Metaphor to Analogy* (Oxford: Clarendon Press, 1992).
2 Keith Ward, *Religion and Revelation: A Theology of Revelation in the World's Religions* (Oxford: Clarendon Press, 1994). Further references to this work are by page number alone.
3 George Mavrodes, *Revelation in Religious Belief* (Philadelphia: Temple University Press, 1988).
4 Swinburne, *Revelation: From Metaphor to Analogy*, 95–7.
5 However, Swinburne is in fact well aware of the complexity of other religions and has elsewhere expressed a generous attitude as to the truth that might be expressed in them. See his *The Existence of God* (Oxford: Clarendon Press, 1979), 266. This whole issue is pursued in the wake of some of Swinburne's central ideas, in detail and with great sophistication, by Caroline Franks Davis in *The Evidential Force of Religious Experience* (Oxford: Clarendon Press, 1989).
6 Ward explicitly asserts this in respect of primal religions (73), but the argument can surely be extended beyond these to the traditions which build on the ideas and practices of primal religions.
7 In the text Ward begins from Christian premises but there is more than a hint that the argument is an a priori one: 'When one considers the many thousands of years for which humanoid beings have existed on this planet, it is incredible to suppose that God had no concern to relate them to the Divine in knowledge and love at all' (73).
8 Particularism is here contrasted with methodism, a distinction made famous by Roderick Chisholm: see 'The Problem of the Criterion', in his *The Foundations of Knowing* (Minneapolis: University of Minnesota Press, 1982), 61–75. In particularism, one begins with what one thinks one knows and works from that to find an appropriate method of knowing. In methodism, one begins with what one thinks is the right method for knowing and then finds out what one knows.

9   The failure here may lie in not fully recognising that issues of epistemology need not in the first instance involve casting around for an account of the relevant evidence. The latter move tends to arise within epistemologies that are internalist in orientation; externalist epistemologies operate within a very different thought-world.

10 It is a very striking feature of Ward's work as a whole that where he finds differences between Christianity and other religions he invariably tries to find a way to reconcile them, but when it comes to differences between himself and other Christian theologians, he is much less apt to look for a way to reconcile the opposing views. There is a significant difference of tone and outlook when he switches from inter-religious disagreement to intra-religious disagreement.

11 Ward brings up the subject in *Religion and Revelation* (44) but does not explore it in any detail. Happily he does address it at greater length in *Religion and Community* (Oxford: Clarendon Press, 2000), 144–51. He even suggests that there is some 'possibility of convergence' between his own view of revelation and the Roman Catholic tradition (148–9).

12 Elsewhere Ward proposes that 'the wider one's perspective, the more reliable one's religious judgements might be': *Religion and Revelation*, 38.

13 Ward conducts his study of other religions on the assumption that God has actually provided revelation in those traditions. He operates essentially as a methodological theist rather than a methodological atheist or methodological agnostic.

14 I have argued this case at length for the history of theology in my *Canon and Criterion in Christian Theology* (Oxford: Clarendon Press, 1998, repr. 2002).

15 Avery Dulles, *Models of Revelation* (Garden City, NY: Image Books, 1985; Dublin: Gill and Macmillan, 1992).

16 Compare p. 318, where Ward conflates canon and canonical revelation.

17 The issue of the epistemology of Christian theology also lurks in the neighbourhood of both these enterprises.

2

Ward on Revelation: Inclusivism or Pluralism?

PETER BYRNE

I

In *Religion and Revelation*,[1] Keith Ward commends and practises something he styles 'comparative theology'. Comparative theology is defined as 'an enquiry into ideas of God and revelation, of ultimate reality and its disclosures to human minds, as such ideas arise across the full spectrum of human history and experience' (RR 50). Comparative theology is opposed to confessional theology. The latter is reflection on God rooted in faithfulness to one exclusive and privileged revelation (RR 39–40).

The comparative theology defended and practised in *Religion and Revelation* does not depart from the principle that theology should be the disciplined reflection on the data of revelation. But it modifies the customary import of that principle by taking 'revelation' to include the religious history of the entire human race. *Religion and Revelation* can thus be seen as being heir to a long tradition in European religious thought – going back at least to the writings on culture and history of Lessing and Herder. It is a tradition which sees the history of the human race as one of divine education. It is one which sees revelation at work in all cultures and epochs and because of that denies the exclusivity of the revelation contained in the Christian Scriptures (RR 73). That both the primal and the 'founded' religions contain revelation yet differ markedly in the accounts they give of the Divine is to be explained by another idea familiar to students of the Romantic account of revelation which is rooted in Herder: the Divine everywhere filters disclosures of itself through the diverse cultural categories and perceptions of the human race (RR 93). This view of the mediation of human–divine encounters via human cultures is so far from being exclusivist as to yield the conclusion, in Schleiermacher, that each form of religion in history is one that at that time, at that place, humankind had to accept given its cultural and historical development at that point.[2]

II

The comparative theology set forth in *Religion and Revelation* sees the primal religions and each of the major, global religions as all alike containing revelation, that is, disclosure by the supreme, suprasensory reality to human beings. It can cope with divergence and conflict between these revelations by the 'error theory' outlined above and by stressing the multi-faceted character of the Real. I can find no arguments in *Religion and Revelation* to show that confessional theology, which takes its stand on one supposed authentic revelation, is incoherent, but it does contain a case for concluding that it is religiously and philosophically arbitrary. One possibility open to the defender of a particular revelation's exclusive claim to truth is apologetic argument: some sort of proof that the favoured tradition makes religious claims that are true, and opposing traditions claims that are false. Ward uses the term 'natural theology' to denote 'the attempt to show that there is a God and that God has been truly revealed in a specific tradition' (RR 41). It is fair to say that Ward dismisses natural theology, so defined (which is not to say that he dismisses attempts to argue from the world to the existence of deity). The possibility of a contemporary apologetic enterprise of this kind is ruled out by the development of historical criticism (RR 41–2). A central argument in Richard Swinburne's apologetics for Christian revelation is said to be hopelessly circular (RR 245–6). In the absence of a successful apologetic, natural-theological strategy of that kind, assertions by conservative theologians such as Barth and Brunner that the Gospel is simply to be accepted as distinct from the mass of human religion on the testimony of its inner truth or the guarantee of the Spirit are set aside as presupposing what they seek to establish: namely that the Christian revelation is the only true one. They may make a show of distinguishing human words and books (as one and all relative and contingent) from the Gospel (as coming from God alone). But they can only access the Gospel via human words and books and end up simply privileging one set of words and books above others. Ward concludes of Barth and Brunner that 'On this question [. . .] they are a positive hindrance. They insist that reason cannot judge revelation, though they themselves judge all revelations and decide that the Christian is alone true' (RR 21). I cannot disagree with Ward in this judgement. Granted that apologetics is ruled impossible (though Ward's case on this score is in truth very thin), we cannot in effect appeal to the authority of Christian revelation (or its Scriptures or its church) when the question at issue is precisely which of the many competing claims to revelation, if any, is valid. In the absence of a successful apologetics, confessional theology does not appear to take seriously the problem that there are competing claims to revelation.

What scope does Ward's account of the aims and basis of comparative theology give for affirming the absoluteness and uniqueness of Christianity and its revelation? Very little, you might think. The Evangelical tactic of appealing to the internal witness of the Spirit or the Gospel itself is ruled out. An apologetic proof of Christianity, and disproof of other faiths, is rejected. Ward, it seems, must then adopt some form of religious pluralism in which Christianity is but one form of human encounter with the Divine amongst others and claims no privilege as such. But, contrary to all expectations, *Religion and Revelation* contains a resounding affirmation of the uniqueness, finality and absoluteness of the Christian revelation. In a section entitled 'The Idea of a Final Revelation', Ward defines a final revelation as 'one that does state what the Supreme Value really is, what human destiny is and what the proper way to it is' (RR 279). Christianity is the final revelation. What Ward picks out as its key claims – that God is redemptive love, that the end consists in personal union with God and is to be achieved through participating in the divine love itself – are stated to be 'irreformable'. All affirmations which are not consistent with them are ultimately false. Ward sums up his absolutism as follows:

> Christianity is absolute in the sense that its basic view of the nature of God [. . .], of the ultimate human goal [. . .], and of the way to it [. . .] is simply true[.] (RR 279)

This view of Christian affirmations fits in with a perspective on Jesus whereby his life is the turning point of history and the source of its meaning. The end of history is prefigured in the glory of the risen Christ (RR 280).

Ward's commitment to the absolute and final status of Christian revelation entails a corresponding commitment to the historicity and faithfulness of the Gospel records. He explores in some detail the challenges historical criticism makes to such a commitment. He accepts that the records can never be historically certain. Faith in the absolute truths contained in revelation is nonetheless possible on the basis of a 'principle of trust' which balances out the doubts arising out of critical history (RR 243). Moreover, though faith in Christ is in one sense grounded in history, the present fruits of the life of faith provide warrant for accepting the historical claims bound up with faith. The present witness of the Spirit provides reassurance that the historical trust placed in ancient documents is not misplaced (RR 277–8).

Ward's absolutisation of Christianity is not meant to exclude the possibility and reality of other faiths containing genuine ways of gaining access to the goal of life – personal union with supreme value. Nor is it meant to exclude the fact that there are religious truths and insights outside the Christian tradition which Christians need to be aware of and take on board. It is part of the stance of comparative theology, as we have seen, to regard divine disclosure as operating in all peoples and all authentic religious traditions. Christianity is final and absolute truth but it is not the only truth and it is not therefore true to the exclusion of other traditions and faiths. There is a universal human–divine relationship which is authentically present in both primal and founded religions, but it reaches its definitive statement in Christianity.

III

We are now in a position to state the obvious: in *Religion and Revelation* Keith Ward has confronted the diversity of religions and revelations and produced a Christian inclusivist account of that diversity. We need to place that kind of response to diversity on a map of possible responses.

When we confront religious diversity we have to face the fact that religions implicitly or explicitly claim cognitive successes and achievements of various kinds. Thus they claim to have a true account of the nature of transcendent, sacred reality, or of the way human beings must act toward that reality, or of human nature, or of how human salvation or liberation from evil is to be achieved. They hold that their spiritualities capture genuine encounter with and experience of the transcendent and/or that they have genuine revelation. Since these claims to cognitive success appear to conflict with one another, we are called upon to determine which, if any, of these cognitive successes are genuine. *Religion and Revelation* rejects the obvious naturalist response to diversity and conflict, which is that diversity and conflict is clear testimony that human religion is merely the work of the imagination influenced by cultural and historical factors. In contrast to naturalism, confessionalism and pluralism are both agreed on the point that religion succeeds in relating human beings to religious reality in some mode or other (be it through salvific success, doctrinal truth, genuine religious experience or whatever). So in this respect they can all be said, in contrast to forms of naturalism, to be realist interpretations of religion.

Confessionalism finds cognitive success in religion but locates it solely or primarily in one confession. In exclusivist confessionalism the ethics or salvific scheme or revelation or doctrines of one religion have cognitive merit to the exclusion of merit in all others. So it holds a deeply divisive view of the human religious scene. Confessional inclusivism modifies this divisive picture while accepting that the prime measure of cognitive achievement is provided by the elements of one faith. Other faiths (or at least a considerable number of other faiths) achieve cognitive success because at some level they approach the success of the favoured faith. Both forms of confessionalism, then, maintain that one religion is sufficiently certain in its dogmatic formulations to be the means of interpreting the whole that is human religion. The exclusivist interpretation holds that the other religions are cognitive failures in the light of the dogmatic structures of the favoured religion, the inclusivist that the other religions are cognitive successes when interpreted in the light of the favoured religion. The crux here is the belief that one confession has the correct account in some detail of what right relation to transcendent, sacred reality consists in (say, that it is defined through the belief that Jesus is the Son of God and the redemption for human sin). Confessionalism then seeks either to exclude other religions from that right relation or to include them.

Religion and Revelation embodies confessional inclusivism, though of an extremely liberal sort. The 'final truth' that is in Christianity is stated in a somewhat minimalist way (see §II above) and every opportunity is taken to stress the fact that other primal and founded religions contain ways of relating human beings to the Divine, important religious insights, and genuine divine–human experience. Ward states that there are three ways of doing comparative theology: neutrally, in a collaborative way with people from different faiths, and from a confessional point of view. He affirms that his version of the enterprise embodies the last approach. He is attempting to interpret all faiths 'comprehensively and justly' from his own avowed faith standpoint (RR 108).

IV

There is a fundamental problem with the confessional inclusivism that characterises *Religion and Revelation*: it does not cohere with the overall argument of the book. The epistemology of revelation contained in *Religion and Revelation* does not allow Ward to adopt a confessional inclusivist approach to the diversity of religions and revelations. The outline argument for this conclusion is easily stated. Ward rejects the apologetic enterprise he styles 'natural theology'. There is no apologetic case which is capable of demonstrating one of the religions to be true, or of showing it to be more probable than not. Ward offers no apologetic strategy for demonstrating the absolute and final truth of Christianity in comparison with the other faiths. The reliance that the likes of Barth and Brunner place on the internal witness of the Gospel and of the Spirit to establish that Christianity is exclusively true is rejected as intellectually arbitrary. Yet he appeals to just such internal testimony, linked to a trust in the witness of the early Christian communities, to ground his claims about Christian finality and absoluteness. He cannot consistently criticise conservative Christian perspectives on religious diversity.[3]

If conservative theologians are allowed the kind of internal 'proofs' of their brand of Christianity which Ward allows himself for his own, then there is a logic to their rejection of comparative theology which Ward fails to take into account. They will say that salvation, right relation to the God of the Gospels, can only be accomplished through the particular means supplied by Christ. Kenneth Surin makes this point when he stresses the specific Christian claim that salvation cannot be produced by human effort but is dependent on the salvific action of Christ. In particular, the project of comparative theology must run head on against the 'scandal of particularity' arising out of the Christian claim that only in and through the life and death of Jesus is salvation made possible.[4] Surin's objection is more important than a simple assertion of confessional superiority. Human nature is characterised by sin and evil and they cannot be removed by human effort because they condition that effort. Only divine action in history can cancel out human sin and that necessitates a single, unique and pivotal intervention by the sacred in history, whereby God takes on and defeats the power of evil and sin. Surin offers what is in effect a general, philosophical argument for the necessity of the Incarnation as it is conceived in Christianity. The argument is general and philosophical in being drawn from an understanding of the concept and character of evil and its place in human life.[5] Evil in human beings can only be defeated if God defeats it by assuming the person of a human being. Such efforts are intended to show on a priori grounds that a Christian philosophy of history is true. Note that these more traditional Christian accounts have a different understanding of 'revelation' to Ward's. We are not talking about a gradual disclosure of the nature of supreme value to human beings rooted in diverse cultures. We are not talking about an evolving divine–human relationship. We have in view instead a decisive intervention of the Divine into history which may be seen as a disruption of culture. This kind of outlook is surely behind the accounts of revelation in Barth and Brunner.

If Ward has given Christian conservatives licence to accept a reading of Christianity as true on the basis of trust and internal testimony, he has surely given the same licence to Islamic inclusivist, Buddhist inclusivist and other inclusivist interpretations of human religion. He would not deny this. He states that each religious tradition can quite properly make a claim to be the uniquely privileged and inspired community. The Christian tradition 'is not being unduly arrogant or imperialistic when it claims a unique witness to the nature and purpose of God. It is simply formulating what each tradition must formulate in its own way, as long as it continues to exist' (RR 217). This claim reinforces the point that Ward has little room to criticise the confessional theologian who simply stands on the uniqueness of his or her own tradition and scriptures as containing the sole revelation of God to human beings. Ward contends that it is impossible to understand the Christian revelation without seeing it in the context of human religious activity in general (RR 37). It is clear why he says that. He thinks there is a general, continuing revelation of the Divine to the human. So it is natural he should affirm that the wider the Christian theologian's perspective, the more reliable his or her judgements will be (RR 38). But if confessional Christian theologians think that the Gospel witnesses to a truth and a way which is qualitatively different from those provided in other traditions, if they think that the Gospel judges human culture rather than being integrally bound up with it, then Ward has no good case against them.

V

The affirmation of Christian absoluteness and uniqueness in *Religion and Revelation* is not merely out of step with its rejection of confessionalist, exclusivist attitudes toward the Christian Gospel, it also faces the charge that it is not a serious response to the challenge of religious diversity. The key challenge diversity provides is to the warrant and truth of the claims to cognitive success in any given tradition in the light of the similar, conflicting claims in other traditions. Diversity could promote the search for inter-religious apologetics in favour of one faith, and against others, as advocated strongly by Paul Griffiths.[6] It does not do so in Ward. Failing that, it should surely lead one to question the claims for uniqueness and absoluteness made by the varied traditions. That means exploring pluralism.[7]

Pluralism can take many forms. Common to them all must be the ascription of cognitive success to a great many of the world's religious traditions. (Neither inclusivism nor pluralism need attribute such success to everything that has counted as a religious tradition in history.) The essential minimum to pluralism must be the assertion of *one* kind of equality among religious traditions, namely that of each providing folk with real contact with a single transcendent focus. Such contact enables all faiths covered by the pluralist thesis to be vehicles for salvation or liberation: the journey to the ultimate human good. Without this basic equality and achievement, others pertaining to religion are worthless.

This way of putting the matter does not as yet secure a distinction between pluralism and confessional inclusivism, for the latter maintains this basic equality while of

course making a decisive judgement of cognitive superiority in favour of one confession. To a minimal definition of pluralism we must add the element of scepticism or
agnosticism with regard to the detailed dogmatic or mythical structure of any
specific form of faith. The pluralist must be someone who, on reasoned grounds,
doubts whether the detailed dogmatics of any particular religion can be known with
sufficient certainty to enable such a faith to be the means of interpreting human
religion. That is to say, pluralism must take its stand on a grand negative: there is not
the certainty in any particular religion to enable its world-view to be the basis of a
viable interpretation of religion.[8]

This agnosticism need not be an a priori, external imposition on the religious
sphere. Nor need it be based on a hopelessly rigorous criterion of certainty. We find
many religions giving, as Ward so clearly describes for us, accounts of a supremely
valuable, suprasensory ground and goal for the human good. They differ markedly
on points of detail. In the absence of reasons for judging one account to be more
reliable than another, we should assume that they all offer some insights into the
nature of this reality. All are to some, substantive extent reliable and unreliable at the
same time (like conflicting but overlapping human testimonies to a road accident).
We can claim superiority for one against the others only if we can show by comparison of that one against the others that it is more reliable. Perhaps we can argue that
where all the non-Christian traditions agree with one another, those points are
found in a more profound form in Christianity. Ward's *Religion and Revelation*
repeatedly stresses a major point in favour of the agnosticism which characterises
pluralist responses to diversity. Ward affirms that revelation is to human beings
rooted in culture. All traditions are therefore 'affected by culturally derived forms of
human response and acceptance', including one's own (RR 187). The one Supreme
Reality behind the continuing religious history of the human race is therefore seen,
according to Ward, through the prisms of many different human cultures. This gives
pluralism the error theory for the agnosticism characteristic of it. Given this error
theory, Ward's 'exceptionalism' – the assertion that Christianity has a uniquely
reliable, authoritative revelation from God to human beings – looks odd once more.

Ward's exceptionalism in favour of the Christian revelation is even more odd
when seen in the light of his argument in *A Vision to Pursue*.[9] Here Ward contends
for the human, error-prone character of the New Testament. It contains, as at
Matthew 24.34, a false belief which is fundamental to its outlook. This is the belief
in an imminent end of history and an imminent Second Coming. Ward argues that
we cannot but accept that this false belief was held by the Jesus described in the
Gospels. The presence of an error of this scale means that the classical doctrine of the
Incarnation must be rethought (VP 16ff.). In *A Vision to Pursue* Ward is clear about
the implications of this view of the Christian revelation as errant and limited: Christ
cannot be said to be *the* mediator between the Divine and humanity. To be sure he
argues that there are facts about Jesus as an 'icon' of the Divine that are unique (VP
85), but there is 'little point' in trying to decide which of the many mediators religious traditions present us with is the final or best one (VP 86). Each great tradition
has a paradigm of divine action. Jesus is one such paradigm amongst others, not the

one normative paradigm. Each paradigm captures a perspective on ultimate reality. None is at all likely to be finally, unrevisably true (VP 131–2).

Exclusivism and inclusivism posit an epistemological divide between parts of humanity, but the problem created by Ward's account of revelation in *Religion and Revelation* is that *all* religions seem to be historically and culturally conditioned in their forms of understanding. Forms of confessionalism will contend that one normative tradition escapes such conditioning to the extent that it can produce a dogmatic structure which is detailed and certain enough to be the means of interpreting religion as a whole. Proponents of inclusivism and exclusivism must contend that their favoured tradition is an exception to a general rule which applies to all other religions. *Religion and Revelation* contains no grounds for making such an exception.

So far we have in pluralism three minimal elements: a fundamental realist commitment to the existence of a transcendent, sacred reality; a basic cognitive equality between faiths in putting human beings in contact with this reality and enabling them to be vehicles of salvation; and finally agnosticism toward, and therefore disengagement from, the specifics of any confessional stance toward religion. Refining pluralism, we get a viewpoint on religions defined by three propositions:

1. All major religious traditions are equal in respect of making common reference to a single transcendent, sacred reality.
2. All major traditions are likewise equal in respect of offering some means or other to human salvation.
3. All traditions are to be seen as containing revisable, limited accounts of the nature of the sacred: none is certain enough in its particular dogmatic formulations to provide the norm for interpreting the others.

How do these three theses hang together? This question cannot be answered properly until the main reasons for advancing religious pluralism are set out. A preliminary account, however, can be given. Central to pluralism as I have defined it is the view of religious traditions as connected, overlapping attempts on the part of human beings to understand and orient themselves towards the sacred. All these attempts are limited to some degree (by the historical and cultural basis of human understanding) and hence none is likely a priori to be more than a stage in the human journey toward understanding of the sacred. Despite their partial and limited character, pluralism maintains, and *must* maintain, that they provide cognitive contact with transcendent reality and enough relational and practical knowledge about it to offer overlapping, connecting ways of living rightly toward it. So pluralism must be built around a conception of reference and a notion of right practice which allows both to proceed in circumstances of partial theoretical understanding of the focus of the human religious quest. This entire strategy can be seen as a means of neutralising the conflicts between religions which the facts of religious diversity throw up: they are to be expected, given the pluralist's reading of the human religious condition, and they do not necessarily deprive at least a range of traditions from achieving, in common, their objects.[10]

VI

There is much in the statement of pluralism provided above that could come straight from the pages of *Religion and Revelation* or that could be supported by its positive and negative arguments. Why then does Ward reject pluralism? The answer to this question is not easily given. Ward distinguishes between soft and hard pluralism. He is unhappy with the latter but content with the former. The distinction between soft and hard pluralism is introduced by Ward in 'Truth and the Diversity of Religions', a critical article on John Hick.[11] Soft pluralism is defined as the belief that the Supreme Reality can manifest itself in many traditions and that human beings can respond appropriately to it in those traditions. Ward espouses soft pluralism. His theory of a general revelation of the Divine to the human is a pluralist thesis on this score. But note that this is a poor way of identifying a religious outlook as pluralistic. A four-square confessionalist interpretation of world religions can accept the soft pluralist thesis. Karl Rahner's perspective on religions in his *Theological Investigations* is avowedly Christian. It views the 'other religions' through the notion that Jesus Christ is the Mediator and the Incarnation of God in human form. Rahner argues that the other religions have opened channels of divine grace to non-Christians. Non-Christians can live out authentic relationships to God, not despite, but through, the forms of their non-Christian traditions.[12] But the non-Christian traditions are, unbeknownst to themselves, preparing human beings for a relationship to God which can only be completed through an explicit confrontation with 'his Christ'.[13] In 'Truth and the Diversity of Religions' Ward seems to be committed to what is implied by Rahner's thesis: that there will be a post-mortem revelation of Christ to non-Christians authentically related to God which will allow them to partake fully of salvation.[14]

Ward's 'soft pluralism', then, is not really pluralism as I have defined it. It is quite compatible with viewing all religions through the dogmatic structures and paradigms of one of them. It merely captures what confessional inclusivism and true pluralism share when they reject exclusivism: the belief that salvation – right relationship to supreme reality – is available in and through many religious traditions.

If Ward's soft pluralism is not really pluralism at all then his hard pluralism is but one version of a pluralistic outlook, namely that of Hick, interpreted after a certain fashion. Ward makes hard pluralism consist of three theses: (1) there is a wholly unknowable religious ultimate; (2) all experiences of it are equally authentic; and (3) all paths to fuller experience of it are equally valid. So defined, pluralism has to incorporate both Hick's assertion that the supremely real is beyond all characterisation, save in formal, non-substantive terms, and the further assertion that there is a complete cognitive equality between all the major world religions. Ward's complaint against hard pluralism is then twofold. He thinks it is incoherent (theses (1) to (3) form an inconsistent triad), and he thinks the agnosticism involved in thesis (1) is so radical as to be destructive of religious life and thought.[15]

What the distinction between soft and hard pluralism does is present us with a wholly false set of alternatives in support of the argument of *Religion and Revelation*.

We are to choose either a standpoint which is quite compatible with confessional inclusivism or the hypotheses of Hick's *An Interpretation of Religion*. But it is quite evident that one can espouse pluralism as I have defined it, leaving confessionalist theories of religious diversity behind as one does so, without embracing Hick's version of pluralism.

Pluralism is not as such committed to saying that all major religions are equal in every aspect of cognitive endeavour or that no judgements of superiority of any kind between religions or their component elements are possible. If a writer claims a thoroughgoing equality of this sort, that appears to reflect his or her own concerns and arguments rather than the essence of pluralism itself. All that is required as a matter of definition is a positive equality in some effective cognitive contact with the transcendent capable of supporting a thesis about religions as vehicles of salvation or liberation, combined with a negative equality consisting in the absence of sufficient certainty in the dogmatic structures of any one faith for it to be the means of interpreting all the others. Inter-religious judgements can still be made. For example, we may be impressed by the following fact: all the major traditions, bar some schools of Buddhism, testify to the existence of a metaphysical absolute, albeit they give different accounts of its nature. We may then conclude that the weight of human religious experience is against the Buddhist claim that there is no metaphysical ground to reality. This does not entail that Buddhism must be interpreted as failing to put its practitioners in touch with the divine substratum or that Buddhism has no insights to offer into its nature. A pluralist theory of religion will make full use of the idea that folk can refer to and be in cognitive contact with an object despite being mistaken in how they describe it.[16]

Pluralists do not have to fall into complete agnosticism about the divine, supreme reality when faced with the incompatible portrayals of its nature in the primal and founded religions. Here Ward has shown us the way. In *A Vision to Pursue* and *Images of Eternity*[17] he has explained with clarity and great insight how we can avoid such agnosticism while honestly facing up to divergent accounts of supreme reality in the world faiths. We appeal to the idea that these divergent accounts are so many symbolic, metaphorical portrayals of the Divine: 'Different metaphors might be necessary to present a view of supreme reality, even though they seem to contradict, taken literally' (VP 171). This appeal to the symbolic can be strengthened by the thought that what the different metaphors do is present different facets of a supreme reality which has more than one aspect (VP 165–7). We can get out of this point a, dare I say it, syncretistic account of a multi-faceted divine reality of which each tradition only has a partial insight. We can put the insights of different traditions together, using our culture-based error theory to explain why they are partial, revisable attempts to fasten onto the one focus.[18]

VII

Here then is the paradox. In *Religion and Revelation* Ward presents us with the choice we are first offered in 'Truth and the Diversity of Religions': either an extreme, highly sceptical pluralism of the kind Hick is alleged to offer, or a form of confessional inclusivism which still gives us one tradition as containing absolute, unique, final revelation. *Images of Eternity* and *A Vision to Pursue* provide us with arguments to show that this is a false choice.

Let us remind ourselves of Ward's self-confessed aim in *Religion and Revelation*: to interpret all faiths comprehensively and justly from one's own confessional stand-point (RR 108). In this book Ward sees no real alternative to a religious, non-naturalist interpretation of religion that is confessionally based. Other religious alternatives are rejected as false because they will be based on the unrealisable attempt to see religions from a neutral point of view (RR 42). They may lead us into the 'hard pluralism' of Hick, which is alleged to be incoherent. I have argued that Ward's aim is conditioned by a vision of false alternatives. There can be genuine pluralist outlooks that are not committed to Hick's version of the pluralist hypothesis. Their accounts of supreme reality can be constructed by looking at overlaps and convergences between faiths – without being imposed from outside by a priori theorising.

A genuine comparative, pluralist theology will have to accept that the fact of the diversity of world religions throws up much greater challenges to the uniqueness, finality and absoluteness of one's own faith than *Religion and Revelation* acknowledges. Strange though it may be, Keith Ward has shown us what a genuine pluralist interpretation looks like in *A Vision to Pursue*. An intriguing and highly relevant fact about Ward's argument therein is that it points to ways in which the challenge of diversity and the development of pluralist thought need not lead to the formal abandonment of first-order religious symbols, doctrines and modes of worship. The Buddhist notion of 'skilful means' is invoked to explain why doctrines, symbols and practices which are central for a given religious community are nonetheless but temporary helps and resting places in pursuit of right relationship with supreme reality (VP 10). Authentic worship is still possible for the Christian revisionist, says Ward (VP 58–9), but the outcome of this kind of pluralism is convergent forms of spirituality across the traditions (VP 203).

VIII

This chapter has highlighted the extent to which Ward's vision of a general revelation of the Divine to humanity through continuing religious history has an honoured place in modern Christian interpretations of religion and history. His vision gives rise to the pursuit of a comparative theology which is allegedly opposed to confessional theology. This opposition would suggest that *Religion and Revelation* will develop a pluralist theory of religion. It does not, but stays inside a confessional inclusivist interpretation. I have contended that Ward fails in his efforts to ground such an interpretation. Confessional interpretations of religion demand what Ward rejects: either a robust apologetic strategy in the manner of Richard Swinburne or a defence of reliance on internal forms of testimony to the truth of a religion. There is little in the book to defend the 'exceptionalism' which characterises his treatment of the Christian revelation beyond an appeal to the necessity of plumping for one starting point in the theory of religion rather than another. His refusal to embrace pluralism is also in part supported by an inadequate understanding of the options for pluralist theory, evident at least as far back as his paper on 'Truth and the Diversity of Religions'. That understanding did not control the argument of *A Vision to Pursue*. The final conundrum is: what happened to the argument of that book when *Religion and Revelation* came to be written? Ward notes in *Religion and Revelation* that his views have changed but states, quite implausibly in my opinion, that the Christian orthodoxies of the later book can be derived from the pluralist analysis of the earlier 'given relatively small amendments of the previous analysis' (RR 240 n. 75).

NOTES

1   Keith Ward, *Religion and Revelation* (Oxford: Clarendon Press, 1994). Further references in the text to this work, abbreviated RR, are given in parentheses.

2   See Peter Byrne, *Natural Religion and the Nature of Religion* (London: Routledge, 1989), 161.

3   Mark Wynn has suggested to me that one difference between Ward, on the one hand, and Barth and Brunner, on the other, is that Ward operates with a kind of 'meta-pluralism'. He implicitly allows other traditions to privilege themselves when they view the world of faiths from their standpoints. They are entitled to their forms of confessional inclusivism, as much as Christian theologians are to theirs. If Barth and Brunner will not extend this liberty to non-Christian theologians, then there is at least one difference between them and Ward.

4   Kenneth Surin, 'Revelation, Salvation and the Uniqueness of Christ and Other Religions', *Religious Studies*, 28 (1983), 336.

5   Ibid., 331–2.

6   Paul Griffiths, *An Apology for Apologetics* (Maryknoll, NY: Orbis Books, 1991).

7   I leave aside here the side-stepping of the diversity problem in the externalist epistemology of Alvin Plantinga's *Warranted Christian Belief* (New York: Oxford University Press, 2000), ch. 13.

8   See Peter Byrne, *Prolegomena to Religious Pluralism* (London and Basingstoke: Macmillan, 1995), 5.

9   Keith Ward, *A Vision to Pursue* (London: SCM Press, 1991). Further references in the text to this work, abbreviated VP, are given in parentheses.

10 Byrne, *Prolegomena to Religious Pluralism*, 12–13.

11 Keith Ward, 'Truth and the Diversity of Religions', *Religious Studies*, 26 (1990), 16–17, and restated in *Religion and Revelation*, 317.

12 Karl Rahner, *Theological Investigations*, vol. xviii (London: Darton, Longman and Todd, 1984), 290.

13 Ibid., 295; cf. Karl Rahner, *Theological Investigations*, vol. xvi (London: Darton, Longman and Todd, 1979), 217–20.

14 See Ward, 'Truth and the Diversity of Religions', 18.

15 Ibid., 16–17.

16 For a fuller account of this point, see Byrne, *Prolegomena to Religious Pluralism*, ch. 2.

17 Keith Ward, *Images of Eternity: Concepts of God in Five Religious Traditions* (London: Darton, Longman and Todd, 1987).

18 As Ward does superbly in *Images of Eternity*. For a discussion and defence of approaching the description of the Divine via metaphor, see Byrne, *Prolegomena to Religious Pluralism*, ch. 6.

3

Theology of Religions versus Philosophy of Religions

JOHN HICK

Those British theologians today who do systematic, or constructive, theology are still for the most part doing it as though Christianity were the only religion in the world, rather than seeing it as part of the world-wide religious life of the whole human race. There is a certain appearance of progress in that the main focus changes from time to time: a few years ago it was the doctrine of the Incarnation, now it is the doctrine of the Trinity. But new thinking occurs only within the limits of traditional orthodoxy, and the result can be of interest only within the shrinking western ecclesiastical world. Within the universities there is, however, also a customer-led development, alongside theology, of programmes of religious studies which open up a wider view of the religious life of the world. But this lies outside what is usually still regarded as the proper business of the theologian.

Within this theological scene Keith Ward shines out as a bright light amid the encircling gloom. There are, happily, a number of other lights as well, but Ward is the most outstanding in intellectual stature, weight and influence. More than any other British theologian he has addressed the religious issues of the contemporary world – not only the science–religion debate, which others also have very actively and profitably entered, but the more radically challenging problems posed by the fact of the other great world religions. Because in this he explores some of the same ground that I have also tried to explore in the philosophy of religion, this chapter will continue the dialogue in which we have been both partly agreeing and partly disagreeing over many years. We agree in a commitment to work for harmonious relations between the different faith communities, in a recognition of the many striking analogies between the different world belief systems, in an appreciative awareness of the spiritual profundities of the other great traditions, and in a desire to bring all this much more fully to the attention of our fellow-Christians. At the same time – within the context of a long-established friendship – we disagree about the extent of the theological and philosophical implications of this.

In his Gifford and Selwyn Lectures, *Religion and Revelation*, Ward has contributed to what he calls a comparative theology, in which 'each tradition [. . .] may hope to preserve the main elements of its own distinctive witness, while engaging in an open, and in some important ways convergent, interaction with others',[1] and he does this from an explicitly Christian standpoint. Central to Christianity, as also to

Judaism and Islam, is the concept of revelation, and in this book Ward examines the role of revelation in each of the major world religions, not only the 'western' monotheisms, in which this means an active disclosure of truths and laws from a personal God to humanity, but also the eastern religions. And so the first question that Ward's project raises is whether the Abrahamic concept of revelation can properly be stretched to cover those traditions – particularly Buddhism, Taoism, Confucianism and some forms of Hinduism – which do not think of the Ultimate as a personal God. He points out that these also have their authoritative sacred scriptures and, in the case of Buddhism, the crucial truth-discovering experience of the Buddha at a particular place and time in history. So I suppose that in a very broad sense of 'revelation', going far beyond its established connotations in the western mind, it is permissible to use the concept globally.

However, it remains a potential problem for Ward's project that the Christian connotations both of 'revelation' and of other key terms may cling to them in ways that exclude, or are at least unable to do justice to, the great non-theistic faiths. Thus he recommends 'an acceptance that the Supreme Reality has not been silent in the other religions of the world, which delivers one from a myopia which confines God to one small sector of human history'.[2] Such an acceptance does indeed make it possible to see God at work throughout the world, but in so doing does it not establish an assumed identity of the Supreme Reality with the God of western religion? For only a personal deity can be said to be either silent or not silent. We can see that the outcome is likely to be that, 'as many of the Church Fathers thought, there may be many forms of manifestation of the Word who was truly incarnate in Jesus of Nazareth'.[3]

Ward's explicit commitment to 'western' monotheism is clear also in his very considerable work on the science–religion front, much of which is summarised in the view that the universe 'exists, as a whole and in every part, as intentionally produced by a wise, powerful, and fundamentally good being',[4] who influences the outcome of natural forces so that miracles can occur as 'revelatory acts of the underlying spiritual basis of nature, not violations of a closed system of nature'.[5] And his more specific commitment to the distinctively Christian form of monotheism is evident again when he says that 'The resurrection is the Christian paradigm of revelation, as the appearing of the suprasensory in the realm of the sensory, disclosing the final goal of human existence in its unity with the spiritual source of all things.'[6] As will be evident, I am here only drawing out aspects of Ward's thought on which I wish to comment, not providing a full and balanced picture of a position which is worked out in his texts in impressively rich detail and with highly coherent argumentation.

Looking at Ward's work, then, from a different and yet in many ways closely related point of view, I see him as being as open to the reality and profound value of the other world faiths as is possible whilst remaining within the borders of basic Christian orthodoxy. I hope that the rest of the theological world will in due course catch up with the wider vision which he pursues, accepting the challenge to go beyond the endless restating and elaborating of the ideas of Trinity, Incarnation and Atonement (which are ecclesiastical constructions going far beyond the teachings of

Jesus himself) to Christian thinking in a global context. For Jesus and his influence
are not separate from, but part of, the complex religious life of the world. Ward and I
both want a religious, as distinguished from a naturalistic, interpretation of religion
throughout history and around the world. But we diverge in that I do not believe
that it is possible to achieve this within the credal framework of any one of the great
traditions, including Christianity. I therefore hold that we have to turn from
theology, as usually understood, to the philosophy of religion.

Within the philosophy of religion a basic epistemological question is whether
religious experience can rationally be trusted, by those who participate in it, as
genuinely responsive to reality beyond us whilst at the same time, as is obvious, it is
clothed in our own images and concepts. If you come to an affirmative answer to that
question you then face the task of seeking a religious interpretation of religion in its
world-wide and history-long variety of forms.[7] Ward has considered this idea of a
tradition-neutral philosophy of religions and has critically discussed my own
proposed version of it, and in what follows I shall briefly outline my pluralist
proposal and then discuss Ward's criticisms as they occur in *Religion and Revelation*
and *Religion and Creation*.

The philosophy of religions project starts from three main premises, two epistemological and one empirical. The first epistemological premise is that it is as rational
to base beliefs on religious experience as on sense experience, except when we have a
positive reason not to (and in the religious case the pervasive western assumption of
naturalism, which is no more than an assumption, does not constitute a valid
reason).[8] We must append to this premise the recognition that whilst sense experience, as the awareness of value-free matter, is compulsory for us if we are to survive as
physical organisms in a material environment, religious experience, as awareness of
value-laden suprasensory reality,[9] is not likewise compelled.

The other epistemological premise is the critical realist principle, first developed
in relation to sense perception as the position that there is a real material world
existing independently of our awareness of it, but that this awareness is always
mediated through our own specific cognitive equipment and conceptual systems.
This involves a distinction between the world as it is in itself, unobserved, and as it
appears to us humans. Applying the critical realist principle to religious experience,
the corresponding distinction is between what Ward calls the Supreme Reality as it is
in itself, and as we humans are conscious of it in the forms provided by the conceptual systems, imaginative resources and spiritual practices developed within our
formative culture and our individual life experience.

And the empirical (in the sense of observational) premise is that the moral and
spiritual fruits in human lives of the different great world faiths seem, so far as we can
tell, to be of more or less equal value. That is to say, it does not seem to be the case,
under the common criterion of transcendence of self-centredness into loving
concern for others, that Christians in general, or Muslims in general, or Hindus in
general, etc. stand out as better human beings than the rest of the human race. I do
not think that Ward would disagree thus far.

However, it is this empirical premise that, for me, calls for a pluralistic interpretation of religion by rendering implausible the privileging of one particular tradition (namely one's own) as providing the sole or the best path to the salvific transformation of human life from natural self-centredness to a new orientation centred in the Supreme Reality.[10]

Given these premisses, the problem is to make sense from a religious point of view of the fact that there is a plurality of sometimes very different faith traditions with their different conceptions of ultimate reality, giving rise to their different forms of religious experience, which in turn give rise – together with many other influences – to their different (and often mutually contradictory) belief systems and their correspondingly different spiritualities and forms of individual and social life. My first premiss, the cognitive validity of religious experience, points to a Supreme Reality transcending ourselves, which is of limitless importance to us and which is the object of the religious attitudes of awe, wonder, ultimate trust, worship. The second premiss points to the possibility of the great historical religions constituting very different but possibly equally valid human responses to the sacred reality. And my empirical premiss turns that '*possibly* equally valid' to *actually* so.

If we take as common ground the reality of what I shall variously call the Transcendent or the Real or (using Ward's term) the Supreme Reality, then the critical realist principle offers a solution to the problem of religious diversity. The principle was definitively presented by Thomas Aquinas in his brilliant statement, 'Things known are in the knower according to the mode of the knower,'[11] although he did not apply this to our present problem. (This is a case of 'Everything has been said before, but often by people who did not know that they were saying it.') It is also the basic Kantian distinction between a reality as it is in itself, unobserved, and its phenomenal appearance to us in terms of the form-giving and organising categories of the human mind. In the case of religious, as distinguished from sensory, awareness, the 'mode of the knower' differs significantly among the different ways of being human that are the great cultural streams of earthly history. And so the pluralist hypothesis, as I see it, is that there is an ultimate transcendent reality which is differently conceived, and therefore differently experienced, and therefore differently responded to in life within the different great religious traditions.

At some points Ward seems to be thinking along somewhat similar lines. But a major difference emerges when I conclude that the ultimate reality in itself must be, from our human point of view, ineffable or, as I would rather say, transcategorial, not falling within the scope of our human categories of thought.[12] For my third premiss tells strongly against its identification with any one of the phenomenologically different and unique personal gods and non-personal absolutes of the different traditions. We are therefore led, I suggest, to think of it as a limitless reality, universally present to and (because universal) within us, whose presence comes to consciousness in the many different forms described in the history of religions.

In *Religion and Creation* Ward refers to this hypothesis that the Real is ineffable, but adds that '[Hick's] words show that he does not really believe this. He does claim to know some things about the Real – that it is a supremely valuable reality; that it makes possible, and is thus causally effective in bringing about an "unlimitedly good end-state"; that it manifests itself to human experience in a number of ways which are not wholly misleading.'[13] Again, Hick 'believes that there is a reality of supreme value, love, and power'.[14] His conclusion is that Hick 'is a theist who is concerned to show how God may be experienced in many traditions, which partially show aspects of the divine being'.[15] And he gives references to my *An Interpretation of Religion* in support of this. However, I do not think that the passages to which he refers can bear the weight he places on them.

My phrase 'an ultimate unity of reality and value',[16] the one which Ward equates with 'a supremely valuable reality',[17] occurs in a discussion of the axial age in the first millennium BCE, in which there was a gradual shift from religion as maintaining the stability of the present order of human life in the world, to the idea of a limitlessly better possibility based in the new 'awareness of an ultimate unity of reality and value'. The context is not a discussion of the concept of the Real (which is introduced at a much later stage in the book) and is not meant to refer to it. Again, the reference to 'an unlimitedly good end-state' occurs within a discussion specifically of theism, not of the concept of the Real: 'any acceptable theory of the eschatological verification of theism must make this distinction between an "unlimitedly good end-state in communion with God" and the various concrete pictures of such a state produced by our human traditions'.[18] I do accept what I call the cosmic optimism of the great traditions, affirming what from our human point of view will be an unlimitedly good final future, although its nature is unknown to us. But cosmic optimism does not necessarily entail a being of 'supreme value, love, and power'. A structure of the total universe, physical and trans- or meta-physical, that is ultimately serendipitous (from our human point of view) may be just 'how things are'.

The third point, that the Real manifests itself to human experience in a variety of not wholly misleading ways, requires rather more discussion, first about why we should think of the ultimate reality as transcategorial (ineffable), and second about how, in that case, we can hold that there may be forms of human experience of it which are, in varying degrees, not wholly misleading.

We should think of the ultimate reality as transcategorial because, given the cognitively responsive character of human religious experience, and given the parity of salvific power of the different modes of experience of it as the gods and absolutes of the major world religions, we cannot identify the Real in itself with any one of those gods and absolutes. And if the ultimate reality is not any one of these, it must lie 'beyond' or 'behind' them and be mediated through them.[19] We are therefore committed to the distinction between the Real as it is in itself, beyond the range of human experience and description, and the different describable forms in which its presence is humanly experienced. Accordingly, 'It follows from this distinction between the Real as it is in itself and as it is thought and experienced through our religious concepts that we cannot apply to the Real *an sich* the characteristics encountered in its *personae* and *impersonae*. Thus it cannot be said to be one or many, person or thing, substance or process, good or evil, purposive or non-purposive.'[20] We can only make formal statements about it, in the sense of statements that do not tell us anything about its inner nature.[21] And since the Real cannot be said to be 'purposive or non-purposive' it cannot be said to manifest itself (in the active sense) to us. It is manifested to us in the sense in which the physical world is manifested to us, by its presence to us and our awareness of it in the limited ways made possible, in the latter case, by our sense organs and categories and habits of thought. Thus the Real is universally present, and when we are open to its presence we become aware of it, not however as it is in itself but as it appears to us in the ways made possible by our particular religious conceptualities.

The second question posed above is: how, if the Real is transcategorial in its nature, can we claim that some of the *personae* (the god-figures) and *impersonae* (the metaphysical absolutes) of the Real are 'not wholly misleading' manifestations of the Real itself? Surely, 'If nothing at all can be said of the Real, then one cannot say that some expressions are more authentic manifestations of it than others.'[22] But to say that the Real is transcategorial in its inner nature – that its nature cannot be captured in our human concepts – is not to say *nothing* about it. My claim is that we have to postulate it to explain, from a religious point of view, the existence of the world religions as, so far as we can tell, equally effective (and equally ineffective) contexts of the salvific transformation from self-centredness to a recentring in the Transcendent, the sacred, the Divine, the Ultimate. So we can say that the Real is that which there must be if the global range of human religious experience is not purely imaginative projection. It is a necessary postulate, not of the moral life as Kant proposed, but of the religious life in its variety of forms throughout the world. But we can speak of such an ultimate reality without claiming to know what its nature is in itself, beyond the range of human experience. And starting within any one particular tradition, whose form(s) of religious experience we believe to constitute a response to reality, rather than being purely projections of the human imagination, we can recognise the validity of the different forms of religious experience within other traditions and can recognise a common criterion for the authenticity of human responses to the Transcendent. And all this without knowing, or needing to know, the inner nature of the ultimate to which we believe that the religions are responding.

Putting all this in the first person, my innate religious instinct or nature has been elicited by the tradition into which I was born, namely Christianity, and I hold as a basic faith position that Christian experience is not purely imagination but is at the same time a response to a transcendent reality. Within Christianity we distinguish between authentic and inauthentic forms of religious experience by their moral and spiritual fruits in people's lives. I thus already have within my starting point both the belief in a transcendent reality and a criterion of the authenticity of human awarenesses of that reality. I then notice that the same would be true if I had happened to be born within any other of the great religious traditions. They also involve both the assurance of a transcendent reality and essentially the same criterion for the authenticity of human responses to that reality, namely a recentring in the Transcendent shown in increasing openness to others in love and compassion. I also observe that the different traditions produce, so far as we can tell, equally valuable effects in this recentring of life. It thus seems that within each of the world religions, including Christianity, people are responding more or less equally authentically (and of course, sadly, for the most part more or less equally inauthentically) to the Supreme Reality to which Christians are trying to respond. And that Reality could only be identified with the form in which it is known within one's own tradition by an imperialistic assertion of the unique superiority of that tradition, a superiority which is belied by the lack of superior transformative effects in human life.

It is important to note that to say that the Real is transcategorial is not to say that it is a blank, but that its nature lies beyond the range of our human concepts. For ineffability is relative to a cogniser or cognising community, in this case humankind. But can we not then at least say that, whatever its internal nature may be, it is *such that* it appears to us to be good rather than evil, loving rather than hating, wise rather than foolish, just rather than unjust? One can say this, but it would be importantly misleading. For good, loving, just, etc. are all human concepts which have their meaning only in the relationships between persons and groups of persons. What we should therefore say is that *our human nature* is such that the Supreme Reality appears to us, in our human terms, as good, loving, wise, etc. But why, then, do we believe that goodness, love, etc., rather than evil, hatred, etc., are the appropriate ways to think in our human terms of the Real? Because we believe that through our religion – whether it be Christianity, Judaism, Islam, Buddhism, Hinduism, Sikhism, Taoism, Baha'i, etc. – we are responding to transcendent Reality. From within the religious 'circle of faith' embodied in the great religious traditions[23] we therefore believe that some claimed responses to the Ultimate are more authentic than others – Christianity, Buddhism, etc. are more authentic than, for example, the Order of the Solar Temple with its murder and suicide rituals, or the Aum Shinri Kyo sect, who put sarin gas in the Tokyo underground system; and the criterion by which we say this is already given in our starting point within the great traditions themselves.

I am thus suggesting that we can best make sense of the global situation by distinguishing between the Ultimate in itself and our different culturally conditioned modes of conceiving and experiencing it.

I do not claim that this hypothesis is without its difficulties. For example, unitive mysticism claims a direct awareness of the Real in itself without the mediation of any human concepts; and I have indicated elsewhere why I think that what is being experienced is not the Ultimate in itself but one or another of its manifestations to human consciousness.[24] There is also the question, why assume that there is only *one* Real or Supreme Reality? As Ward has pointed out, it does not follow from the fact that the religions speak of an ultimate reality which is in its own inner nature ineffable that they are referring to the same ineffable reality. As he says in *Religion and Revelation*, one cannot move from 'Many religions believe in an ineffable Real' to 'There is an ineffable Real in which many religions believe.'[25] Indeed human religious experience, understood in the naïve rather than the critical realist way, points to there being many different gods and metaphysical absolutes – Jahweh, Vishnu, Allah, Shiva, the Holy Trinity, Brahman, the Tao, the Dharmakaya – each of which is said to be ineffable in its ultimate inner nature. As an explanation of this situation, polytheism, or poly-ultimatism, is clearly a theoretical possibility. But it seems to me to involve much greater problems than the hypothesis of one Ultimate Reality which is being differently thought and experienced through different religious conceptualities and practices. For how would the different gods be related to one another? Does the Holy Trinity preside over Christian countries, the Qur'anic Allah over Muslim countries, Vishnu and Shiva over different parts of India, and so on? But what about the many countries in which several different religions mingle? Even in my own city of Birmingham one can name wards in which the Holy Trinity is predominantly worshipped and others in which Allah is predominantly worshipped. It seems to me that the more one considers the possibility of multiple ultimates the less attractive it becomes as a religious interpretation of religion world-wide. However, in the end even the notion of 'one', as distinguished from two, three, etc., does not apply: the Ultimately Real is 'the one without a second'. But since we only have human language, it is less misleading to use 'one' than a plural number in referring to it.

This chapter has had two aims. The first is to express the very great appreciation and admiration which I share with many others for Keith Ward's work over the years, concentrating here on the problem of the relationship between the world religions. In this area he has, rightly, distinguished his own solution from others, including mine. The second aim of the paper has been to clarify the difference between us in this area. It boils down, I think, to the fact that he has offered a Christian theology of religions, whereas I hold that *any* interpretation of the global religious situation based on one tradition is bound to be inadequate. So on the one hand I hope that other theologians will follow Ward in opening their minds to the problem that he has faced, and will give it the same serious attention, taking the trouble to learn as he has done about the main alternative religious traditions. But on the other hand I also believe that there is another, and more radical, step that awaits both him and them.

NOTES

1   Keith Ward, *Religion and Revelation* (Oxford: Clarendon Press, 1994), 1.
2   Ibid., 324.
3   Ibid., 288.
4   Ibid., 289.
5   Ibid., 293.
6   Ibid., 301.
7   For those who give a negative answer to the basic epistemological question, that project is also on the philosophy of religion agenda, but as an optional topic. For them it is the thought experiment of seeing how religion could best be understood *if* human religious experience were – at least sometimes and in varying degrees – a cognitive response to a transcendent reality.
8   Although assumed as a premiss here, it has been argued for at length, e.g. in John Hick, *Faith and Knowledge*, 2nd edn (Ithaca, NY/London: Cornell University Press/Macmillan, 1966), pt 2; Richard Swinburne, *The Existence of God* (Oxford: Clarendon Press, 1979), ch. 13; William Alston, *Perceiving God* (Ithaca, NY and London: Cornell University Press, 1991).
9   Value-laden, that is, from our point of view and expressed in our human concepts.
10 Cf. Ward's 'Religion is primarily concerned with the transformation of the self, by appropriate response to that which is most truly real': *Images of Eternity* (London: Darton, Longman and Todd, 1987), 153.
11 Thomas Aquinas, *Summa Theologiae*, II/ii, 1, 2.

12   Ward points out that 'If I say, "There exists something of which I can say nothing", I have con-
      tradicted myself' since 'I am saying something about that of which I can say nothing': *Religion
      and Creation* (Oxford: Clarendon Press, 1996), 135. Concerning a postulated transcategorial
      reality we can of course make the purely formal statement that it is able to be referred to. This
      does not even entail that it exists, except notionally, nor if it exists does it indicate what it is
      like. And this not because it is said to be specifically not-loving, not-powerful, etc. but because
      these concepts simply do not apply to it, either positively or negatively – it is transcategorial,
      beyond the range of all our descriptive concepts.
13   Ibid., 133–4.
14   Ibid., 134.
15   Ibid.
16   John Hick, *An Interpretation of Religion* (London/New Haven: Macmillan/Yale University
      Press, 1989), 33.
17   Ward, *Religion and Creation*, 134 n. 11.
18   Hick, *An Interpretation of Religion*, 180.
19   As Ward said in an earlier book, but in a theistic and Christological context, 'If the question is,
      "How can a finite mind meet the infinite God?", the obvious answer is that some finite reality
      must mediate that infinity, in a way not inappropriate to our understanding': *A Vision to
      Pursue* (London: SCM Press, 1991), 79.
20   Hick, *An Interpretation of Religion*, 246.
21   I did however make the mistake, later repudiated, of giving Anselm's definition of God as 'that
      than which no greater can be conceived' as an example of a formal statement – which, as
      several critics have pointed out, it is not, since Anselm's God is defined as having all conceiv-
      able good attributes.
22   Ward, *Religion and Revelation*, 311.
23   I have confined the discussion here to the 'great world religions', but the same criterion applies
      to smaller and newer religious movements.
24   John Hick, *The Fifth Dimension* (Oxford: Oneworld Publications, 1999), ch. 15.
25   Ward, *Religion and Revelation*, 313.

4

Christ, Revelation and the World Religions: A Critical Appreciation of Keith Ward's Comparative Global Theology

GAVIN D'COSTA

I. INTRODUCTION

Keith Ward's contribution to the question of the place of world religions in Christian theology and philosophy of religions is extensive, creative and richly elaborated in at least six major book-length publications.[1] Ward's work reflects massive erudition and sympathetic familiarity with all the major world religions, in terms of their early 'scriptural' texts, main philosophical developments, and modern representations. In England, the only other writers to cover such a vast terrain in analogously constructive and systematic ways are Professors John Hick and Ninian Smart. Smart kept off the theological approaches in this area, while Hick squarely faces them and dismisses them for a number of considered reasons (outlined in his essay in this collection), advancing instead an allegedly neutral philosophical approach to the problem of making sense of religious diversity. Ward has offered robust criticisms of Hick's position, at times claiming there is a covert theism at work in Hick's allegedly neutral approach[2] and at times claiming that there is an indefensible agnosticism at the heart of Hick's project.[3] I think Ward is correct in both these judgements, but only in so much as they apply to different moments in Hick's project and in this respect, Hick's defence of his (present) position in the current volume as not theistic is plausible. Covert theism is only properly predicated of Hick's earlier work in this field, and indefensible agnosticism of his later developments.[4] But the difference between Hick and Ward, as Hick points out in this volume, also concerns methodology. For Hick, Ward does 'theology of religions' (what Peter Byrne, in his essay in the present collection, also accurately calls 'confessional inclusivism'). Hick argues that one should not approach the puzzle of the existence of many religions by privileging one's own religion, but rather one must stand back and propose a neutral theory which could be acceptable to all religions as an account of the religious life of all humankind. Byrne agrees with Hick's methodological starting point. Ward, not without moments of ambiguity, basically argues that confessional theology of religion is the approach for him, for he is a Christian committed to certain absolute truths regarding the nature of God, the ultimate human goal, and the way to it.[5] It is *within* this Christian context that Ward then seeks to affirm the varying truths of revelation within other religions to purify and develop his own Christian tradition, and to embrace and affirm the validity of other religions in specified ways.

There are a number of interesting questions that arise from the account given above. For example, is Ward actually on the wrong track doing 'theology of religions', rather than a neutral 'philosophy of religion' – as both Hick and Byrne suggest? This is the first question I will examine, and my answer will be that Hick and Byrne are actually doing confessional theology/philosophy and are far from neutral. This point relates both to formal methodology and the substantive contents of their doctrine of the 'Divine'. In this respect, Ward is undertaking a vital task. I do not presume to speak for Ward, and what follows is *my* response to Hick and Byrne. Secondly, if Ward is on the right track methodologically, are there basic confessional theological problems that are not properly resolved in Ward's project? Here my focus will be on 'revelation' and therefore Christology. I shall be arguing that while Ward's basic approach is internally coherent, it is not Christological and Trinitarian enough, and Ward appears to drive his project with a form of philosophical process theism. I will suggest that Ward's form of process theism pays little attention to the narrative doctrines of the Incarnation and Trinity and fails to justify properly Ward's account of 'revelation' in the world religions. These arguments, however, do not detract from my basic sympathy with Ward's project.

II. WHOSE NEUTRALITY? WHICH 'GOD'?

Hick's basic objection to Ward's theological approach is that it privileges one tradition at the outset, whereas what is required is the parity of all religions, based on grounds both empirical (they are all equally capable of acts of unselfish love) and epistemological (it is valid to base religious beliefs on one's experience, and this validity extends to all equally). Then, and only then, can we go about trying to explain how each religion may be granted 'validity'. Byrne's objections to Ward's methodological approach bring in additional factors, even if he shares Hick's concerns (as just outlined). Byrne argues that confessional theology must offer arguments for its own grounding. One might use apologetic arguments, showing why the claims made by one religion are true, and other claims are false. Or one might employ natural theology. Byrne argues that Ward cuts off these routes. The other route, when apologetics and natural theology have failed, is the Barthian fideist one, portrayed as relying on the inner truth of Christianity, guaranteed by the Spirit. This is a non-foundational stance. Ward dismisses this approach, arguing that Barth and Brunner falsely insist that 'reason cannot judge revelation, though they themselves judge all revelations and decide that the Christian is alone true'.[6] Hence, Byrne concludes that two problems are left unresolved in Ward. First, 'confessional theology does not appear to take seriously the problem that there are competing claims to revelation'.[7] Second, Ward's own starting point is not properly justified, and akin to that of Barth and Brunner, a starting point already dismissed by Ward.

In response to these types of criticisms, I wish to make two points – elaborated upon in detail elsewhere.[8] First, the terrain of options mapped out by Hick and Byrne should be contested. Hick and Byrne assume that there is a 'neutral' position, a position which is not biased or confessional or tradition-specific. (Ward himself seems, at times, to accept the concept of a neutral approach – but I shall leave this to one side.[9]) Despite the differences between Byrne and Hick, I would contend that they both belong to what Alisdair MacIntyre calls the tradition of 'liberal modernity' or the 'Encyclopaedic tradition', with its assumption of a neutral gaze which can, by the aid of reason, establish truth. MacIntyre argues that this is not a view from nowhere, but one whose historical genealogy can be traced to the Enlightenment: the presumption of universal reason, a refusal of the scandal of particularity regarding Christian revelation, and the primacy of the ethical, even though the latter is incapable of being given thick teleological specification.[10] My point is that Hick privileges a form of transcendental agnosticism, allied to modern western liberal social practices, from which to carry out a covert confessionalist analysis of the 'data' of religious plurality. This leads to his mythologising of *all* religions, such that any claims for final definitive truth are undercut and denied, and also to a methodological refusal to take *any* religion seriously *on its own terms*. The only tradition that comes out unscathed from this immersion in mythologising acid is Hick's own liberal transcendental agnostic modernism, which entails the privileging of his own tradition in his pluralist schema. Byrne's three minimal elements seem no different, especially as the third is an 'agnosticism toward, and therefore disengagement from, the specifics of any confessional stance toward religion'.[11]

Hence, the first point I want to make is that there is no confessionally neutral place from which to carry out the task of making sense of the diversity of religions. One might do this as a Marxist, a feminist, a materialist, a Christian, a Buddhist, a modern liberal with religious sympathies, and so on. It is simply not epistemologically or ontologically possible to occupy the sort of neutral 'high ground' that Hick and Byrne both presume to exist. Reason, practice and beliefs are always part of some existing, even if not unitary, tradition-bound way of relating to the world. I therefore want to conclude that Ward's confessionalism, formally speaking, or Buddhist, Muslim, etc. confessionalism, is the only legitimate way in which one might approach the question of religious pluralism.[12] The notion of neutral objectivity is bogus.

Second, when Byrne calls Ward to task for not properly grounding his position, in one sense he is correct and in another, possibly not. Byrne is perhaps wrong in assuming that the options are fideism (the purported Barthian strategy, which requires no justification from outside itself), natural theology (the use of pure reason to establish the truth), or apologetics (defined as 'proving' one revelation is right and the other is wrong). The Barthian position dismissed by both Ward and Byrne is criticised as undercutting all justification for revelation by claiming that reason cannot judge revelation. However, this is not in fact the Barthian position at all – at least on my reading. The mature Barth was not concerned to discount reason and its role in developing the intellectual coherence of Christian doctrine. He was simply questioning (and rightly so, from my MacIntyrean perspective) the claim that reason could be the arbiter of revelation per se, for reason could only operate within the context of the truth of revelation, such that faith seeks understanding and explication, a task that reason must aid.[13] Thus, from a MacIntyrean historicist Thomist position, it would be proper to argue that a Christian can be committed to the truth of her position, is able to give an account of those claims, and is able to do ad hoc apologetics. She can do the latter only in so far as she is able to show that the internal arguments of a 'rival' tradition are problematic, or that her own Christian tradition might better respond to unresolved lacunae in the other tradition within the terms of that other tradition. However, she has no a priori ability to show she is right and another wrong in terms that are acceptable to all parties. At this point, one must accept that there might be genuinely irreconcilable and differing starting points, authorities, texts, rules of exegesis, philosophical assumptions, and so on that shape each tradition, such that convergence of beliefs might be very difficult, if not impossible. Clearly, there is no a priori incommensurability, but real and potentially non-negotiable differences cannot be discounted. This is far from fideism, but it is also far from a type of correspondence theory of truth that assumes an objective vantage point from which to judge the 'fit' between a religion and the reality to which it relates. There is no such point, only the traditions from within which every enquirer works.

Hence, my second point is that Ward's position might well have the self-contradictory tendencies noted by Byrne (such that Ward criticises the Barthian starting point and then seems to adopt it, in another guise). Ward might well respond to Byrne's criticism and could do so, given that he employs a form of natural theology in other works without hesitation, a fact Byrne acknowledges.[14] However, in terms of the confessionalism I have been defending, I want to suggest that the notion of reason providing foundations for religious truth, as outlined by Byrne, is a requirement that is generated from a modern liberal foundationalism which has been called into question by many philosophers and theologians. This of course does not settle the issue, and there are forms of rationalist foundationalism in the Christian tradition. However, it does suggest that the problems have been construed in contestable ways by 'pluralists' such as Byrne and Hick. What I want to suggest is that the dichotomy between confessionalism and theology on the one hand and philosophy of religion on the other is untenable. I have sought to show that every position on the question of the significance of religious diversity contains an implicit tradition and deity (or absolute ontological commitment) in both formal and material terms.

Ward's project then is a good and methodologically feasible project, at least in the light of my attempt to rebut pluralist claims to the contrary. But what of Ward's project in terms of Christian confessional theology?

III. CHRIST, THE NARRATIVE OF GOD, AND THE QUESTION OF REVELATION

Ward's four-volume project in comparative theology raises the question: how is Christian theology and philosophy enriched by starting with the assumption that insight and wisdom are to be found in the world religions and modern science which might act as helpful correctives to Christian myopia? But this question presupposes that there is knowledge and insight within other religions that will have the *authority* to call into question the Christian tradition. This is in effect the sub-theme of Ward's *Religion and Revelation* and is worth looking at, for the theological strength or otherwise of his entire project depends on the contention that 'revelation' is to be found within the other world religions. Ward attempts to establish this contention in a somewhat a priori fashion. Rather than using the resources of the Christian tradition to establish his claim, he writes: 'It is not enough to accept the canon of Scripture just as it stands as the starting-point of theology. For we will not know just what is authoritatively contained in Divine revelation until we have first decided what the character and authority of that revelation is' (36). It would appear from this that one should look around and choose the most 'attractive' or 'authoritative' revelation, or idea of revelation, and this is confirmed when Ward later writes that the comparative theologian must look at the 'phenomena of alleged revelation [. . .] asking what the best model of Divine revealing action seems to be, in the light of them' (90). Here, as Byrne notes in his chapter, Ward seems to be a philosophical pluralist rather than a confessional theologian. It is not clear to me why one cannot start from the authority of one's own religious tradition, but to be fair to Ward, by the time he comes to the end of the book, there is no trace of this open-ended pluralist methodological approach, and that is also true throughout the subsequent volumes. However, this still raises the question of whether *Religion and Revelation* entirely succeeds in establishing the *theological* validity of the project on theological grounds. Ward seems to miss a splendid opportunity.

I would suggest that 'revelation' is a *sui generis* term formed and shaped by Christ and the Trinity, such that the word 'revelation' cannot be defined apart from this particular story and its performance within the community called the Church. What I am wanting to claim here might easily be misunderstood, so let me briefly make three points to clarify this way of seeing things. First, in saying that revelation is fundamentally Trinitarian I am simply saying that 'revelation' is not a generic term applicable to a range of different things, as 'machine' applies to a car, my computer, a bicycle and a stereo. Rather, 'revelation' theologically designates the reality of the self-disclosure of God who is Trinity: Father, Son and Holy Spirit. If something claims to be revelation, and is not the Trinity, then technically speaking it is not revelation, for it is not the self-revelation of God disclosed in Jesus Christ. Second, such a stipulation is not intended to limit the freedom of God, but rather safeguards the integrity of Christian theological language and practice *as well as* preserving the self-defined integrity of other religious traditions. The latter is achieved by making it clear that Christian theological description of other religions operates in a different framework from that of the self-descriptions found within those religions. It is not helpful to presume that our outsider theological description of another religion is congruent with the insider description of that tradition – although there is no reason a priori why it might not be so. Take for example the claim that revelation occurs in Buddhism. Given the logic of theological discourse, this is to claim that the Trinity is revealed in Buddhism. This is *manifestly not* what Buddhists think, even if this is what a Christian might see in Theravada Buddhism's powerful 'apophaticism' (some Christians have seen here the affirmation of the unknowable Father). Hence, the language rule regarding 'revelation' safeguards the integrity of the other religions in their own self-understandings. Third, in so much as 'revelation' is an intra-Christian term denoting the event of the self-disclosure of the triune God, then revelation in other religions (whatever that might mean, which we can leave genuinely open in so far as it does not contradict truth discovered in God's Trinity) is always an event that must transform Christian practice and theology anew. Hence, revelation is only revelation in so far as the Church is transformed in the process of this identification.

I hope it is clear that I am not wanting to limit or control God's self-revelation, which could only amount to worshipping a God made in our own idolatrous fixed image. God has chosen to act as she is in herself: Father, Son and Holy Spirit. The Spirit leads the Church into a deeper, more complex engagement with God, which cannot be a priori limited or predicted. It may well be the case that the Church discovers it must employ new models and new language to confess to the truth of God's self-disclosure and there is no reason why Advaita Vedanta should not play the role that Aristotle played for Thomas Aquinas. This process has already begun. But this process should not be confused with the notion that Advaita Vedanta per se is 'revelation', just as the early Church did not claim Aristotle's philosophy was revelation. Some of the Fathers saw the Logos's actions behind the wisdom of Greek philosophy, although they were nearly unanimous in condemning all forms of Greek religion.[15] Ward's position seems very close to this at times, as we shall see below, but at other times his use of 'revelation' vis-à-vis other religions has no Christological or Trinitarian anchor.

In *Religion and Community* we see this latter orientation very clearly. He writes:

> Part of the argument of this volume is that Christian faith is essentially a communal faith, but it needs to learn from its own history and from the history of other religious traditions the sorts of limits on power and authority that are needed to counterbalance the *repressive* tendencies which seem inherent in all human institutions. (4–5, my emphasis)

There is no longer an attempt to sift through all views of community and come up with a synthesis of the best, without giving any one of these priority. But there still remains the question: 'repressive' by whose account? The candid answer is found a few lines later: 'in a sense there is here an apologia for a Protestant interpretation of Christianity that is found in, but not restricted to, the Anglican Episcopal church' (5).

If we take this as Ward's starting point we can now move to some further questions regarding Ward's comparative theology project. I have three questions, none of which necessarily call into question Ward's project, but rather require clarification that will, I believe, help advance his important goals. First, there is a decided ambiguity about the role of Christology in Ward's approach. In *A Vision to Pursue* Ward's Christology was decidedly close to that of Hick's, seeming to abandon entirely ontological claims of any sort regarding the divinity of Jesus Christ and presenting Jesus as a sometimes badly mistaken charismatic prophet rather at the mercy of historical criticism.[16] *Religion and Revelation* presents a seriously revised Christological position, in my opinion, despite Ward's comment that it only contains 'small amendments' to his earlier book (240 n. 75). In *Religion and Revelation* Ward argues that historical criticism is untenable in a strong sceptical form, offering an impressive critique of Van Harvey (247–58). Here Ward argues that theological readings must be hermeneutically tempered with 'trust' in the Gospel witness and must take into account the predisposition of the interpreter. Ward then goes on to say that Jesus was sinless and, following the testimony of the apostolic Church, thereby unique in the history of humankind. On this basis Ward defends a high ontological Christology, affirming Jesus to be a unique incarnation of the Word such that the Word is 'identical' with Jesus the human subject. This is exciting, though too brief (two pages of discussion on the meaning of identity), but it allows Ward to proceed to claim that 'Jesus alone, by the grace of God, is both uncorrupt and united to Divinity' (264), and regarding the two natures: 'Their perfect union is the foreshadowing of the future fulfilment of all humanity in the Divine Life' (267). All this serves to correct the impression of *A Vision to Pursue*, but it is difficult to find this high ontological view of Christ *integrated* into Ward's doctrine of God. In other words, the narrative specificity of God's Trinity is not given in Ward's project through thick Christological description, but rather in terms of process philosophy.

In *Religion and Creation* Ward is able to develop an elaborate doctrine of God's action in the world entirely apart from Christology which draws heavily, but critically, on process philosophy. Here Ward develops and defends his earlier position in *Rational Theology and the Creativity of God*.[17] His language about divine action in other religions is not anchored in his high Christology; rather Ward employs words which affirm the truth of their claims in terms of their 'creativity', their 'dynamism' or their 'intrinsic value'. These latter phrases tend to obscure the ontological relation of the 'Word' to these religions and the 'Word' to God in a way that calls for clarification. Are these religions, or parts of them, of intrinsic value, or is their value found in their fuller illumination of the reality of Christ? Or in my earlier terms, are their own self-descriptions revelatory or rather, is it Christian theological description that brings this to light? This problem is rather well represented in a statement made in *Religion and Revelation*: 'being set on the way to salvation does not depend on holding Christian beliefs; but being ultimately saved will depend on acceptance of the basic truths about Christ as Divine self-revelation' (317). Is Ward here subscribing to the traditional *praeparatio evangelica*, as the quote would imply? This takes him far from the soft pluralism that Byrne detects in his position.

Furthermore, it is not clear to me whether Ward would defend an *exemplary* Christology or a *constitutive* Christology. Those holding an exemplary Christology usually view Jesus as an example of holiness, even if the best example. This allows that other religions may also have different examples, possibly varying in degrees of holiness. Hence, these Christologies tend to be non-incarnational. Those holding constitutive Christologies usually insist that prior to Jesus Christ we did not know the meaning of holiness, for in this man, God's self-revelation is made, ontologically and uniquely, a historical event. Hence, constitutive Christologies tend to generate high incarnational Christologies. A clarification on this point from Ward would help because his manner of relating the insights of other traditions often seems to promote an exemplary Christology, which would also account for Ward's lack of Christological description of these traditions. In my view, only a constitutive Christology is capable of resisting pluralism, for only a constitutive Christology refuses to accept the notion that we might have equally plausible but varying descriptions of the world (religions), and the Christian description is the 'best' (confessional inclusivism) or the liberal transcendental agnostic is the best (another version of confessional inclusivism) in terms of a sliding scale. Instead, constitutive Christology requires that this Trinitarian description of the world constitute the world, in a *sui generis* manner, that requires the theological reading of all religions and creation, not in the fashion of a grand imperialistic ideology, but in endless conversation and engagements, whose outcome cannot be predicted.[18]

A second area of questioning revolves around the goal of Ward's project. At times it would appear that he aims at purifying Christian theology of its repressions and perversions. However, at other times, Ward's project seems oriented towards producing a doctrine of God that is 'broadly acceptable to all four traditions [i.e. Judaism, Christianity, Islam and Hinduism].'[19] This latter is akin to Ward's occasional lapses into philosophical pluralism. Please note, I am not denying such commonality, but rather want to resist a theology of religions that has such a goal as its aim. Let me elaborate on this. In *Religion and Creation*, after looking at the doctrine of God and creation in Heschel, Barth, Iqbal and Aurobindo, Ward argues rightly that

> all modify their classical traditions by stressing the affectivity, creativity, relationality, and temporality of the Divine. For all the differences of their scriptural sources, they agree in seeing the Supreme Being as creatively powerful, wise, expressing goodness in relational love, affectively knowing, and blissful. (342)

Now it is one thing to see various overlaps and relationships between these different thinkers which can allow for interesting avenues to be further explored, but quite another to move from there to a position which suggests: (*a*) that these different doctrines can be extricated from their scriptural mooring and social practices; and (*b*) that the synthetic commonality drawn together by one Christian thinker (Ward) should be 'broadly acceptable' to the different traditions. Ward is far too sophisticated to buy into either (*a*) or (*b*) in any naïve sense, but the rhetoric of his position often pushes him into such corners. He acknowledges openly that the positions he deals with are abstracted from the social realities of their practice and that religions are characterised by immense internal diversity.[20] So why does Ward suddenly move to the notion that his synthesis might be 'broadly acceptable' to four different religious traditions – and why should that be important? I think the answer lies in a simple theme that runs throughout these four books: Ward seeks to develop and defend a form of *theism* which is basic to all theistic traditions and is then shaped differently by the various traditions. Crudely put, it is a type of natural theology which then moves on to revelatory theology as a second rung on the ladder of truth. Instead of narrating Christ as the doctrine of God, Ward's strategy seems to narrate God on the basis of differing conceptions of the divine reality found in the different religions, and as a result, this theistic reality then makes its appearance in Christ. This would also reflect the indecision in Ward's work between a constitutive and an exemplary Christology. My sense that Ward is an exemplarist who has his doctrine of God in place prior to Christ is also confirmed in the conclusion of *Religion and Creation*, where Ward summarises his contribution:

> religious faith, in its theistic form, may be understood, not as an irra-
> tional leap into the unknown, or as a satisfaction of some purely
> emotional needs, but as a reasoned commitment to seek personal union
> with a reality of supreme value and power, which gives to the universe
> and to sentient lives within it objective purpose and significance. (346)

Note the dissolution of all language about the Word, the identity of the Word with Jesus Christ, and the self-revelation of 'God' in Jesus Christ. It is precisely the Incarnation that wrecks traditional 'theisms', for it is the reality of the God-man, not theism, that generates the definition of 'God', 'revelation' and 'human' and defines God as *Trinity*. In other words, Ward's desire to affirm such commonalities as 'theism' lies first and foremost in his advancing the project of natural theistic theology, which appears to be independent of 'revelation'. This might amount to nothing more than the fact that Ward is more a process theist than a Trinitarian and Christologically focused Christian thinker. However, it is precisely this 'fact' which seems unclear, but important in understanding the implications of Ward's comparative theology project.

My final question takes up an invitation from Ward: it is a response to his project from one who is in a different 'religious' tradition, albeit a Roman Catholic Christian. I offer these comments as a way of indicating the significance of thick description regarding 'revelation' and its ecclesial character, and to pursue my earlier point regarding what constitutes 'repressive' tendencies. Ward deals with Roman Catholicism in *Religion and Community*, chapter 10. Ward argues against the Roman Catholic view of community as expounded by Thomas Aquinas. Ward takes issue with Aquinas on two counts: Thomas's view of salvation outside the community of the Church, and Thomas's view of the hierarchical nature of the Church. While his depiction of Thomas is accurate, he makes two highly contestable claims regarding 'repressive' tendencies within the Roman Catholic community per se which make it a deformed community. First, he claims that the doctrine of 'no salvation outside the Church' (*extra ecclesiam nulla salus*) is held with such minor qualifications (i.e. excluding those in 'invincible ignorance' and those who have an 'implicit desire for faith' but are not baptised) as to make the qualifications almost useless (260). Second, he asserts that these qualifications 'never become enshrined in a normative teaching' (ibid.). So Ward argues that the Catholic Church is wrong, as it enshrines a false view of its salvific exclusivity.

This analysis is factually incorrect, for in 1949 the Holy Office plainly stated that 'no salvation outside the Church' was *not* to be taken as a literal statement about Hindus or Buddhists (or Anglicans for that matter). Rather, it referred to the more fundamental claim that all salvation, wherever and whenever it took place, was through the grace of the triune God who revealed himself in the revelation entrusted to the Church. Hence, in so much as a person was not culpably rejecting the truth of Christ (invincible ignorance), and was following the good through the grace of God (possibly within their own religion), that person could not be excluded from salvation, for they were seen to have an *implicit* desire for membership of the Church, even though they were not baptised members. This certainly does not mean a salvific equality of religions. This document from the Holy Office was aimed at Fr Leonard Feeney, who had insisted that 'no salvation outside the Church' referred to the fate of Hindus, Buddhists and Protestants. Ironically, when Feeney refused to retract his comments, he was formally placed outside the Church. He was excommunicated. This definition clarified 'normative' teaching. Elsewhere I have tried to show that historically, the *extra ecclesiam* doctrine was never technically applied to non-culpable non-Christians and therefore could never be properly understood in a literal and negative manner.[21] This teaching has been developed explicitly in Vatican II and post-conciliar documents. Ward cites the Vatican II teaching that only those who explicitly know that the Church is the means to salvation and reject it cannot be saved.[22] He calls this a 'virtually platitudinous statement' (251). In effect it is simply reiterating Thomas's distinction between culpable error and invincible ignorance. The force of my concern is that Ward seems to put a lot of weight on his critique of the exclusivity of the Roman Catholic community when that community is not committed to such a view. Hence, some of Ward's urgent concern to develop a Christian approach which is not so exclusive is deeply misplaced.

The second of Ward's points is more serious and while it is summarised in the word 'hierarchy', it actually consists of two elements. First, Ward contests the doctrine of papal authority and secondly, he denies that the kingdom of God is exemplified in a 'group of elderly, unmarried men [who] make all the important decisions and exercise a monopolistic power over ultimate entrance to or ejection from salvation' (261). His critique is from the vantage point of 'anyone who prefers an alternative vision of the church as a set of egalitarian and participatory communities' (ibid.). I am perplexed because I am not alone amongst Roman Catholics who would find themselves in agreement with many of Ward's criticisms and would still defend the notion of papal authority (for there are very many understandings of this, and Ultramontanism is not the only one, as Ward seems to suggest) and the notion of a clerical hierarchy (while agreeing entirely with Ward's protest at the exclusion of women from the priesthood – if that is what Ward's critique of exclusively celibate men is aimed at). Furthermore, the type of liberationist approach he champions is hardly alien to the Roman Catholic tradition.

I am not claiming that the Roman Catholic Church is in no need of reform. It is in desperate need of it. But I do want to ask whether Ward's vision can move forward if it takes, as a test case, Anglican–Roman Catholic relations so lightly. Can one begin to imagine a wider inter-religious ecumenism in the light of Ward's treatment of intra-Christian differences? A more important point is that the *extra ecclesiam* tradition only developed to safeguard the constitutive nature of salvation that took place in the Incarnation, such that 'revelation' could only be properly anchored in that historical triune event. The reality of that event transforms all creation.

In the latter part of this chapter, I have sought to ask theological questions and seek clarification from Ward on certain important issues within his overall project. They are questions from one who remains grateful for, and in awe at, Ward's considerable achievements in this area.

NOTES

1   Most recently in the tetralogy on comparative theology (all Oxford: Clarendon Press): *Religion and Revelation* (1994), *Religion and Creation* (1996), *Religion and Human Nature* (1998) and *Religion and Community* (2000); and previously, in the more philosophical and pluralist *Images of Eternity: Concepts of God in Five Religious Traditions* (London: Darton, Longman and Todd, 1987), followed by the more theological and clearly pluralist *A Vision to Pursue* (London: SCM Press, 1991).

2   See Ward, *Religion and Creation*, 133–4.

3   Keith Ward, 'Truth and the Diversity of Religions', *Religious Studies*, 26 (1990), 1–18.

4   See my *Theology and Religious Pluralism* (Oxford: Blackwell, 1986), 22–51.

5   Ward, *Religion and Revelation*, 279–80.

6   Ibid., 21.

7   Peter Byrne, 'Ward on Revelation: Inclusivism or Pluralism?', this volume, 13.

8   Gavin D'Costa, *The Meeting of Religions and the Trinity* (Edinburgh: T&T Clark, 2000), 1–52.

9   See Gavin D'Costa, 'Whose Objectivity? Which Neutrality? The Doomed Quest for a Neutral Vantage Point from which to Judge Religions', *Religious Studies*, 29 (1993), 79–95, and Ward's response in *Religion and Revelation*, 319–24.

10 See Alisdair MacIntyre, *After Virtue*, 2nd edn (London: Duckworth, 1985), and *Three Rival Versions of Moral Enquiry* (London: Duckworth, 1990).

11 Byrne, 'Ward on Revelation', 19.

12 I say 'Ward's confessionalism, formally speaking' because in substantive terms my own confessionalism differs from his in a number of ways. Ward specifically criticises my approach in *Religion and Revelation*, 319–24. I have tried to give more specificity to my confessional position in *The Meeting of Religions and the Trinity*, 19–52 and 99–142.

13 Karl Barth, *Church Dogmatics*, vol. I, pt. 1, tr. G. W. Bromiley, 2nd edn (Edinburgh: T&T Clark, 1975), 3–24.

14 Byrne, 'Ward on Revelation', p. 13, ll. 11–12.

15 See Chrys Saldanha, *Divine Pedagogy: A Patristic View of Non-Christian Religions* (Rome: LAS, 1984).

16 Keith Ward, *A Vision to Pursue* (London: SCM Press, 1991), 49–117.

17 Keith Ward, *Rational Theology and the Creativity of God* (Oxford: Blackwell, 1982).

18 See D'Costa, *The Meeting of Religions and the Trinity*, 99–172.

19 Ward, *Religion and Creation*, 342.

20 See, for example, Ward, *Religion and Community*, 3.

21 Gavin D'Costa, '"Extra ecclesiam nulla salus" Revisited', in Ian Hamnett (ed.), *Religious Pluralism and Unbelief* (London: Routledge, 1990), 130–47, in which references to the Feeney affair are to be found.

22 'Lumen Gentium', art. 14: Walter M. Abbott (ed.), *The Documents of Vatican II* (London and Dublin: Geoffrey Chapman, 1966), 32–3.

5

Religion and the Revelation of Value: The Emotions as Sources for Religious Understanding

MARK WYNN

[A] revelation which can call forth such a passionate commitment must be more than a set of theoretical truths proposed for our assent. It must enshrine a disclosure of a value which can override all selfish desires and all competing values.

Keith Ward, *Religion and Revelation*, 30

[W]hat is most important is to bring out the distinctive character of religious commitment; to make clear that it is neither some sort of irrational leap of blind faith nor some compelling inference. It is a matter of fundamental vision and response[.]

Keith Ward, *Images of Eternity*, 161–2

Of the many rich themes in Keith Ward's writings there is one that I have personally found particularly nourishing, namely the idea that religious commitment is to be understood in terms not only of belief but also of 'feeling', or in Ward's terms, the idea that such commitment is not a matter simply of 'theoretical truth' or 'compelling inference' but also of 'passionate commitment' and 'disclosure of value'. In this chapter, and in a spirit of tribute to Ward's own explorations in this field, I would like to consider one way in which recent philosophical discussion of the emotions may help to corroborate this general theme. Specifically I shall be interested in the tendency in recent writing to take feelings, as distinct from thoughts or judgements, as contributing to the intentionality of the emotions. I begin by outlining three such approaches, before considering their implications for our understanding of feeling and belief in religious contexts. The general thesis of this chapter is that feelings are intentional in their own right, and accordingly are not mere add-ons to the religious life, but integral to its cognitive significance.

I. SOME RECENT THEORIES OF EMOTION:
FINDING A ROLE FOR AFFECT

In philosophical circles, it has been customary for some time now to think of the emotions as differentiated from one another by virtue of the thoughts which they embody, where these thoughts give rise, at least sometimes, to a bodily response, the awareness of which constitutes the feeling component of the emotion. Following this model, we might suppose that grief, for example, is constituted by the thought that one has suffered some loss, together with a felt response to this thought which involves pain rather than pleasure. Accounts of this kind treat the emotions as intentional on account of the thoughts of which they are formed and, accordingly, they tend to represent the feeling component of the emotion as a kind of addendum, which lacks any intrinsic intentional significance: in so far as the emotion is about anything, this is due to the thoughts that are integral to it, where these thoughts are understood as in themselves feelingless. Summarising this general approach, Geoffrey Maddell comments: 'A dominant view of emotion has been that emotions are essentially evaluations which cause certain bodily changes, and it is our awareness of these which constitutes feeling.'[1] On this sort of view, the felt component of an emotion is assimilated to sensation, in so far as it has to do with awareness of some bodily state, though it remains distinct from mere sensation to the extent that it owes its origins to thought or judgement, rather than mere sensory stimulation.

Several recent treatments of the emotions have sought at least to qualify this model, on the grounds that feelings can themselves be directed towards the world, independently of judgements or beliefs. In the first section of this chapter, I shall set out three such accounts, before building on these accounts to present three models of how the emotions may serve as sources of religious understanding.

John Deigh has argued that the shift towards the thought-based conception of emotion that I have just outlined was underpinned by a concern to acknowledge the intentional character of emotional states.[2] But the belief that this was best achieved by conceiving of the emotions as constituted of thoughts rested, he suggests, on an idea that was assumed rather than established, namely the idea that affects cannot be intentional in their own right. Deigh challenges this idea on various grounds. For example, he distinguishes between being sensible of something and having a concept of it. A person may be sensible of sharps and flats, for instance, while lacking any concept of half-steps in a diatonic scale.[3] (Evidently, on this account, having a given concept involves more than the ability to discriminate things which fall under the concept: what matters for concept possession is the ability to articulate the relevant distinctions in general terms, and perhaps in terms of a certain sophistication.) Developing this thought, Deigh proposes that in 'primitive' contexts, the emotions of fear, horror and disgust can be adequately differentiated from one another without invoking the idea that different concepts and associated thoughts are in play in each case. The differentiae of these emotions are given, he suggests, not by any thoughts of which they are composed, but in immediate experience. Hence he remarks:

> Roughly speaking, one feels fear at what is scary, horror at what is gruesome, and disgust at what is foul. These properties characterise the way things look, sound, taste, and smell. [. . .] the important point is that the scary differs from the dangerous in being at least sometimes a true or direct property of the way something looks and sounds. Something that looks dangerous is something one can infer is dangerous from the way it looks, whereas one need make no inference to see that something looks scary.[4]

On this view, the feelings of being scared or horrified are, at least sometimes, targeted at the world directly, that is, independently of any conceptually articulated judgement about its character.[5] By contrast, to recognise something as dangerous is, presumably, to insert it within some larger causal context, by recognising how it might bring about harm, and thereby to move beyond the immediate phenomenology of one's experience.

A critic might respond that in cases such as these, we should suppose that it is a feelingless perception that engenders the feeling of being scared, so that the intentionality of the emotion resides in the perception, and not in the feeling. If this objection involves the idea that we do not recognise the object as scary, but recognise it as something else, and are thereby caused to feel scared, then Deigh will surely say that this is false to the phenomenology of our experience. As he says, scariness is at least sometimes a 'direct property of the way something looks and sounds'. Alternatively, we could take the objection as saying that while we recognise objects as scary, we do this independently of feeling, so that feeling again lacks any intrinsic intentional significance. But on this point, Deigh will presumably appeal once more to the phenomenology of our experience: in at least some cases, our recognition that something is scary is realised in an affectively toned perception of the thing, and not in a non-affective appreciation of its scariness which then gives rise to the feeling of being scared.

There is one further element of Deigh's discussion that bears on our current concerns. He notes that, to some extent, 'primitive emotions' such as fear and disgust may be responsive to reason. For instance, as a child develops it will in the normal case learn to differentiate the harmful from the merely scary, and the rotten from what is merely foul, and as a consequence the sensory presentations associated with scariness and foulness may lose some or all of their power to excite an affective response. In such cases, the model of the emotions as constituted by thoughts will come to apply after all, in so far as fear, for example, is constituted by the thought of danger, and not by some direct, affectively toned apprehension of an object's scariness. However, on occasions, Deigh observes, emotions prove relatively impervious to reason (think for example of lust), and sometimes they seem to combine both reflection and an element of affectively toned perception (think for example of romantic love).[6] In the latter case, we might suppose that feeling can retain its status as intrinsically intentional even when embedded within a larger emotional complex which depends in part for its character on conceptualisation or judgement.

Here then is one line of thought which lends support to the thesis of feeling's intrinsic intentionality. Geoffrey Maddell has endorsed this same thesis for rather different reasons.[7] Maddell takes issue with the suggestion of Eduard Hanslick and others that music may give rise to feelings but not emotions, since it lacks any intentional object. This suggestion seems to involve once more the idea that the emotions are necessarily intentional, and that their intentionality cannot be understood by reference to their status as feelings. As Hanslick puts it, music evokes at most 'an indefinite state of mind' (one which fails to be targeted at an object or state of affairs).[8] Maddell also opposes those critics of Hanslick who allow that music is capable of evoking emotions, but add that these emotions are unusual in being objectless or mood-like. Against both of these views, he maintains that the appreciation of music typically involves feelings of tension and correlative desires for resolution, and that these affective states pick out an object independently of any thought or evaluation:

> hearing the dominant seventh evokes a desire, and sometimes something akin to a longing, for its resolution. That is a state of consciousness directed to an intentional object; it is also an affective state of consciousness. It is *not* the entertaining of an evaluation which (magically) leads to certain bodily disturbances. One may, if one is so disposed, regard the desire for the tonic resolution as ground for the evaluation that such a resolution would be 'a good thing', but it would be a total distortion to suppose that the desire, or the longing, *is* an evaluation, one which inexplicably leads to certain physical effects. It is a mode of 'feeling towards' its intentional object.[9]

Here again we can imagine a critic proposing that the intentionality of the emotion is rooted in perception: it is hearing that identifies the music's character, and feeling is then engaged as a consequence of that perception. In reply, Maddell might appeal to considerations similar to those cited earlier on Deigh's behalf: he could argue that this is false to the phenomenology of our experience, which involves an affectively toned perception of 'tension' in the music. And in keeping with the passage just cited, Maddell would presumably say that the affective state of consciousness he is describing is anyway targeted at a 'resolution' which is not (as yet) accessible to sense perception.

Maddell extends this account to cover the emotions in general. In all cases of emotion, he maintains, including emotions which are structured in terms of thoughts, there is an element of feeling-towards. On this view, my fear of a stock market crash will be constituted in part by my thought of the stock market crashing, but also in part by my feeling-towards this event in the requisite way. On this point, Maddell's approach seems to differ from Deigh's, since Deigh concentrates on the case where an emotion's object is picked out independently of any 'concept' or thought, and his suggestion that feelings are intrinsically intentional remains undeveloped outside of this context.

I would like to introduce one further account of these matters before turning explicitly to the question of the emotions' role in religious contexts. In his book on the emotions, Peter Goldie maintains that feelings have an intentional content which is not reducible to that of the beliefs or desires with which they may be associated.[10] Hence like Deigh and Maddell, Goldie is also opposed to the 'add-on' theory of emotion. He suggests, for example, that before falling on ice, a person may well have an intellectual grasp of the dangers presented by ice; but afterwards, they will appreciate its dangerousness in a new and richer way. Resisting the add-on theorist's construal of this development, he writes:

> Coming to think of it in this new way is not to be understood as consisting of thinking of it in the old way, plus some added-on phenomenal ingredient – feeling perhaps; rather, the whole way of experiencing, or being conscious of, the world is new [. . .]. The difference between thinking of X as Y without feeling and thinking of X as Y with feeling will not just comprise a different attitude towards the *same* content – a thinking which earlier was without feeling and now is with feeling. The difference also lies *in* the content, although it might be that this difference cannot be captured in words.[11]

Here it is suggested that what is revealed in feeling may not be fully intelligible in any other way. This thought marks a departure from the models of Deigh and Maddell. Their concern, it appears, is simply to establish the possibility of feeling carrying intentional significance in its own right. Goldie is advancing the more ambitious claim that this sort of intentionality may offer our only mode of access to certain kinds of intentional content.

Goldie makes the same sort of point by means of other examples. For instance, he notes how a visitor to a zoo might understand in a purely intellectual way that the gorilla before her is dangerous, and might also understand in a purely intellectual way that its cage door is open. But apprehending this state of affairs affectively is not merely to grasp the same content in a new, affectively laden way, but to be related to a new content, albeit one that is most naturally reported in the same terms (the gorilla is dangerous and able to escape). It is noteworthy that in this example (as in the example of falling on ice) Goldie maintains that affects are revelatory of danger; by contrast, Deigh draws a sharp distinction between the recognition of danger and of scariness, seeing only the second as requiring the intrinsic intentionality of feeling. But these accounts need not be in competition with one another. Deigh's interest is in the possibility of affects operating independently of any conceptualisation, whereas Goldie seems to be interested in the possibility of affects adding to the intentional content already grasped by way of conceptual thought (where this addition may escape verbalisation). It is significant that in Goldie's examples, the further content that is embedded in the feeling component of the emotion has to do with helping us appreciate the character of our circumstances in existential terms: it is action-guiding content, which enables us to respond to the world in ways that are practically appropriate.[12]

Next I want to apply these three accounts of the intentionality of feelings to the question of the emotions' relevance in religious contexts.

II. FEELING AND BELIEF IN RELIGIOUS CONTEXTS

The theories we have been considering seem to carry somewhat different implications for the character of religious understanding, so I shall consider their import in this connection by examining each in turn. Deigh's account of the inherently intentional quality of feeling turns on the idea that certain 'primitive' emotions may be realised in various feelings-towards the world which are free from any conceptual grasp of its character. This suggests the possibility of apprehending a religious content prior to any verbal articulation of that content. There are various understandings of religious belief which might be related constructively to this thought, but I shall confine my comments to one author. Here is his profession of the idea that feeling is the source of religious belief:

> I do believe that feeling is the deeper source of religion, and that philosophic and theological formulas are secondary products, like translations of a text into another tongue. [. . .] When I call theological formulas secondary products, I mean that in a world in which no feeling had ever existed, I doubt whether any philosophic theology could ever have been framed.[13]

This is, of course, the voice of William James. Elsewhere James gives rather more precise form to the idea that 'theological formulas' are 'secondary products', for example in his proposal that metaphysical outlooks such as idealism or materialism arise from a prior affective response to the world. He describes the idealist in these terms:

> At [*sic*] this very day, all sentimental natures, fond of reconciliation and intimacy, tend to an idealistic faith. Why? Because idealism gives to the nature of things such kinship with our personal selves. [. . .] To say that the universe is essentially thought, is to say that I myself, potentially at least, am all. There is no radically alien corner, but an all-pervading *intimacy*.[14]

Here James suggests that a metaphysical belief may follow on from an affective apprehension of the world's significance, where the belief serves to represent the world in terms that legitimise this initial, affectively laden sense of things. Hence to take James's example, for a person of appropriate affective orientation, idealism will ring true in so far as it represents reality in terms that suggest the appropriateness of a feeling of intimacy towards the world.

James does not specify the conceptual structure, if any, of the emotions which serve to ground metaphysical and religious world-views, though it is implied that these emotions do not depend for their intentionality on the technical concepts which are embedded in the world-views to which they give rise. Deigh's account provides one way of giving further definition to James's discussion on this point. Following Deigh, we may say that certain qualities can be apprehended in states of feeling and independently of any conceptualisation or judgement. Extending this thought beyond what Deigh himself envisages, we may add that where such feelings are deeply entrenched in our experience (if they recur, for example, or prove unusually enduring), then they will identify the world as, say, scary or an object of intimacy in some relatively pervasive way.[15] And for the reasons cited by James, feelings of this sort may in turn help to generate a metaphysical world-view. I am not proposing that James's remarks on intimacy and other such feelings as the sources of world-views depend for their plausibility on precisely this explication, according to which feelings of this kind operate independently of any conceptualisation. But at any rate, Deigh's model suggests one way, a particularly radical way, of spelling out more exactly how feelings may run ahead of any developed, conceptually articulate metaphysic.

Deigh's model involves one further notion which may help to shed light on the relationship between the globalised feelings James postulates and the metaphysical world-views which he takes to be grounded in those feelings. The supposition that there is some such relationship has an obvious counterpart in everyday life; for we often come to think of our circumstances in ways which help to make an already established emotion seem rationally appropriate. As Robert Stocker notes, states such as anger and self-pity can be mood-like, and accordingly 'they seek out and collect, even create, sustaining or concordant facts (or "facts"), which they then use to justify and sustain that emotion, which then leads to further seeking, collecting, creating and coloring'.[16] This way of putting the matter suggests, of course, that the beliefs which arise out of our prior affective commitments may be little more than rationalisations. There is, however, a more benign interpretation of the power of affective states to generate beliefs. Take for instance Ronald de Sousa's proposal that the emotions can play a role akin to that of scientific paradigms: 'paying attention to certain things [as we do when our emotions are engaged] is a source of reasons, but comes before them. Similarly, scientific paradigms, in Kuhn's sense, are better at stimulating research than at finding compelling and fair reasons for their own adoption. They are too "deep" for that, too unlike specific, easily formulated beliefs.'[17] Here too we find a conception of the emotions as in some way prior to belief and the giving of reasons. This suggests that deep-seated affects of the kind postulated by James and others may be regarded as supra-rational: they do not merely generate rationalisations of themselves, but help to establish something like a research programme of metaphysical dimensions, one which is at least prima facie innocent, since we need some such programme to provide an initial orientation in the world, in the light of which our more specific enquiries can get started.

At this point, we can appeal once more to Deigh, to give further definition to this broadly Jamesian account. Drawing out Deigh's comments on romantic love and the idea that growth in understanding may condition our felt responses, we should suppose that the relationship between a primal affective stance and articulated belief may well prove to be two-way: such a stance may help to engender a certain metaphysical conception of the world, as James supposes, but the metaphysic, as it is developed in the light of conceptual and evidential pressures, may then sponsor new forms of feeling in its turn, and feeling and theory may react back on one another in this sort of way over and over, until some sort of equilibrium is reached. Sometimes this interplay may involve an attenuation of feeling, rather as the feeling of being scared by something may be eroded once we have developed a richer, conceptual account of its nature; but in other cases, it may be a matter of feeling being deepened and refined.

In these various ways, then, Deigh's theory suggests an understanding which gives to feeling a primary, generative role in religious contexts, while also allowing a role for belief and the giving of reasons. And accordingly, his model offers one way of articulating Keith Ward's proposal that religious thought is to be understood against the background of a non-discursive, affectively structured disclosure of value.

Goldie's examples of the caged gorilla and falling on ice suggest that affects may play a part in relating us to the world existentially, so that the bearing of our environment on our well-being is appreciated not in purely cerebral terms, but in ways that help to elicit an appropriate behavioural response. This approach recalls some recent work in ethics which has emphasised the role of affective responses in giving salience to certain aspects of our environment, and helping thereby to direct our conduct.[18] For instance, Rai Gaita writes of how some psychiatrists with whom he once worked strove to live up to the idea that their patients were fully their equals. However, the superficiality of their understanding was revealed one day when a nun visited the ward:

> In her middle years, only her vivacity made an impression on me until she talked to the patients. Then everything in her demeanour towards them – the way she spoke to them, her facial expressions, the inflexions of her body – contrasted with and showed up the behaviour of those noble psychiatrists. She showed that they were, despite their best efforts, condescending, as I too had been. She thereby revealed that even such patients were, as the psychiatrists and I had sincerely and genuinely professed, the equals of those who wanted to help them; but she also revealed that in our hearts we did not believe this.[19]

The implication of this account is that the nun's behaviour is grounded in something she believes 'in her heart' – and it is because the psychiatrists lack this affectively toned appreciation of their patients' significance that their conduct falls short of hers, whatever high-minded beliefs they may formally and sincerely profess. Moreover, Gaita goes on to suggest that an adequate recognition of the value of such people as these patients depends upon the revelatory force of affective responses of this kind (or less directly, upon the behaviour of people, such as the nun, whose actions speak of that sort of response).[20]

In Goldie's terms, we could make this point by saying that the nun's affective response to the patients implies a different and richer content than any which can be captured by verbal means, so that even when the psychiatrists sincerely profess the equal worth of their patients, they fail to grasp what is revealed in, and only in, such an affective apprehension of their worth. In turn, this suggests one way in which Goldie's model can be applied to the question of feeling's role in religious contexts. For if we follow mainstream Christian teaching in supposing that my relationship to God is internally related to my regard for my neighbour, where this regard is to find expression in action, then it becomes at any rate intelligible to suppose that a person's religious life may depend for its fulfilment upon the quality of their felt responses to other people, where these responses pick out a content that cannot be specified in purely verbal terms.

This model is somewhat different in its implications from Deigh's. Here it is not so much that feeling provides a pre-theoretical orientation from which beliefs may spring. In fact, the psychiatrists in Gaita's example already have a fairly sophisticated credal understanding of their patients' worth, but this understanding falls short – and, on Gaita's view, necessarily so – of what is revealed in feeling. So on this account, feeling's part is not so much to invite articulation or legitimisation in credal terms as to identify a content deeper than any which can be expressed in such terms. Hence this model and Deigh's model provide rather different ways of expounding the fundamental role in religious contexts of affect in relation to belief, but both point towards a broadly Wardian understanding of the importance in such contexts of 'passion', 'vision' and the 'disclosure of value'.

Deigh's approach allows us to accord a measure of independence to feeling vis-à-vis belief, in matters of religion, by thinking of feeling as coming before belief. It is striking that certain other accounts achieve this same effect by thinking of feeling as coming after belief. For example, there is a well-known tradition of spiritual formation, common in Catholic circles at least until the middle years of the twentieth century, which represents the spiritual life as a progression that begins with discursive forms of thought and culminates in a state of wordless, affective contemplation. (In general terms, this transition corresponds to the movement from the purgative to the illuminative and then to the unitive phase of spiritual development.) Expounding this tradition in a standard spiritual handbook of the early years of the twentieth century, Adolphe Tanquerey writes that as souls develop, they 'experience great difficulty in making their mental prayer in a purely *discursive* fashion' and accordingly 'the Holy Ghost inspires them to give less time to considerations and more to affections and petitions'.[21] On this view, the will or the heart is accorded an intentionality which is distinct from that of the intellect. In Tanquerey's words, 'The will attains its object in a manner different from that of the mind: the latter knows an object only according to the representation [. . .]; the will or the heart tends towards the *object* as it is *in itself*.'[22] Hence not only can the heart be directed towards an object independently of any verbal representation of that object, but this kind of directedness is superior, as befits a later stage of spiritual development, since it points towards the object as it is 'in itself'. However, it is worth emphasising that on this general approach, the soul is only ready to cultivate a wordless, affective relationship to God once it has mastered a more discursive understanding of God and God's relationship to the world.

Goldie's model offers one way of making sense of this proposal: what is revealed in these mystical states of feeling eludes, and runs deeper than, what can be articulated in verbal terms. However, Goldie's model provides no direct counterpart for the idea that feeling's role is to complete what has been understood initially by verbal means. Maddell's account of feeling's role in our appreciation of music suggests a more direct parallel with Tanquerey's scheme on this point. As we have seen, Maddell suggests that as a person listens to a piece of music, feeling may direct her towards a 'resolution' which has yet to be consummated in experience, but which is identified by way of her desire and longing in the present. By analogy, we could suppose that instruction in Christian doctrine (of the kind that Tanquerey takes to be required before we can progress to a non-discursive, affectively toned apprehension of God) may engender certain desires for fulfilment, where these desires pick out the object of that fulfilment (God himself) by means of an intentionality that is distinct from the kind of intentionality that is characteristic of 'representational' thought. This leaves open the question of why this non-representational intentionality should be taken to be superior. Again, Goldie's model offers one response to this question, but alternatively, to persist with the musical analogy, we might suppose that just as we may be able to identify the character of the music's resolution in abstract musicological terms, and independently of feeling, so we may be able to identify the object of our religious fulfilment in abstract, doctrinal terms, and independently of feeling; but in the musical as in the theological case, it might be said, such an apprehension of fulfilment is qualitatively inferior to one which consists in an affectively toned apprehension of its character.

Perhaps it will be objected that in Tanquerey's account the emphasis falls upon God as closely related to the believer (after all, the state he is describing belongs to the unitive stage of a person's relationship to God), whereas this model suggests that our mind is directed to God as one who is removed from our experience. However, even in Tanquerey's scheme, our relationship to God falls short of what will be possible in the beatific vision, and accordingly we may suppose that even on his scheme, there remains an element of longing. So, tentatively, I suggest that the understanding of affect that is found in the tradition represented by Tanquerey can be explicated, in part, within the framework of Maddell's theory: just as in the case of musical appreciation, where feeling is able to take us beyond a certain sensory input so as to pick out a reality that is not yet fully revealed in sensory terms, so in relationship to God, we might suppose, feeling is able to take us beyond a certain doxastic input, to relate us to a reality that has yet to be fully revealed in doxastic terms.

III. CONCLUSIONS

In this chapter, I have tried to show how Keith Ward's characterisation of religious commitment as grounded in 'passion', 'vision' and a 'disclosure of value' resonates with certain themes in recent philosophical discussion of the emotions. The upshot of this discussion is perhaps that modern secular philosophy is rediscovering, in its own terms, and in a variety of ways, a truth that has long been understood, at least implicitly, in religious practice, namely, that in some cases at least, affects are intrinsically intentional. We have seen that this idea can find expression in a number of ways in religious contexts. We may think of feelings as offering a pre-conceptual appreciation of the world's significance, which may then be elaborated in credal terms (as suggested by Deigh's model), or as a way of grasping an intentional content (of a value-laden, action-guiding kind) that cannot be grasped in purely verbal terms (drawing here on Goldie's model), or as a way of moving beyond what is given in sensory or discursive terms, so that our attention is fixed on some as yet unrealised consummation (here applying Maddell's model). These approaches offer different, though compatible, accounts of the relationship between feeling and belief in religious contexts. But together they point to the thought that just as affects should not be considered as mere add-ons in a theory of the emotions, so they ought not to be considered as mere add-ons in any developed account of the religious life. On this last point, I would like to suggest, Keith Ward is importantly and perceptively right.[23]

NOTES

1 Geoffrey Maddell, 'What Music Teaches about Emotion', *Philosophy*, 71 (1996), 76.
2 John Deigh, 'Cognitivism in the Theory of the Emotions', *Ethics*, 104 (1994), 824–54.
3 Ibid., 840.
4 Ibid., 842.
5 Some commentators have taken all perceptual experience to have this character, where what is given is in principle distinguishable from any conceptualisation of that given. See for example William Alston, *Perceiving God* (Ithaca, NY: Cornell University Press, 1991), 27, 37–9.
6 Deigh, 'Cognitivism in the Theory of the Emotions', 851–2.
7 Maddell, 'What Music Teaches about Emotion', 63–82.
8 As quoted ibid., 63.
9 Ibid., 78, emphasis in the original.
10 Peter Goldie, *The Emotions: A Philosophical Exploration* (Oxford: Oxford University Press, 2000).
11 Ibid., 59–60, emphasis in the original.
12 There is an interesting parallel here with the role Antonio Damasio gives to 'somatic markers' in guiding action: see his *Descartes' Error: Emotion, Reason and the Human Brain* (London: Picador, 1995), ch. 8.
13 William James, *Varieties of Religious Experience* (Harmondsworth: Penguin, 1982), 431.
14 William James, 'The Sentiment of Rationality', in William James, *Essays in Pragmatism* (New York: Hafner Press, 1948), 20–1, emphasis in the original.
15 For a defence of the possibility and importance of such feelings, see Quentin Smith, *The Felt Meanings of the World: A Metaphysics of Feeling* (West Lafayette, Ind.: Purdue University Press, 1986).
16 Robert Stocker with Elizabeth Hegeman, *Valuing Emotions* (Cambridge: Cambridge University Press, 1996), 94.
17 Ronald de Sousa, 'The Rationality of Emotions', in Amélie Rorty (ed.), *Explaining Emotions* (Berkeley: University of California Press, 1980), 139.
18 See for example Lawrence Blum, *Moral Perception and Particularity* (Cambridge: Cambridge University Press, 1994), 32.
19 Rai Gaita, *A Common Humanity: Thinking about Love & Truth & Justice* (Melbourne: Text Publishing, 1999), 18–19.
20 Ibid., 21.
21 Adolphe Tanquerey, *The Spiritual Life: A Treatise on Ascetical and Mystical Theology*, tr. Herman Branderis, 2nd edn (Tournai: Desclée et Cie, 1930), 455, emphasis in the original.
22 Ibid., 654, emphasis in the original.
23 I am very grateful to the Editor and Professor Peter Byrne for helpful comments on an earlier draft of this chapter.

Part II
CREATION

6

Creation and its Alternatives

DAVID BROWN

In the second of his volumes on comparative theology Keith Ward tackles the theme of creation. In that work he contends that incoherence results from the type of interplay between freedom and necessity employed by some contemporary theologians.[1] If I understand him aright, Ward's own position is that, while there remains a divine openness to the future that leaves many of the world's specific forms as yet undetermined, Christianity may well need to concede a necessity in the divine nature that leads to the initial creative act as such.[2] Rather than engaging directly with Ward's own position or his criticism of others, what I would like to do here is examine the terminology commonly employed by Christian theologians to discuss creation and its alternatives. My hope is to illustrate how in general the contrasts are not nearly as sharp as often supposed, and thereby provide some indirect confirmation for Ward's more limited moves in this direction.

In rough, the conventional Christian claim can be characterised as the view that the world originated from divine will without necessity, and it is a world that is therefore wholly distinct from him, and upon which he is in no sense dependent. Emanation, pantheism, monism and immanence are all thought to threaten such a contention in one way or another. But how far is this so? In my view modern discussion usually stops too soon, as though each of the terms had a single, precise sense, whereas in fact their varied historical applications suggest not only a quite different account of the matter but also significant overlaps with what are often portrayed as uniquely Christian emphases. Inevitably, given my competence, most of my examples will come from the western tradition.

I. CREATION AND EMANATION

'Emanation' stems from the Latin verb *emanare*, which means 'to flow' or 'pour out'. Here God is conceived of as somewhat like a bubbling cauldron of infinite being, so rich in abundant existence that he overflows into progressively lesser levels of being until the lowest possible level of such reality is reached. A serious competitor to Christianity in the later patristic period, the Neo-Platonism of Plotinus (d. 270), envisaged the divine One flowing out into the Divine Mind and that in turn into the World Soul and so the material world being eventually generated. Although the extent of the influence of such a triadic structure of divinity on the doctrine of the Trinity can be contested, what cannot be disputed is that at least within the Godhead Christianity developed a notion closer to emanation than to creation, and so it would be wrong to see emanation as an entirely alien concept. Likewise, the later influence of Neo-Platonism ensured that emanation also played a role within Islam and Judaism. If Avicenna (Ibn Sina) provides an example from Islam in the eleventh century, a famous example from Judaism is the thirteenth-century Kabbalistic document, the Zohar. Here the world is depicted as a flame from the divine coal and as the divine garment beneath which God will be found. If the imagery could be read as pantheistic, attention to the wider context indicates that it is emanation which is being explored.

So far as contrasts with creation are concerned, these may be considered under three heads: the necessity of the process, the connected theme of the absence of a personal dimension, and the alleged negative consequence of divinising nature. Necessity in this context is, I think, often misunderstood. For, though emanation certainly implies the necessity of the world, it does not in fact make it necessary to God's existence. That is to say, the world only exists in virtue of the fact that it has flowed out of God, but God himself (or the One) is held to be complete even apart from this overflow. God's perfection is held to be infinite and so nothing is lost through the overflow: a finite sum taken from an infinite still leaves an infinite sum. An analogy sometimes used (though the physics is erroneous) was that of the sun and its rays: light pours out, but takes nothing away from its source. It would certainly, therefore, be unfair to criticise the view on the grounds that it detracts from the aseity or independence of God and so undermines the traditional definition of him as that upon which all else depends, himself depending on nothing. It is worth observing that in this respect at least emanation is quite unlike pantheism or even the proposal of many modern Christian theologians who posit some requirement on God's part to create the world based on reciprocal notions such as love or expressiveness.

Even so, some find the kind of necessity postulated less than satisfactory. In the course of suggesting that making and emanation should be treated as complementary models of creation, John Macquarrie sums up what he sees as emanation's principal advantage and disadvantage: it avoids the impression that creation could be considered like an arbitrary act, but it does this by moving too far in another direction and suggesting that creation is like a natural process.[3] But can the issue be decided quite so summarily? Is there not something distinctly mythic in the Christian assumption that God might have to make a decision about such a matter? Even in the human case we think that there is something defective in a person's character or goodness if he has to think before he does some good deed – for instance, tell the truth. With God that oddness would seem still further heightened, not least because the most obvious reasons for legitimate hesitation in our case, uncertainty about the quality of the end or the best means to achieve it, are clearly absent in his case. Again, pure generosity is usually polluted in our case by the need to resolve to act (to let down our self-defences), whereas God surely has no such need to steel his resolve.

So, if it is good that the nature of one's being should be shared, one might argue that it is not only natural but even inevitable that it should be shared. Indeed, so plausible is this argument that, so far from patristic theology rejecting it, it was actually accepted but confined to within the Godhead itself in accounts of the Trinity, though with one key modification in the claim that the effects (the Son and the Spirit) could be as great as their cause.

Some, though, may protest that I am still missing the heart of the issue, which is the absence of a personal dimension as compared with the stress on will in the creation model, however mythically this may be expressed in terms of actual decision-making. By way of response two key factors must be stressed. The first is that, although historically emanation has tended to exclude the personal, its application to the Trinity shows that this is not inevitable, while even where the personal is excluded it should be noted that (as in Neo-Platonism) this is because it is believed that there is a higher form of reality than the personal beyond the divisions and pluralism of decision-making. So from that perspective the problem only arises because Christianity is too anthropomorphic in the way it customarily speaks. Then, secondly, emanation presents itself as appealing to a higher justification than any need for reciprocal or experiential love. If personalised, the ground lies in the generosity of pure gift; if expressed impersonally, in the overflowing riches of the inexhaustibility of divine being. So there is no lack that needs filling as in so much contemporary Christian exposition; instead, a fulfilled being gratuitously shares its being.

Finally, we come to what is often regarded as the crunch objection, that emanation divinises the world. This is an objection which will need to be considered in more detail when we turn to pantheism. But for the moment two observations may be made. The first is that, though in confining emanation within the Godhead there were undoubted gains in securing human independence and responsibility within this world, Christianity also paid a price in that it raised the very question of the intelligibility of God's relation to matter, if it is indeed something totally other than himself. Significantly, in trying to circumvent this difficulty, Karl Rahner seems to come close to an emanationist model: 'Theologians proceed from the assumption that absolutely everything that is not God is created by one and the same God. [. . .] Materiality must be understood as the lowest stage of this spirit. [. . .] Otherwise, materiality cannot be conceived as originating from an absolute spirit, since this spirit cannot create something that is absolutely disparate from itself.'[4] If Christian theologians are seldom quite so explicit, the more common focus on divine expressiveness in matter betokens a similar kind of anxiety.

If such concerns argue for matter not being totally other than God, equally nothing necessarily follows which requires matter to be of great religious significance, far less divine. For, if Plotinus was as a result led to defend the goodness of the material world, this certainly did not prevent him from according it a very lowly status.[5] Indeed, it is worth observing that emanation of itself tends to generate a quite different kind of spirituality from pantheism. For it declares that, though the world derives from the being of God, the best clue to his nature involves, not as in pantheism turning towards the world in awe and wonder, but rather away from that

world and towards the higher levels of divine existence, not in themselves constituted by the world. So, instead of celebrating the presence of God in a flower, for
instance, the recommendation becomes that one should try to strip off the world, to
retreat into one's own spiritual core, so that thereby one can achieve identity with
what God is most like when unencumbered by the world, and so we have Plotinus's
famous phrase describing what is involved – 'the flight of the alone to the Alone'.[6]

II. PANTHEISM AND PANENTHEISM

Rather surprising to relate, 'pantheism' as a term originated during the deist controversy. One leading advocate of the deist, non-interventionist God, John Toland, first
used the word in 1705 in one of his lesser works, *Socinianism Truly Stated*. Four years
later it was taken up by one of his critics, and henceforth the term passed into
common use, Toland himself in 1720 publishing a work entitled *Pantheisticon*, a
pagan celebration of the identity of God and the world. Literally the term means 'all
is God' or 'God is all', but to use the term in that wide sense would, I think, fail to
draw out significant differences which exist between what is now most commonly
acknowledged as pantheism, a celebration of the world as divine as in Toland's
original use, and variants such as emanation, where 'God is all' but by no means
confined to the world. Under such a narrower definition – the equation of God and
the world – perhaps the most obvious modern example would be New Age
theology's equation of our world with the goddess Gaia or 'Mother Earth'. But of
course the phenomenon is much older than this. The Romantic poets and the early
Schleiermacher with their ready equation of the Universe, the All and God must also
be seen in the same light, as must the philosopher whose rediscovery by Lessing
ensured the popularity of pantheism in the late eighteenth and early nineteenth
century, namely Spinoza. His famous formula, *Deus sive Natura*, could scarcely be
more unequivocally pantheistic, the Latin *sive* as distinct from *aut* indicating the
absolute indifference of whether we refer to Nature or God, both alike having extension and thinking predicated of them. Stoicism (rather than Platonism in any of its
forms) then becomes the most obvious classical version.

Widely adopted in contemporary theology as a response is the notion of panentheism. So it is worth noting its earlier history. First coined by a now-forgotten
theologian, K. C. K. Krause (1781–1832), to describe his own system, the term was
intended to imply that (compatible with pantheism) the being of God includes and
penetrates the whole universe, so that it all exists in him but that (incompatible with
pantheism) nonetheless the divine being is more than and not exhausted by the
universe. Putting it at its simplest, the universe is part of God but not the whole of
him. It is a term which has been enthusiastically adopted by process theologians to
describe their own approach, and clearly it does this quite well, as one of their
favourite analogies is to suggest that the world should be viewed as God's body,
distinct from but interacting with the divine mind. However, with so many modern
theologians abandoning the classical attributes of God which guaranteed his
independence of the world it is clearly a term capable of much wider applicability.

It is a conception with which, for instance, John Macquarrie declares that he 'has a good deal of sympathy',[7] but Jürgen Moltmann is perhaps the best example of a contemporary theologian employing the term. In *God in Creation* Moltmann explicitly endorses its use while attacking the process theologians' denial of *creatio ex nihilo*.[8] Even so it is not clear that he has completely disengaged himself from his earlier Blochian Hegelianism in *The Theology of Hope*, according to which focus on the existing created order was seen as an endorsement of the status quo, and so God's involvement had therefore to be tied exclusively to the world's future rather than its past.[9] In an intermediate work he had declared: 'If God is love, then he does not merely emanate, flow out of himself; he also expects and needs love; his world is intended to be his home. He desires to dwell in it.'[10] If Moltmann is more cautious in his choice of language in *God in Creation*, the same basic sentiments continue,[11] and it is significant that even in more recent work it remains unclear in what sense God is really independent of the world, since God's Trinitarian life is held to be intimately bound up with the future of the world, and that world, it is held, will, though transformed, never in fact end.[12]

It is therefore all the more surprising that he is so severe in his criticisms of both process theology and Schleiermacher, for what seems in dispute is a matter of degree and not kind, in as much as all three abandon divine aseity for some notion of divine dependence on the world. In the case of Schleiermacher, it is often suggested that the later *Christian Faith* represents a decisive move away from the earlier pantheism of the *Speeches*.[13] Certainly, gone is the more explicit use of 'the Universe', 'the Whole' and 'the All' of the earlier work. Yet creation is still in effect reduced to preservation,[14] while the relevant divine attributes are analysed as expressive simply of the way the world is. So, for instance, omnipotence is cashed out purely in terms of the actual causal laws of the universe rather than the potentiality of God to do otherwise: 'since divine omnipotence can only be conceived as eternal and omnipresent, it is inadmissible to suppose that at any time anything should begin to be through omnipotence; on the contrary, through omnipotence everything is already posited which comes into existence through finite causes, in time and space.'[15] Again, omniscience is analysed out into what he calls 'the absolute spirituality of divine omnipotence', by which he appears to mean that, so far from ascribing to God knowledge of all potentialities and their implications, it is a matter of believing that the actual totality of causes in the world is not just a matter of 'a lifeless and blind necessity'.[16]

Yet, if we turn to ask what it is that might make the panentheism of Moltmann acceptable and the pantheism of Schleiermacher not, it is hard to see what it is that really divides them, apart of course from the more sympathetic use of the latter word by Schleiermacher. To illustrate how Moltmann's objections reduce to caricature, let me measure them against a very early version of pantheism: Stoicism.[17] Moltmann objects that pantheism 'makes everything a matter of indifference' because all things become God; he suggests that 'if there is no creation in the beginning, there cannot be a new creation either'; and he objects to the resultant 'divinisation of the world'.[18] But, like Schleiermacher, Stoicism in fact claimed a larger, decisive significance for the pattern of natural causation as a whole, detecting in it certainly a necessity but a necessity based on an inherent divine principle, the Logos or Reason, and indeed its advocates were prepared to go rather further than Schleiermacher in a 'panentheistic' direction in their insistence that the activity of the Logos should not be too closely identified with this present world but rather with a number of such recurring worlds (or new creations). One notes too that the resultant spirituality can scarcely be said to have led to the worship of nature. Rather, respect was due to all nature as part of a cosmic design, with, however, some aspects more closely reflecting the Divine than others, in particular human beings. Even human beings, though, were expected to accept a cosmic purpose larger than themselves. It is thus possible to speak of a transcendent dimension to Stoicism, and indeed this is reflected in its most famous religious work, Cleanthes' 'Hymn to Zeus'.[19]

One suspects that in contemporary theological writing there is a tendency to equate pantheism too quickly and too readily with popularised forms of the sort found in Romantic poetry or New Age writing. The reality, I suggest, is otherwise, with pantheism and panentheism not only on a sliding scale but sometimes the latter further from classical Christianity than the former. Intriguingly, Moltmann himself elsewhere uses the terminology of divinisation for his own views,[20] while at times one finds him speaking of a degree of divine dependence on the world that would be rejected in at least some versions of pantheism: 'from eternity God [. . .] wanted to communicate himself to the one who is other than himself [. . .]. That is why the idea of the world is already inherent in the Father's love for the Son.'[21]

III. MONISM AND DUALISM

Monism might seem initially too remote from the concerns of Christian doctrine to merit consideration here. Why very much the reverse is so will emerge shortly, but first some brief remarks on the history of the term. It was invented in the eighteenth century by Christian Wolff, the populariser of Leibniz, as a way of characterising the two opposed theories of idealism and materialism, that is to say the view that everything is mental and the view that everything is material. It then came to be widely used of the *Identitätsphilosophie* of Schelling and Hegel in the next century, with their claim that matter and mind are ultimately identical, Schelling for instance describing matter as 'congealed spirit'. Put like this it need not of course be a religious claim at all; thus Marx's turning of Hegel's philosophy on its head could equally be described as monism, though in his case it is the reduction of all reality to matter. As such Marx and Hegel, despite the enormous religious difference between them, could philosophically be set on one side as monists with Descartes on the other as a typical dualist, someone who believes that the mental and the material are fundamentally two different kinds of reality.

But in considering the range of options regarding God's relation with the world, it will be more helpful to narrow the definition somewhat. We may say that religious monism is the view that nothing exists except a single (non-dual) divine reality; in other words we have a monism that not only chooses between mind and matter but also insists that all of the one or the other is God. On such an analysis most forms of pantheism would not in fact be monistic since their exponents are content to speak of the world as exhibiting the features of both spirit and matter. There would, however, be some exceptions. Thus Spinoza would certainly emerge as a monistic pantheist since on his view all reality is reducible to a single substance, matter which thinks. Similarly, this would hold for Stoicism, since on its view only matter exists, though with the proviso that only one form of matter is quintessentially divine (fire).

So there will be an overlap with pantheism. Nonetheless the analysis does offer a great gain. For in general monism does suggest a very different form of piety from pantheism. Thus while Schelling in his writings did take nature seriously, it is hard not to detect in Hegel's analysis the conviction that it is just an insignificant element on the way to the true realisation of *Geist* or Spirit, as this works itself out in the history of the human consciousness. It is a contrast which emerges with equal force if we turn to an eastern variant in the ninth-century Hindu philosopher Sankara. Brahman is the only true reality, in relation to which the plurality of material phenomena must be seen as illusory. To use his analogy, we perceive what we take to be a serpent, but it is in fact a rope. Clearly none of this is compatible with according a high value to the variety of the world, in which the typical pantheist so often takes delight.

Much the same might be said of Muslim versions. Since in the following passage Sufism is analysed as monism yet distinct from pantheism, it is worth quoting:

> The basic doctrine of Islamic mysticism, which later came to be termed Oneness of being, and which western scholars term monism, is implicit in the divine name al-haqq (truth, reality). [. . .] If God alone is absolutely real, God alone *is*, whence the term Oneness of Being. But this does not mean that God is the sum of all existing things [. . .]. That would be pantheism, whereas on the contrary [. . .] the doctrine of the Oneness of being means that appearances are deceptive and that each apparently separate object is, mysteriously, nothing other than the indivisible plenitude of the absolute, infinite and eternal truth.[22]

I hasten to acknowledge that such an analysis does not apply to all versions of Sufism, al-Ghazali's bridge to orthodoxy being for instance very different from the position of al-Hallaj or Rabi'a.

Nowadays hostility to dualism is a common theme in Christian theology. What is meant, though, is not dualism in general but the perceived negative influence of Platonic dualism in diverting historical Christianity from the biblical view of human beings as psychosomatic unities and towards a narrow emphasis on soul that despised enmattered reality. I have not the space to indicate why I think such an account unfair to Platonism. More relevant in any case to note here is the way in which such discussions usually bypass a far more important issue, namely the principal reason why Plato and his successors moved in that direction. Because of the not implausible Greek principle that like can only know like, it was thought essential to place human beings at least in part on the side of divine and thus of immaterial reality. Nor has Christianity been immune from such considerations in its earlier history. One might think of the philosophies of Berkeley or Malebranche, or indeed the way in which both Protestant and Catholic theology moved towards giving dogmatic endorsement to belief in the immortality of the soul.[23]

Nor has this principle been absent in materialistic monism. If Tertullian is a rare example of a Christian theologian willing to think of God as material, Stoicism adopted the principle wholesale. It is all too easy to give short shrift to their notion of the divine as fire and forget the neurons firing in our brain that make such a thought possible. Like Plato, it was an attempt to ensure continuity and thus connections between the human and the Divine. So, when engaging in dialogue in the modern world with eastern religious systems that are monistic, our first thought should not be that crucial distinctions are dissolved (though sometimes this is so), but rather the importance of that underlying religious motivation, the desire to make links possible between ourselves and the Divine.

IV. TRANSCENDENT AND IMMANENT

The above reflections can perhaps be most conveniently brought together under the contrast between transcendent and immanent. For contemporary theology often uses these two words to demonstrate what is supposedly unique about Christianity, that it portrays God as both transcendent and immanent. But no less than the terms discussed above, these too are in fact quite slippery. Literally, they should mean that God is 'beyond the world' and that he 'remains within it', yet as an immaterial being he clearly does not quite do either, being equally related to all places as to none. So in talking of the Christian God's transcendence to the world one must guard against supposing that really more has been said than is in fact the case, for, as I have tried to indicate above, without endorsing *creatio ex nihilo*, emanation through its hierarchy of divinity offers a greater sense of transcendence than Christianity, while without having a God beyond the world both pantheism and monism can still sometimes succeed in ensuring the transcendence of deity, in the directional control of the whole over its parts.

As that last sentence indicates, though, meaning can still sometimes be conveyed without explicit definition. But it is important to note that the process often conceals hidden ambiguities. Thus in this case if the transcendence of emanation is one of lack of involvement (the world is not the result of any 'interest' on the part of the One), clearly with pantheism this cannot be so; rather, in the nature of the case there is inevitably considerable interaction, but still with the divine element remaining in overall control (at least in versions such as Stoicism). But, equally, immanence should not be assumed to entail some sort of dependence simply because the Divine is now portrayed as being 'within' the world. So, for instance, however widely believed in the past, all would now agree that the immanence of eucharistic presence should not be seen as subject to human control. Indeed, given our own situatedness within the world, any knowledge of a transcendent reality will inevitably be heavily dependent on immanent action. A purely interventionist model may well sometimes be appropriate (as in a conventional reading of miracles), but its very occasionalism would force God to the margins if left on its own. So, not surprisingly, other sorts of appeal are commonly made, but what is seldom noted is their heavy prior dependence on immanence. Take, for example, appeal to conscience summoning the individual to a radically new and challenging form of conduct, or to the experience of wonder before the majesty of an awe-inspiring landscape.[24] Conscience is in fact an 'inner' prompt, while even mountains and seas only function in this way in virtue of the immanent reality they are. Apart from the inevitably highly episodic intervention, any acknowledgement of transcendence would, therefore, seem to be inescapably parasitic on a prior immanence. So the fact that the Transcendentalism of mid-nineteenth-century America turns out to constitute a strong claim to immanence is not as absurd or paradoxical a notion as it may first appear. Mediated through Kantian 'transcendentals', it simply carries further Kant's insight into the extent to which all experience is conditioned by the way the world is.

V. CONCLUSION

Long before process theology, J. R. Illingworth had suggested that we get our sense of immanence and transcendence from our own relation to our bodies, as both intellectual spirits and active through matter. In his case the suggestion was deployed as a means of offering a curt dismissal to deism, pantheism and monism.[25] But the way in which half a century later process theology could use the same image to justify its panentheism illustrates well how slippery all these terms can be. None of this is intended to argue for rejection of the traditional Christian doctrine, but it is to suggest that contemporary theologians often 'win' the discussion too easily, forgetting that others with quite different views can be no less subtle than themselves. It is the great strength of Keith Ward's own innovative work on comparative theology to insist that great care should be taken not to misrepresent rival views, and instead due acknowledgement should be given of the vitality and complexity of positions different from characteristically Christian options, yet sometimes much closer than an initial, casual look might suggest.[26]

NOTES

1   Keith Ward, *Religion and Creation* (Oxford: Clarendon Press, 1996), 177–9 (criticising Paul Fiddes).
2   For the former, see ibid., 236–8, 257–61; for the latter, ibid., 224–5 and, more tentatively, 319–21 (cf. esp. 320).
3   John Macquarrie, *Principles of Christian Theology* (London: SCM Press, 1966), 200–5, esp. 201.
4   Karl Rahner, *Theological Investigations*, vol. xxi (London: Darton, Longman and Todd, 1988), 34–5.
5   See Plotinus, *Enneads*, II, 9 for the former (his attack on the Gnostics); for the latter, e.g. *Enneads*, II, 4, 16.
6   Ibid., VI, 9, 11.
7   John Macquarrie, *In Search of Deity* (London: SCM Press, 1984), 54.

8   Jürgen Moltmann, *God in Creation* (London: SCM Press, 1985), 72–103, esp. 78–9, 98, 103.
9   Jürgen Moltmann, *The Theology of Hope* (London: SCM Press, 1967), 42–5, 84–94. What worried Bloch and Moltmann was the type of natural theology which seemed to imply a given, unalterable blueprint.
10 Jürgen Moltmann, *The Trinity and the Kingdom of God* (London: SCM Press, 1981), 99; cf. 58.
11 Moltmann, *God in Creation*, 79–86.
12 Jürgen Moltmann, *The Coming of God* (London: SCM Press, 1996), 267–79.
13 For Schleiermacher's own hesitant comments, see *The Christian Faith*, ed. H. R. Mackintosh and J. S. Stewart (Edinburgh: T. & T. Clark, 1928), 38–9 (§8, postscript 2); for a strong assertion of the counter-view, making good use of the *Dialektik*, see Richard Brandt, *The Philosophy of Schleiermacher* (Westport, Conn.: Greenwood Press, 1968; 1st publ. 1941), 232–52.
14 Schleiermacher, *The Christian Faith*, 142–56 (§§36–41) and 170–84 (§§46–7), esp. 143 (§36, 2).
15 Ibid., 212 (§54, 1).
16 Ibid., 219 (§55, 1). While both passages could be read in a manner compatible with classical theism, this seems to me unlikely as an interpretation, for not only does Schleiermacher nowhere use the language of the traditional formulae, it is also part of his overall strategy to ensure experiential understandings of all aspects of Christian doctrine.
17 For an excellent collection of relevant texts in both Greek and English, see A. A. Long and D. N. Sedley, *The Hellenistic Philosophers* (2 vols.; Cambridge: Cambridge University Press, 1987), §§43–55 in both vols.
18 Moltmann, *God in Creation*, 78, 79, 103.
19 For both the original Greek and an English translation, see C. A. Trypanis (ed.), *The Penguin Book of Greek Verse* (London: Penguin, 1971), 283–5.
20 Moltmann, *The Coming of God*, 272–5.
21 Moltmann, *The Trinity and the Kingdom of God*, 108.
22 Trevor Ling, *A History of Religion East and West* (London: Macmillan, 1968), 295, emphasis in the original.
23 It was declared a dogma of the Catholic faith at the Fifth Lateran Council in 1513, while it was also included in the Calvinist Westminster Confession in 1646.
24 In *Painters of Faith* (Washington, DC: Regnery, 2001) Gene Veitch interprets nineteenth-century American landscape in artists such as Thomas Cole and Frederic Church as a Calvinist expression of divine transcendence at the opposite pole to the immanent mediation of saints and miracles in Catholic Baroque, forgetting that the landscape is no less a mediator: cf. 13–34, 82–3.
25 J. R. Illingworth, *Divine Immanence* (London: Macmillan, 1898), 65–72.
26 I am grateful to Tom Hamilton and Ann Loades for help with an earlier draft of this chapter.

7

How May We Compare Ideas of Transcendence? On the Method of Comparative Theology

HENK VROOM

I. INTRODUCTION

How might we legitimately compare different ideas of transcendence and draw valid conclusions about the similarities, differences and contradictions that exist among them?

The reflection of thinkers from various religious traditions forms the subject matter of comparative theology, and these reflections in turn must be understood against the background of the rituals and holy texts of those traditions. Practically speaking, this implies that most comparative theologians are quite heavily dependent on the work of other specialists: Islamologists, Indologists, Sinologists, Africanists and others. However, those of us who wish to compare different religious beliefs also need to face some methodological questions. In order to make comparisons, we must first establish what should be compared. As far as ideas of eternity are concerned, we should first decide what is truly analogous between respective traditions. To designate the category that includes ideas of God, the Divine, emptiness, *ch'i*, etc., I prefer the term 'transcendence'. This category may be viewed as a kind of empty receptacle in which to collect a variety of ideas that we consider worthy of comparison – although, following certain other scholars in this field, I will also refer to God, the Real and eternity. In using these terms, I am not suggesting that in the end all traditions proclaim the same message, or that they all point to the same referent. The term 'transcendence' denotes a category – a human construct – and not a being, let alone Being itself.

The process of categorisation itself inevitably anticipates the comparisons that we wish to draw, because we must make comparisons in order to decide which ideas belong in our category. We cannot escape this hermeneutic circle. We therefore have to decide which characteristics determine whether or not an idea may be categorised as an idea of transcendence. We should be careful to leave room for the possibility that some ideas are ultimately incomparable, so that we can speak about 'gods' without necessarily implying that there is a common denominator, in much the same way that one can speak about 'salvations' without necessarily intending a common point of reference. Perhaps the identification or equation of all the ideas of the Real in various world-views has been premature.

Once we have established the ground that justifies our subsuming these ideas within the same category, the next issue we must face is the method of comparison. Here also the hermeneutic circle is unavoidable, because every proposal for a method of comparison requires experience with actual comparisons. With regard to this issue I will consider a distinction Keith Ward has employed in his interesting initial study in comparative theology, *Images of Eternity*, a distinction which lies at the root of his so-called 'dual nature' conception of the Divine. On the basis of his description and analysis of five classical religious traditions, he concludes that in each case the Divine has two aspects – the Divine in itself and the Divine as related to the universe.[1] I will try to extend this approach.

At the end of this chapter, I will return to the question of the grounds that are needed for the belief that all ideas of the Real have the same referent, and whether or not such grounds are forthcoming. Are all the various ideas of the Real incompatible or do they perhaps converge at certain points? I shall begin, however, with the prior topic of whether it is even possible to compare ideas of the Real.

II. ARE IDEAS OF TRANSCENDENCE COMPARABLE?

The first question Ward considers in *Images of Eternity* concerns the grounds on which we may say that images of transcendence are comparable, and so can be placed into one and the same category. Thus, the question is what items may be compared with each other. In this case, 'comparable' does not mean that all such images are more or less identical, but only that, technically speaking, their status within religious traditions is more or less the same. For example, persons are not comparable to things. The Buddha, Krishna, Jesus and Muhammad, however, may be compared, although nobody would consider these persons to be identical. Therefore, the very fact that these persons can be put in the same category is fully compatible with the suggestion that ideas about them as well as their referents might differ. Comparisons can be helpful here because they highlight the particularities of, and the similarities between, traditions. We must, however, have good reason to compare these persons, just as we must also have good reason to refrain from comparing them with others. We may compare the Buddha with Jesus, for example, but not with Martin Luther or John Calvin. The same line of argument is valid in the case of salvation(s). While it may be acceptable to compare various ideas of salvation or conversion (or, more neutrally, transformation), the fact that they are comparable (in the technical sense) does not imply that these different ideas ultimately converge. Yet if they did not have something significant in common, it would not be legitimate to compare them. Therefore it is legitimate to speak about salvations if and only if there is a plausible category of salvation, and this requires significant similarities between the contents of the various ideas of 'salvation' and the meaning that salvation has for people who are longing for fulfilment. Furthermore, salvation is an open-ended category into which we can put several different ideas. Such ideas can compete and may exclude each other if the paths that lead to salvation really do differ and the situations in which salvation is attained are exclusive. It is also possible that various ideas of salvation overlap, because the miseries from which religious traditions try to liberate their adherents are to a large extent 'the same' (although this does not mean that valuations of the shortcomings of human life are the same). The very possibility of comparing ideas of salvation and the paths which lead to it presupposes that there is a way of coming to understand ideas that we do not ourselves hold.

The method used in comparisons such as these is often decisive for an author's conclusions. Those of us who conceive of religious traditions as coherent entities and like to accentuate differences will be more inclined to believe in the incomparability of 'gods' and of 'salvations', while those who like to stress commonalities and have a more fragmentary view of religions are more apt to equate ideas of the Divine and ways of salvation. Temperament plays a role here, but so too do different theories of religion.[2] In every substantive discussion in theology and the philosophy of religion, the difference between a holistic and a more fragmentary view of religion is decisive, and so it is in the case of images of eternity.[3]

I must therefore respond to the objection that the results of religious studies do not permit us to use the category 'images of transcendence'. This methodological objection resonates with nominalist and deconstructionist thought: every tradition is specific and particular, and therefore ideas of a divine being, emptiness, etc. are particular to different groups, and thus contextually specific. Anyone who lumps them together in the one category 'ideas of transcendence' is comparing apples and oranges. General terms such as 'Hinduism' and 'Buddhism', let alone 'eastern culture', are western constructs which betray a serious neglect of the variety within those cultures. The same applies to those who think that all human beings worship the same 'god'. This idea stems from the natural theology of the (western) Enlightenment, which in turn stems from the influential Greek philosophical idea that concepts are universal. This desire for universally valid concepts and rules can also be found in discussions on global ethics and in the idea that images of eternity must have a common core (and not just a common structure). In fact, this 'identifying way of thought' (Adorno) is inevitably linked with a neglect of the *altérité* of the other (Levinas) – and for many writers respect for the *altérité* of the other is the most important requirement for inter-religious dialogue and comparative studies.[4] On the basis of the western presupposition of a common, natural 'theology' – or for that matter, on the basis of a Hindu view of the Divine and of religious plurality – the comparative study of religion forces all ideas of the Divine into the one category 'images of the Divine' and a comparative philosophy then concludes that they have a common core – thus changing the presupposition into a conclusion. Anyone who has a healthy respect for details and differences will resist this urge to universality and commonality and will refuse to posit an essence common to all ideas of this kind. A category of 'gods' is not a thing. The only things that exist empirically are quite divergent images of heavenly and cosmic powers and of interconnectedness in the universe. This objection, if valid, is disastrous for the thought of Wilfred Cantwell Smith and John Hick, and for Keith Ward as well.

But this objection can be refuted as follows (although this refutation will necessitate a fundamental revision of certain views, such as Hick's). In much the same way that, under the category of 'religious building', a Hindu *mandir* may be compared to a synagogue, a cathedral and a mosque, a student of religious studies may also compare the Buddha's ideas concerning the deepest ground of our being, *shunyata*, with ideas of Adonai, the Trinity and Allah – without prematurely equating them. *Shunyata*, however, should not be compared to a local rabbi, priest or imam, let alone to a holy text or a building. In this sense, the aforementioned ideas of transcendence belong to the same category. Therefore, even the scholar who defends the thesis that Buddhas and creators are not identical has already classified them as phenomena that admit of comparison, although the conclusion of such a comparison will be that, despite some similarities, there are such profound differences between these notions that they and their referents should not be identified. Because of these profound differences, the question of which Buddhist ideas should be compared with the idea of a creator admits of debate.[5] Those who think that Adonai and *shunyata* are both images of the ground of all reality should give arguments to substantiate this claim. And anyone who accepts the idea that all such images are depictions of the ground of all existence has to admit that in principle any one of these traditions could be true, even though they may refer to different kinds of realities that cannot possibly be identified. Perhaps Mahayana Buddhists are right in thinking that the ground of the world is emptiness, and in that case there would be no creator.

Given this line of thought, John Hick's identification of a plurality of images of transcendence with 'the Real' is problematic. Peter Byrne has rightly pointed out that different people can refer to the same thing with different words – even if the expressions they use are only partially true.[6] For example, if I am with a child in the countryside and she sees a bird and says 'Look, a flying banana,' she can succeed in attracting my attention to a yellow bird. If, however, I see only a blackbird, the likelihood that we are experiencing different objects is much better than the likelihood that we are referring to the same thing.

The reason why some do equate the referents of various ideas of transcendence is that there could be only one ground of reality. Therefore, it is said, the bird analogy does not explain how different names may refer to the same thing, because there are many sorts of birds, but only one real referent of the various images of eternity. On this point, many thinkers agree that there can only be one ground of reality, and it is with reference to this ground that one must categorise these ideas as ideas of transcendence and compare them (e.g. Copleston, Smith, Hick). Some images, however, may simply be mistaken, as when I see a swan and think it is a crane.

The main objection against the view of Hick and his followers – that all the various ideas of the Divine are equally justifiable and refer to the same reality – is that it takes seriously neither the differences and contradictions between those ideas nor the actual disagreements between members of various traditions. For this reason one must not postulate that all these ideas of transcendence refer to the same 'thing'. Because the truth-claims of various traditions seem to exclude one another, one has to give reasons for thinking that some or all of them refer to 'the same reality'. Therefore, because there can be only one ground of reality, we may group these ideas into one category, but because there can be only one member of that category, some images may be wrong and so they will not refer to 'the same reality' as that of other ideas.

Hick, Byrne and others state that, in spite of their great differences, divergent images of eternity are all ideas of 'the same', and so they equate their referents (though Byrne issues a caveat in relation to *shunyata*[7]). This identification is, so far as I can see, motivated by three arguments:

1. a moral argument: why should one group (mine!) be right and the others mistaken?;
2. a religious argument: I am convinced that the religious experience of the other person is an authentic experience of transcendence, and not just an imaginative projection;
3. a comparative argument: on the basis of the similarities between the various images of eternity, we may justifiably conclude that people are speaking about the same ultimate reality.

I think that the first and second arguments are logically dependent upon the third. The first argument is a sincere and plausible reason to immerse oneself in the thoughts of others and to try to look for the truth in their ideas as well as in one's own. It is not, however, a valid argument for the claim that the other person refers to the same reality or that both her ideas and mine are equally true. In fact, the moral problem arises once we begin comparing both sets of ideas. Therefore, the moral argument logically depends upon the comparative one. The religious argument also gives us a proper motive for taking the ideas of another tradition seriously. Yet, however regrettable it may be, human beings can dedicate themselves to unworthy causes. In order to ascertain whether the other person is authentic and is serving a good cause (as in Hick's 'transformations'), we must confront the moral question. However, in that case too we have started to compare another tradition with ours and have found enough similarities to take the other one seriously. Therefore the third, comparative motive is decisive. In the absence of valid reasons, however, 'comparability' (i.e. membership in the same category) does not imply identity.

In this section I have argued for two conclusions. The first is that different images can be grouped into a single category as ideas of that which grounds and interconnects all that exists. The second is that arguments must nonetheless be given for identifying some or all of the referents of these ideas. Such ideas are found in stories, rituals and images. In what follows I restrict myself to predicates of the Divine, which, as I noted earlier, should not be separated from their background in these stories and practices.

III. METHOD OF COMPARISON

How can we compare predicates from different traditions and different languages that seem to signify 'transcendence'? When is there enough similarity to conclude that various ideas of transcendence refer to the same 'reality'?

First, we must ask whether divine predicates in the various ancient languages are equivalent to those in a modern language such as English. Consider one of the main characteristics of Brahman, in Sanskrit *sat-cit-ananda* – being (*sat*), intelligence (*cit*) and bliss (*ananda*). I shall restrict the discussion to *sat*. Immediately we face the problem that this term, as many have observed, has two meanings: 'truthful' and 'being'.[8] However, why grant this distinction between two meanings and two philosophical disciplines, epistemology and ontology? The concept of *sat* transcends the distinction between being and knowledge so commonly made in modern western philosophy. Like the concepts of emptiness, Buddha-nature and the Trinity, *sat* is a highly complicated idea that has no meaning in itself apart from the context of a specific historical tradition. It follows that it is not possible to analyse and discuss this 'concept' in terms of modern western thought. So a philosopher who is not also an Indologist must make use of the work of Indologists. Can we nonetheless understand an idea which, when compared to western thought, means both being and truth? One way to solve this problem is to remember that in the western tradition some schools of philosophy hold views of being and truth that are in some ways similar to Vedantic thought. Another way is to note a parallel in Hebrew thought. In Hebrew the term *emeth* means truthfulness: sometimes it is used simply to mean that one correctly asserts something to be the case, but it is also often used to say that someone can be trusted and meets the requirements for being a good person (or perhaps one should say: is as a person is meant to be). Here too a western distinction is transcended – the one between ontology and ethics. Just as in biblical thought it can be said that in God there is no darkness and no evil, so in Hindu thought it can be said that in Brahman there is no karma. In each tradition the difference between ontology and ethics is transcended or overcome, but in different ways. Now these differences may encourage some people to go so far as to conclude that these belief systems are incomparable, for the reason that the two ways of overcoming this distinction differ widely from each other. If, however, we follow the line of argument set out in the previous section, we are entitled to place the terms *sat* and *emeth* into the same category and explore their differences and similarities. Indeed, this is the only way to compare the ideas of different philosophical schools.

I will cite one more example, from ethics. According to the Buddhist tradition, one of the most important virtues is *mahakaruna*, which is usually translated as 'great compassion'. The expression *maha*, 'great', warns us against the hasty identification of *karuna* with compassion. So what kind of compassion is this? And what does it have to do with love in biblical thought, *agape*? One difference could be that *karuna* is detached while *agape* is purified from egoism but not detached. Hate, the Buddhist thinker says, is a negative attachment and love a positive one, but attachments both belong to the chain of karma and are causes of suffering, while *mahakaruna* is detached and is accompanied by pure awareness, a purified mind, and a natural state in which one's acts are wise and appropriate. That is, *mahakaruna* is accompanied by *prajna*, wisdom, while love veils one's eyes from the truth. Clearly, then, the Christian confession 'God is love' may not be readily understood by Buddhists, who at first sight will suspect that love is an attachment we should overcome. Here again we encounter words that derive their meaning from a cluster of concepts. Words from clusters as different as these can indeed be compared, but they should not be identified. It is not difficult to multiply examples which could be used by those who would like to escape the difficulties of intercultural comparison by affirming that 'East is East and West is West' and that the world-views they embody are nothing more than 'ships passing in the night'. Yet this may be too quick, for there are Buddhist philosophers who say that 'God is love', and the Hindu theologian Ramanuja asked himself how Brahman can be full of bliss and have knowledge of imperfect human beings – a problem with which Anselm of Canterbury (and many others) also wrestled.[9]

These examples may clarify the reasons why we should reject two views commonly found in comparative theology. On the one hand, the problems that arise throughout the variegated world of religious thought are too analogous to be called incomparable. On the other hand, these various ways of thought are also too divergent to be identified.

In relation to the problem of the comparison of divine predicates, it follows that similar predicates can be compared without neglecting the variations in the meanings of the terms used in various traditions. It is remarkable to note, for example, that in English translations of Christian, Islamic and Hindu treatises similar predicates are attributed to the Divine, such as 'eternal', 'omniscient', 'blissful', 'gracious' and 'unchangeable'. This similarity provides a firm ground on which to defend the claim that two or more traditions have the same idea of transcendence. If there are indeed enough commonalities, it would be right to conclude that these traditions are referring to the same 'god'. When comparing images of eternity, it is also helpful to distinguish between various categories of divine attributes. Characteristics like the ability to create, power, knowledge and will can be seen to compose one group. Other characteristics, such as grace, love, mercy and justice, form another group. Thus, we can attribute various kinds of qualities to divine acts, and assign them to different categories – although the second group of qualities is dependent upon the first because it is difficult to be just and merciful without knowledge, wisdom and power.

A classical distinction in attributes predicated of the Divine is that between metaphysical and relational attributes. As noted earlier, Keith Ward employs this distinction in his 'dual nature' view of the Divine: he points to a distinction in the thought of classical representatives from five religious traditions between attributes of the Divine *in se* and *quoad nos*. He concludes that this distinction belongs to the very idea of the Divine and he also stresses the paradoxical unity between both of these natures.[10] Ward's approach seems promising to me and I shall now attempt to elaborate it, beginning with some remarks on the distinction.

Those who try to sort divine attributes into these two groups face several problems. In the first place, some attributes have to be predicated of the Divine *in se* on the basis of divinity's relation to the world. In order to be able to bring the world into existence, the Divine must have those characteristics which are needed to ground the world, such as knowledge, power, wisdom and the capacity to make choices. According to those religious traditions that affirm a relationship between God and the world, God also has all these predicates in relation to the world. Although the potential to be a creator is an attribute *in se*, these attributes are at the same time relational because power, knowledge and wisdom do not make sense without a relation to something other than oneself. The attributes needed to secure the potential to become a creator are in themselves relational in some sense, and certainly not fully *in se*. In the second place, attributes like love, kindness and mercifulness would lose their meaning if God did not have those characteristics *in se*. While it is possible to think that God's love develops in relation to humankind, it is not consistent with the nature of righteousness and mercifulness to think that God only became righteous and merciful after creation. Thirdly, this distinction suggests that God cannot be known *in se* and so nothing can be said about the Divine. As a consequence, attributes that are predicated of God *quoad nos* would not be real attributes of the Divine but just imaginative human projections.

These problems push us toward the path that John Hick and Peter Byrne have taken: to claim that many traditions refer to the same divine reality and everything that is said about the Divine is relative and contextual, with the exception of a few predicates that refer to features of the transcendent.[11] The question therefore arises as to whether it is possible to draw some other distinction which would be helpful in our effort to compare ideas of transcendence.

In comparisons of different treatments of the Divine and in discussions of divine predicates, one can distinguish various functions of the Divine. I think that progress in comparative theology might be facilitated by distinguishing some of these functions and then comparing ideas of transcendence in relation to them. Whether or not 'the Divine' in different religious traditions has the same functions might determine whether or not different ideas of the Divine have the same referent. I tentatively posit the following six categories of divine characteristics (each of which may be found in treatises on the Divine from different religious traditions):

I. expressions of the idea of transcendence, considered in abstraction from the existence of the world (as far as possible);
II. preconditions for the generation of (*a*) the world and (*b*) eventually, relations with the world;
III. attributes in relation to the perpetuation of the world;
IV. attributes in relation to processes in the world as a whole;
V. attributes in relation to the guidance or redirection of the course of nature, particular peoples, and persons in general;
VI. attributes in relation to special events in nature, history or the lives of individual persons.

Perhaps after further study we might wish to make further distinctions within some of these categories. On the basis of this more refined division of characteristics and functions of the Divine, we could draw some conclusions about the relations between various images of the Real and also about the possibility of identifying some of the realities to which these traditions refer. I think that there are strong reasons to identify the referents of those ideas of transcendence that share all six of the foregoing categories. If they do not, I doubt, to at least some extent, that the referents are equivalent.

The divine characteristics in categories V and VI point to a personal or more than personal idea of God: God as distinct from the world (hence its creator), as providential, and (in VI) as having special relations with specific peoples and persons. These elements of the idea of God presuppose certain characteristics, such as the potential to make 'himself' known and the ability to know human thoughts, and also leave room for other characteristics. So the conclusion that the various ideas of a creator point to one and the same creator is much more plausible than the conclusion that all ideas of God which share fewer of the functions of transcendence refer to the same transcendent reality.

In the idea of an ultimate reality which grounds the world but does not create it, and in which the Divine has a restless, comprehensive and immanent relation to the world as a whole (categories IIa, III and IV), the cosmos and the transcendent are one. This idea could be called cosmic pantheism, though the element '-theism' in 'pantheism' is rather misleading. I prefer to use the expression 'cosmic religion' or 'cosmic idea of the Divine'. As I explained in the preceding section, I think that we need some comparative arguments for the identification of the referents of the various divergent ideas of the Divine.

In some Hindu schools, Brahman is seen as the ground of all reality (category III) – though, since Brahman is also understood to be without attributes (category I), we are not allowed to predicate attributes that constitute the preconditions for Brahman's being the ground of everything. Relations between Brahman and the world are denied. The 'non-dualism' of Advaita philosophy, for example, prohibits speaking of divine attributes at all. In another school of Hindu thought, this refusal has been criticised quite sharply (although this school presupposes that both they themselves and the Advaita Vedantists are referring to the same reality, Brahman – the ground of all reality, of which the Vedanta Sutra speaks). While the Purvapaksha school holds to a kind of a cosmic pantheism, believing that the divine ground of the world is absolutely transcendent, Ramanuja teaches a qualified theism.[12] Yet because Ramanuja rejects the view of the Purvapaksha as heretical, he nevertheless takes them seriously as pointing to the same transcendent reality. Obviously, he thinks that both views within the Vedantic tradition have so much in common – such as their respect for the authority of the Vedanta Sutra, their belief that Brahman is the ground of all reality, and many more ideas concerning humankind and the world – that, in spite of all their controversies, both parties are discussing the nature of the same divine reality. The question of whether or not one can defend the notion that the Hindu *bhakti* traditions and the Abrahamic religions refer to the same divine reality, however, requires more consideration.

There is some wisdom, then, in distinguishing three different understandings of transcendence: cosmic, acosmic and theist. To me, it seems premature to identify these three transcendents – emptiness, the Brahman of the Advaita Vedanta, and the creator. Seen from the human side, these three interpretations are all candidates for transcendence, but they exclude each other. Yet in the formal sense employed in such categories as 'the idea of transcendence' or 'the ground of reality' we can still say that these religions all refer to the ground of reality – but that is to speak about a formal category, and not 'one and the same reality'. Thus, we leave room for discussion and disagreement concerning which 'candidate' is the real transcendent.

IV. CONCLUDING REMARKS

Lists of divine predicates can serve as points of departure in comparative theology and inter-religious dialogue.[13] I have claimed that thinkers like Hick and Byrne who too easily equate all referents of ideas of the Divine relativise the differences and controversies between various religious traditions. However, anyone who wishes to reject the more sweeping judgements of comparative theology – 'All religions refer to the same reality' or 'Every religion is its own universe of thought and their referents cannot be identified' – has to compare the religious phenomena carefully and then argue for their conclusions. As I have suggested in this chapter, I think that a list of functions of the Divine can help in making such comparisons. From these comparisons we can proceed to critical discussion of the various ideas of transcendence, thus carrying forward the project of Ward's *Religion and Creation*.[14] Drawing on the work of Indologists, Islamologists, Sinologists, biblical scholars and historians of western and eastern philosophy, comparative theology can study the differences and similarities between various traditions, and also give arguments for ascribing some attributes to the Divine and for modifying others. Hence we could move further along the path which Wilfred Cantwell Smith has urged us to follow: to learn from other traditions while at the same time adhering to one's own. One could therefore combine a maximal receptivity towards other traditions with a deep loyalty towards the tradition that one believes to be most worthy of one's assent.

NOTES

1 Keith Ward, *Images of Eternity: Concepts of God in Five Religious Traditions* (London: Darton, Longman and Todd, 1987), 158ff.
2 See S. Mark Heim, *Salvations: Truth and Difference in Religion* (Maryknoll, NY: Orbis Books, 1995).
3 See my 'The Unity and Diversity of Religions: The Controversy between Holistic and Non-Holistic Theories of Religion', *Studies in Interreligious Dialogue*, 8 (1998), 99–112. An example of an antithetical approach to relations between religions is William A. Christian, *Oppositions of Religious Doctrines* (London: Macmillan, 1972).
4 See Theodor Adorno, *Negative Dialektik* (Frankfurt am Main: Suhrkamp, 1966), 15. However, the pretence of identity is ineradicable because it is fundamental to thought itself. To think means to identify. Self-satisfied conceptual order is already present before thought attempts to understand the other.

5   In discussions between western thought and the Buddhist Kyoto philosophy, the idea of emptiness has been taken as the main point of comparison to the idea of a creator, but religious scholars have also argued that the Buddhist idea of *dharma* is the proper analogue of God. See Wilfred Cantwell Smith, *Faith and Belief* (Princeton: Princeton University Press, 1979), 24ff.

6   See John Hick, *An Interpretation of Religion* (London and Basingstoke: Macmillan, 1989), 233–51, and Peter Byrne, *Prolegomena to Religious Pluralism* (London and Basingstoke: Macmillan, 1995), 42–52.

7   Byrne, *Prolegomena to Religious Pluralism*, 158, 163.

8   See S. Radhakrishnan and C. A. Moore (eds), *A Sourcebook in Indian Philosophy* (Princeton: Princeton University Press, 1973), 59, 625. *Satya* means truth. See my *Religions and the Truth* (Amsterdam/Grand Rapids: Rodopi/Eerdmans, 1989), 117ff.

9   See Anselm, *Proslogion*, 6, and Ramanuja, *The Vedanta Sutras with the Commentary by Ramanuja*, ed. and tr. G. Thibaut (Delhi: Motilal Banarsidass, 1984), 607ff.

10 Ward, *Images of Eternity*, 156ff.

11 Byrne speaks of a severely agnostic analogical description: *Prolegomena to Religious Pluralism*, 164; see also 150–2.

12 For the Purvapaksha school, see Ramanuja, *The Vedanta Sutras*, 20ff.; for his criticism of that school, see 39ff. See also Ward, *Images of Eternity*, 37.

13 See my 'Do All Religions Worship the Same God?', *Religious Studies*, 26 (1990), 73–90, and Byrne, *Prolegomena to Religious Pluralism*, 31–53.

14 Keith Ward, *Religion and Creation* (Oxford: Clarendon Press, 1996).

8

Metaphor and the Reality of God

VINCENT BRÜMMER

I. THE DILEMMA OF TALK ABOUT GOD

In the second part of his *Religion and Creation*, Keith Ward discusses a fundamental conceptual problem which theists in all traditions have to face when suggesting ways in which to conceptualise the reality of God: 'is it possible to speak of such a reality in language which, after all, is primarily suited to refer to more mundane finite things?'[1] This suggests a dilemma: either we have to talk about God in human language and risk doing so in anthropomorphic terms that contradict the infinity, transcendence and otherness of the Divine, or we have to admit the inadequacy of human language as a medium for talking about God and risk an agnosticism that denies all knowledge of the reality of God. Ward points out that it has become widespread in modern theology to deal with this dilemma by claiming on the one hand that it is possible to talk about God in human language but on the other hand that all such talk is metaphorical. According to him there are two powerful objections to this view.

First of all, the claim that all language about God is metaphorical is based on a misunderstanding of the nature of metaphor: 'A metaphor is a figure of speech which describes one thing in terms which primarily describe another. One has to understand the primary use before one can understand the metaphorical use; and one has to realize that a straightforward, or literal, description is not being attempted. It is essential to the function of metaphor that there must be a literal description, which in this case is negated. Metaphor is parasitic upon literal description.'[2] Although metaphor is essential in religious language, not all talk of God can be metaphorical.

Ward's second objection is that this view entails a non-realism that rules out claims about the real existence of God. Thus he argues that Sallie McFague's claim to be a critical realist with regard to God is incompatible with her view that all talk of God is metaphorical.[3] Similarly he argues that the view defended by Kant and John Hick, that God is a noumenal reality about which we cannot speak in literal terms, entails a form of apophaticism which necessarily undermines their attempts to defend a realist ontology with regard to God.[4]

In my contribution to Keith Ward's festschrift I would like to reflect further on the points raised by these objections. Does the nature of metaphor indeed exclude the view that all language about God is metaphorical? And does this view necessarily rule out claims about the real existence of God?

II. METAPHOR IN THOUGHT AND IN LANGUAGE

The term 'metaphor' is ambiguous. For our purposes we can distinguish two senses in which it is used in the theoretical literature on metaphor. On the one hand it is used, especially in literary theory, to refer to a specific figure of speech which is distinguished from the literal use of language. It is clear that Ward is using the term in this sense. On the other hand the term is also used to refer to a pervasive feature of all human thought and experience. In this context the distinction between metaphoric and literal does not apply. We could say that all human thought and experience is metaphorical in this sense.[5] Let me first say something about the sense in which we can call *thought and experience* metaphorical and then see what light this throws on the distinction between literal and metaphorical *uses of words*.

Metaphorical thinking

Sallie McFague defines metaphor in this sense as 'seeing one thing *as* something else, pretending "this" is "that" because we do not know how to think or talk about "this", so we use "that" as a way of saying something about it. Thinking metaphorically means spotting a thread of similarity between two dissimilar objects, events, or whatever, one of which is better known than the other, and using the better known one as a way of speaking about the lesser known.'[6] In this sense the term 'metaphor' is used to refer to the conceptual activity in which we understand things by comparing them to each other.

   This is an essential feature of all human thought and experience. One of the most basic conceptual activities characteristic of human thinking is the classification of entities according to the characteristics they have in common.[7] If we wish to gain a hold on the chaos of our sensory impressions, we must recognise the similarities and differences between the things we perceive and classify them according to these similarities and differences. In perceiving the world we do not merely register chaotic sensory impressions, nor do we perceive random undefined objects. We always perceive objects *as belonging to a kind* (people, chairs, tables, houses, trees, etc.) and therefore having recognisable characteristics in common and differing in recognisable ways from other objects. This classificatory organisation of experience constitutes our horizon for understanding the world: we seek to understand things by comparing them to similar things with which we are already familiar. I try to understand how *A* works or what value I should attach to *A* by comparing it to *B*, whose working or value I already understand. Understanding the world around us would be impossible without such metaphorical comparison.

   On the other hand we know that comparisons are odious since they tend to ignore individuality and to treat things that are analogous as though they were identical. After all, everything is itself and not another thing. Hence McFague warns us (in terms derived from Paul Ricoeur) that our generalising metaphorical concepts 'always contain the whisper, "it is *and it is not*"'.[8] The danger of metaphorical thinking is that we can become so used to the generalising 'is' that it becomes part of our intuitive pattern of thinking or mental set and we become deaf to the whispered 'and it is not'. It is therefore important to remember that the meanings of the generalising concepts we employ in our metaphorical thinking are open-ended in the sense that they contain a penumbra of associations, suggestions and implications. When in our metaphorical comparisons we use the same concept in two different contexts or with reference to two different entities, it does not necessarily follow that the whole penumbra of meaning is transferred from the one context to the other. We therefore need critical reflection in order to determine what part of the penumbra of meaning is transferred in each case. Thus in thinking and speaking of (our relations with) God we use the same concepts we also use in our thinking and speaking about (our relations with) each other even though we know very well that God is not like other people. Central to theological reflection on the way the community of believers think and speak about God is the task of sorting out critically what part of the penumbra of meaning can and what part cannot be transferred to our thinking and speaking about God. Such reflection does not eliminate the metaphorical nature of our thinking about God, but tries to illuminate its meaning by determining the limits between 'it is' and 'it is not'. All our thinking about God remains metaphorical in the sense that we think and speak about (our relations with) God in terms which derive from our thinking and speaking about (our relations with) each other.

Metaphor as a figure of speech

What light do these remarks on metaphorical thinking throw on the nature of metaphor as a figure of speech and the difference between the metaphorical and the literal use of words? In modern Greek the word *metaphora* can be used to refer to a city bus as a vehicle for transferring people from point A to point B. In an analogous way we could say that metaphor as a figure of speech is a 'vehicle' used to transfer meaning from context A to context B. Terms with which we usually say something in one context are used metaphorically to say something in a different context. This transfer of meaning is based on the analogy between what we do with our words in the one context and what we do with the same words in a very different context. Clearly this analogy is not identity. Because of the difference between the contexts only part of the penumbra of meaning and implications can be transferred from context A to context B. In this way words which are used *literally* in A can be used *metaphorically* in B.

What is the difference between the literal use of a term in context A and its metaphorical use in context B? Some would say that the literal use is factual and the metaphorical use figurative or non-factual. In A the term is used to make a factual claim whereas in B it is used figuratively and no claims about reality are made. Ward's criticism of McFague and Hick seems to suggest that he supports this view. In some circumstances this could be true, but not always. It all depends whether making reality claims is or is not part of the analogy between what we do in the two contexts with the same terms. Thus in talk about Ward's father or my father, the term 'father' entails claims about reality. This point does not carry over to talk about Father Time, Father Christmas or the father of the Prodigal Son. However, it is quite possible for metaphors to be 'reality depicting', as Janet Soskice argues.[9] Thus, as I shall argue below, the claim that all talk about God is metaphorical does not necessarily entail a non-cognitive or anti-realist view on religious belief.

Another view is that the literal use of words is primary or proper and the metaphorical use secondary or improper. For example, Paul Ziff considers metaphor a species of 'deviant discourse'.[10] The question is: deviant from what? An essentialist would say that metaphors deviate from the true or essential meaning of the word. Mary Hesse points out that this view on metaphor follows from the Aristotelian theory of universals: 'The implicit postulates of an Aristotelian model of metaphor may be summarised as follows: there is a distinction between proper and improper naming, derived from the theory of natural kinds and essences; a metaphor is a word borrowed from an alien context; its use is therefore deviant.'[11] Elsewhere she argues that this view entails 'a two-tiered view of language in which some usages are irreducibly literal and others metaphoric'. This contradicts the dynamic nature of language: 'An expression initially metaphoric may become literal (a "dead" metaphor) and what is at one time literal may become metaphoric (for example the Homeric "he breathed forth his life", originally literal, is now a metaphor for death).'[12]

A more plausible view is that metaphor deviates from the usual use of words to which participants in the linguistic community have become accustomed through a process of linguistic socialisation. Hesse expresses this view as follows:

> The literal/metaphoric distinction is properly a pragmatic, not a semantic use. That is to say, it concerns the way in which speakers learn, use, and if necessary define the words of their language. Literal use is the most frequent use in familiar contexts – that use that least disturbs the network of meanings. Thus literal use is the easiest to manage, to learn and to teach. [. . .] It is the use that is least open to misunderstanding and mistake. It is the one generally put first in dictionary entries, where it is followed by comparatively 'dead' metaphors, and perhaps the more novel and interesting live ones are omitted altogether.[13]

By thus deviating from our customary uses of words, metaphor functions as an iconoclastic technique which helps us break through our mental set of 'literal' forms of thinking and speaking, and reminds us of the unavoidable selectivity and one-sidedness of all our conceptual forms. As a figure of speech metaphor turns up the volume in order that we might hear the whispered 'and it is not'. This explains the evocative nature of metaphor to which Ward refers,[14] and also the way in which metaphor can facilitate the revelatory role of religious language by opening our eyes to new perspectives on reality and helping us to look on ourselves and on the world with the eyes of faith.

III. THE REALITY OF GOD

I have argued that all our thinking about God is metaphorical in the sense that we think and talk about (our relations with) God in terms derived from the way we think and talk about (our relations with) each other. However, since God is not like other people, we cannot transfer the whole penumbra of meaning and implication of these terms to our thinking and talking about God. Are the reality claims entailed by our thinking and talking about ourselves part of the meaning transferred to our thinking and talking about God? Or is our talk about God to be understood in a non-cognitive and non-realist sense? Before we can answer this question we first have to see how we can determine what part of the penumbra of meaning can be transferred to our thinking and talking about God. How do we determine the limits of the metaphors we use for God?

God is not like other people

Following Anselm's definition of God as 'that than which nothing greater can be conceived', so-called perfect being theology argues that all perfections or 'great-making properties' which can be ascribed to human beings also have to be ascribed to God, albeit to an infinite degree. While humans can be wise, powerful, loving, knowing, etc., God is infinitely wise, powerful, loving, knowing, etc. In the words of Paul Helm, in his inaugural lecture as Ward's successor at King's College London, 'perfect being theology thus invites us to think of God [. . .] as a Herculean figure, able, as it were, to out-lift and out-throw and out-run all his opponents, and to perform such activities maximally. [. . .] Whatever the most powerful of his creatures can do, God can do it to an infinitely greater degree.'[15] In this way the great-making qualities of human beings have to be maximised in order to apply to God.

This kind of perfect being theology is flawed in two important respects. First, it reduces the difference between God and human persons to one of degree and therefore fails to account for the qualitative difference between the Divine and the human. God becomes merely Superman. Secondly, divine perfection is the standard or ideal by which our contingent and fallible ideas of what counts as perfection have to be judged and therefore cannot simply be the maximising of these ideas. Roger White points out that this approach fails to recognise 'the extent to which natural man may have either no idea, or a perverse misconception of what the ideal alluded to by the word may be like'.[16] Karl Barth is therefore right in saying that we have no a priori knowledge of divine perfection. Christians claim that we can only come to know it a posteriori in light of the way God reveals himself to us in his dealing with the people of Israel and in the life and teaching of Jesus Christ. This revelation often contradicts the ideals of perfection maintained by natural man: 'What the believer calls "success" will be failure in the eyes of the world, what he calls "joy" will seem like grief, what he calls "victory" will seem like certain defeat. So it was, Christians believe, at the Cross of Christ.'[17] From this it is clear that we can only transfer the penumbra of meaning of our human concepts to our talk of God to the extent that it is consistent with the way in which God reveals himself to us, as Christians believe, in Christ and in the Bible.

In spite of these objections, perfect being theology can also be interpreted in a more qualitative and less quantitative way and thus provide us with a useful rule of thumb complementing the appeal to revelation. God is perfect, not in the sense that his perfections are the maximisation of ours, but in the sense that he is free from the limitations of human finitude. Thus our knowledge is always limited, whereas God knows everything that it is logically possible to know. Our capacities are limited and we cannot do just anything, whereas God can do anything that is logically possible to do and that is consistent with the divine character as revealed to us.[18] Our weakness of will (*akrasia*) limits our ability to do what is good, whereas God is free from *akrasia* and therefore perfectly good in the sense that everything he does is good.[19] As spatio-temporal beings our capacities are limited by our finite spatio-temporal location, whereas God is eternal and omnipresent and therefore free from such spatio-temporal limitations. This difference between the divine and the human has far-reaching implications for all the characteristics that we can ascribe to God and thus for the extent to which the penumbra of meaning of our human concepts can be transferred to our talk of God.[20] How does this affect the meaning of the claim that God really exists?

Does God really exist?

According to Ward, Christian believers 'are more likely to be concerned with coping with problems of suffering, guilt, and meaninglessness in their daily lives, and with whether there is a power to give strength, affirmation, and meaning to their lives. Religion is a primarily practical affair, a matter of value-commitments and of a personal search for happiness and fulfilment.'[21] Some philosophers of religion argue that this entails a non-cognitive interpretation of religious belief. Religion is a form of life and not a theory about the facts: 'Coming to see that there is a God is not like coming to see that an additional being exists. [. . .] Coming to see that there is a God involves seeing a new meaning in one's life, and being given a new understanding.'[22] Ward correctly questions this conclusion and argues that religious belief as a form of life *presupposes* metaphysical beliefs about reality: 'The factual beliefs in question will most likely just be taken for granted by me. Nevertheless, it is an important fact that some such beliefs are presupposed in my practical commitments.'[23] Religious belief is indeed a form of life, but as Wittgenstein reminds us, forms of life and the language games expressing them are constituted by tacit presuppositions about reality.[24] We have to assume that reality is such that the form of life is possible within it. Thus the religious form of life of fellowship with God is logically unattainable if God does not really exist as the kind of personal being with whom such fellowship can be enjoyed. We cannot have fellowship with a non-existent or fictitious God. The real existence of God is in this sense a 'necessary truth' for believers who are com-mitted to a life of fellowship with God. Clearly the factual claims involved in talk of human fellowship do in some sense carry over to talk of fellowship with God. This does not mean, however, that God really exists in exactly the same sense as human persons really exist. Let us reflect on the penumbra of meaning of the concept of 'real existence' and see to what extent this is carried over to those claims about the real existence of God that are constitutive of the religious form of life.[25]

J. L. Austin maintains that 'real' is a so-called 'trouser word': 'With "real" it is the *negative* use that wears the trousers. [. . .] The function of "real" is not to contribute positively to the characterisation of anything, but to exclude possible ways of being *not* real.'[26] For our purposes two senses of '*un*real' are relevant here: unreal in the sense of 'fictitious' and in the sense of 'illusory'. Since we cannot have fellowship with a fictitious or an illusory God, this part of the penumbra of meaning of 'really exists' does carry over to our talk of the real existence of God. The difference therefore lies with 'exist' rather than with 'real'. What does it mean to claim that something 'exists' in a non-fictitious and non-illusory sense?

According to John Stuart Mill,

> a thing is said by us to exist, even when it is absent, and therefore is not and cannot be perceived. But even then, its existence is to us only another word for our conviction that we should perceive it on a certain supposition, namely, if we were in the needful circumstances of time and place, and endowed with the needful perfection of organs. My belief that the Emperor of China exists, is simply my belief that if I were transported to the imperial palace or some other locality in Pekin, I should see him. My belief that Julius Cæsar existed, is my belief that I should have seen him if I had been present in the field of Pharsalia, or in the senate-house at Rome. When I believe that stars exist beyond the utmost range of my vision, though assisted by the most powerful telescopes yet invented, my belief, philosophically expressed, is, that with still better telescopes, if such existed, I could see them, or that they may be perceived by beings less remote from them in space, or whose capacities of perception are superior to mine.
>
> The existence, therefore, of a phenomenon, is but another word for its being perceived, or for the inferred possibility of perceiving it.[27]

For many people in contemporary culture Mill's empiricist analysis sounds plausible. It can account for the reality claims we make regarding the existence of empirical objects with which we deal in our daily lives and which we study in the empirical sciences. It is doubtful, however, whether reality claims regarding the existence of God can be understood in this way. Very few people today think of God in accordance with Michelangelo's fresco as an old man with a beard floating on a cloud where we could observe him 'if we were in the needful circumstances of time and place, and endowed with the needful perfection of organs'.

Although it is false to claim that God exists as a possible object of empirical observation, it is clearly also incoherent for believers who participate in the theistic form of life to claim that God's existence is a fiction or an illusion. But then we are back with our initial problem: what is meant by the claim that God 'really exists'? At this point Heidegger's critique of Husserl is illuminating.[28] As phenomenologists they both tend to 'humanise' the concept of reality in the sense that for them reality constitutes the limit to what we can know and what we can do. While Husserl emphasises the limit to what we can *know*, Heidegger emphasises the limit to what we can *do*. Contrary to Husserl, Heidegger maintains that our primary relation to reality is not that of objectifying knowing. Such objectifying knowing is a derived form of knowing and is preceded by an affective and practical relation to reality. The revolution in phenomenology brought about by Heidegger consisted in replacing the concept of *consciousness* with that of *existence*. This move affects our concept of reality. If we look upon ourselves not in terms of 'knowing consciousness' but rather in terms of 'acting existence',[29] then reality will not be understood primarily as the object of our knowing but as the context of our action. The claim that something 'really exists' will then not be merely, as Mill argued, an assurance about the limits of what we can *perceive* 'if we were in the needful circumstances of time and place, and endowed with the needful perfection of organs', but rather an assurance about the limits of what we can *do*, the limits of the context of our actions. That something 'really exists' means that it determines the limits of our possibilities of action and not merely of our possibilities of perception. To unpack the meaning of 'x exists', we need to specify the circumstances under which the existence of x would make a difference to what we could *do* rather than the circumstances in which x could be *perceived*.

This distinction would become minimal if we were to adopt the kind of behaviouristic view of action in which 'action' is reduced to 'observable behaviour'. If on the other hand we presuppose a more intentional view of action[30] according to which our actions are partly defined by the intentions with which we perform them, then the difference becomes much more significant. This can be illustrated by the following example.[31] The *observable behaviour* of Barry and Brendon is the same and could be described as 'taking food to the refugee camp'. If, however, we ask them what they are *doing* (that is, what *actions* they are performing), the descriptions are quite different. Brendon says: 'In taking food to the refugee camp, I am meeting the needs of the politically oppressed masses, and in this way preparing the peasants physically for the coming revolutionary struggle, in accordance with the teaching of Chairman Mao.' Barry describes his actions very differently. He says: 'In taking food to the refugee camp, I am meeting the needs of my fellow-creatures, and in this way creating signs of the coming Kingdom of God on Earth in obedience to his will.' Although the observable behaviour of Brendon and Barry is the same, they are nevertheless performing very different actions, because the intentions with which they act are very different. The limiting conditions of their *behaviour* are formed by the observable context within which they act. The limiting conditions of their *actions*, however, extend much further. Brendon's description of his actions can only make sense if he presupposes the reality of the coming revolutionary struggle and the truth of Mao's teaching, while Barry's description of his actions can only make sense if he presupposes the reality of God and of God's kingdom. Although the real existence of the coming revolution is not logically constitutive of Brendon's observable behaviour, it is for his actions, and although the real existence of God is not logically constitutive of Barry's observable behaviour, it is for his actions. For believers God's existence is therefore neither a fiction nor an illusion. For them God really exists as the logical limit to their intentional actions within the context of the theistic 'form of life'.

Realist claims regarding the existence of God differ, therefore, in two ways from realist claims about the empirical world. First, as Ward points out, God's existence is not an empirical hypothesis:

> theism is not primarily postulated in order to explain observed events. [. . .] It does not help one to predict anything in particular. Atoms were postulated because they help to explain why events happen as they do; and their postulation enables predictions to be made about what will happen in specifiable circumstances. God is not postulated to explain why things happen (although some accounts of religious belief by non-believers construe it as such). No precise predictions follow from the postulate of God.[32]

The claim that God exists is therefore not open to empirical verification or falsification, since it cannot be unpacked in terms of predictable possibilities of perception. Secondly, although belief in the reality of God does not determine what we observe, it does determine how we understand what we observe and thus what attitudes and actions we adopt toward observable reality: 'It will not predict what is going to happen; it will rather empower one to face whatever happens with patience, courage, and hope.'[33] Thus, as I have argued, the real existence of God is a tacit pre-supposition constitutive of the theistic form of life and therefore a 'necessary truth' for believers committed to this form of life. As such it cannot be separated from the believer's commitment and is thus an 'existential' claim. Unlike empirical hypotheses, 'It is not adopted in a speculative, dispassionate spirit.'[34] In these ways claims about the real existence of God differ from those about the empirical world and the penumbra of meanings and implications that the term 'really exist' has with reference to the empirical world does not carry over to the believer's claims about God. It is now clear that, although the theistic form of life necessarily presupposes realist claims about the existence of God, these claims, like all claims about God, are metaphorical.

I hope that these reflections will remove, or at least alleviate, Keith Ward's doubts about the view that all talk about God is metaphorical and hence contribute to the further development of his illuminating ideas on these matters.

NOTES

1   Keith Ward, *Religion and Creation* (Oxford: Clarendon Press, 1996), 129.
2   Ibid.
3   Ibid., 149–50.
4   Ibid., 131–5.
5   Elsewhere I have dealt with metaphor in this sense more extensively than is possible here. See ch. 1 of my *The Model of Love* (Cambridge: Cambridge University Press, 1993).
6   Sallie McFague, *Metaphorical Theology* (London: SCM Press, 1983), 15, emphasis hers.
7   David E. Cooper points out the metaphorical nature of classification in *Metaphor* (Oxford: Blackwell, 1986), 139. See also the examples in George Lakoff and Mark Johnson, *Metaphors*

We Live By (Chicago: University of Chicago Press, 1980), and my *Theology and Philosophical Enquiry* (London: Macmillan, 1981), 57–63.

8   McFague, *Metaphorical Theology*, 13, emphasis hers.

9   Janet Martin Soskice, *Metaphor and Religious Language* (Oxford: Clarendon Press, 1985), ch. 7.

10 Paul Ziff, *Semantic Analysis* (Ithaca, NY: Cornell University Press, 1960), ch. 1.

11 Mary Hesse, 'The Cognitive Claims of Metaphor', *Journal of Speculative Philosophy*, 2 (1988), 3. Her paper contains a useful critique of this view on metaphor.

12 Mary Hesse, *Revolutions and Reconstructions in the Philosophy of Science* (Brighton: Harvester Press, 1980), 116–17.

13 Hesse, 'The Cognitive Claims of Metaphor', 3.

14 Ward, *Religion and Creation*, 142, 147.

15 Paul Helm, *The Perfect and the Particular* (London: King's College, 1994), 18.

16 Roger White, 'Notes on Analogical Predication and Speaking about God', in Brian Hebblethwaite and Stewart Sutherland (eds), *The Philosophical Frontiers of Christian Theology* (Cambridge: Cambridge University Press, 1982), 223.

17 D. Z. Phillips, *Faith and Philosophical Enquiry* (London: Routledge and Kegan Paul, 1970), 83. See also Helm's detailed analysis of this point in *The Perfect and the Particular*, and White, 'Notes on Analogical Predication'.

18 On divine omniscience and omnipotence, see ch. 3 of my *What Are We Doing When We Pray?* (London: SCM Press, 1984).

19 On this point see ibid., 33, 40, and ch. 4 of my *Speaking of a Personal God* (Cambridge: Cambridge University Press, 1992).

20 In chs 7–9 of *The Model of Love* I give a detailed analysis of the penumbra of meaning of the human concept of love and show how God's freedom from the limitations of finitude determines the extent to which this penumbra of meaning can be transferred to our talk of the love of God.

21 Ward, *Religion and Creation*, 118.

22 Phillips, *Faith and Philosophical Enquiry*, 17–18.

23 Ward, *Religion and Creation*, 118.

24 Ludwig Wittgenstein, *Philosophical Investigations* (Oxford: Blackwell, 1958), §§179–80. For a more detailed discussion of the way such tacit presuppositions are constitutive for language games and forms of life, see my paper on 'Wittgenstein and the Anselmian Project', *Bijdragen*, 60 (1999), 436–55.

25 For a more extended discussion of these issues than is possible here, see my paper 'Does God Really Exist?', in Timo Koistinen and Tommi Lehtonen (eds), *Philosophical Studies in Religion, Metaphysics, and Ethics* (Helsinki: Luther-Agricola Society, 1997), 15–34.

26 J. L. Austin, *Sense and Sensibilia* (Oxford: Oxford University Press, 1962), 70, emphasis his.

27 John Stuart Mill, *A System of Logic*, 8th edn (1886), III, xxiv, 1: J. M. Robson (ed.), *Collected Works of John Stuart Mill*, vol. vii (Toronto/London: University of Toronto Press/Routledge and Kegan Paul, 1973), 604–5.

28 On this point see Theo de Boer, 'Fenomenologie, een Lied van Schijn en Wezen', in R. C. Kwant and S. IJsseling (eds), *Filosoferen: Gangbare Vormen van Wijsgerig Denken* (Alphen aan den Rijn: Samson, 1977), 84–6.

29 See also John Macmurray's *The Self as Agent* (London: Faber and Faber, 1957), where this move is explained and defended in detail.

30 See, for example, G. E. M. Anscombe, *Intention* (Oxford: Blackwell, 1957), and Anthony Kenny, *Will, Freedom and Power* (Oxford: Blackwell, 1975).

31 Taken from S. R. Sutherland, 'Religion, Ethics and Action', in Hebblethwaite and Sutherland (eds), *The Philosophical Frontiers of Christian Theology*, 160f.

32 Ward, *Religion and Creation*, 112.

33 Ibid., 124.

34 Ibid., 112.

9

Theistic Compatibilism: Better Than You Think

T. W. BARTEL

I. INTRODUCTION

Whatever the divagations of Keith Ward's thought, he has always maintained that theists should leave compatibilism well alone – that belief in God cannot be rational if universal causal determinism is compatible with human freedom or moral responsibility.[1] And Ward is anything but eccentric in holding this view. Indeed, among theists these days who are English-speaking philosophers or theologians, it is virtually an article of faith: despite the long list of major figures throughout the ages who have defended theistic compatibilism, almost no one now thinks this worth the effort.[2]

Despite the undeniable popularity of theistic incompatibilism, however, there is a sobering, and insufficiently appreciated, fact about it which cannot be brushed aside: it exposes any remotely traditional theism to a grave risk of decisive empirical refutation. For it remains very much an open scientific question whether human choices and actions are wholly determined by antecedent causes. For all we know, this could be true, and we could discover that it is true. We cannot dismiss determinism by a priori argument, or by invoking our introspective feeling that our choices are not predetermined; for those choices might be necessitated by unknown causes. Nor can we dismiss it by invoking quantum indeterminism, since indeterminism at the quantum level does not guarantee that the operation of any macroscopic entities, including the human brain, is fundamentally indeterministic. Nor can we dismiss it by invoking any of the revolutionary discoveries of twentieth-century physics which have so thoroughly discredited 'clockwork' models of the natural world – chaos, emergence, top-down causation, etc. For universal macroscopic determinism is simply the thesis that, given the laws of nature, there are no two possible worlds exactly alike in their macroscopic features up to a particular time, but which differ thereafter, without some violation of these laws. And this thesis can accommodate the anti-mechanistic phenomena unveiled by the new physics – but according to incompatibilists, it cannot accommodate human freedom or moral responsibility, and therefore cannot accommodate traditional theism.

I do not object in principle to submitting belief in God to the risk of empirical refutation – that is nothing more than a fideist failure of nerve. Theists who reject compatibilism, however, are not just incompatibilists, but also libertarians. They believe not only that free will and moral responsibility are incompatible with determinism, but also that we *are* free and morally responsible – and at least as free and morally responsible as their own kind of theism presupposes us to be. And it is far from clear that we can find a libertarian account of freedom and moral responsibility which is much more satisfactory than anything available to compatibilists. It must be admitted that compatibilism does violate some forceful intuitions. For instance, we clearly have no control over the laws of nature and the state of the world before our births, and it does seem very plausible to believe that whatever is entailed by something over which we have no control is itself something over which we have no control. So since, if determinism is true, what we do is entailed by the laws of nature and the state of the world before we were born, it does seem that we would have no control over what we do. But such intuitions are not immune to challenge, and in any case there are powerful countervailing intuitions in favour of the compatibility, at least, of determinism and moral responsibility.[3] Moreover, libertarianism faces disquieting difficulties of its own. How, for example, can very many of our significant choices be free and subject to moral appraisal when we always could have chosen some other option even if our own deliberations had proceeded in precisely the same fashion right up to the moment of choice? Suppose a child is drowning at the shallow end of a swimming pool, right in front of me, and, after quickly coming to the conclusion that she will survive if and only if I pull her out and that I can do so perfectly safely without having to call on anyone else, I lift her out of the water. Even supposing that I am not worthy of moral approbation for my act if it was determined, am I any the more worthy of moral approbation if I could have left her to drown after having gone through exactly the same process of thought? Why should freedom and moral responsibility require the possibility of choosing so capriciously – and on so many occasions?[4]

In brief, it is time to look again at theistic compatibilism. Is it really as bad as its current reputation? I shall argue that it is not. Indeed, I shall try to make a useful start toward arguing that, while theistic compatibilism might not be plausible if we discover that none of our choices and actions are determined, Christian theists, if not orthodox theists of other religions, may well have overwhelming reasons to hope that we discover, to the contrary, that *all* of our choices and actions are determined. There can be few terms more abused in academese these days than 'paradigm shift'. But if my argument can be sustained, then a paradigm shift is precisely what ought to happen: one of the most firmly established paradigms in philosophy, let alone philosophical theology, for the past half-century – libertarian accounts of divine providence and human freedom – ought to be shelved.

II. THEISTIC COMPATIBILISM DEFENDED

But of course it has been repeatedly argued that, whatever the merits of compatibilism when God is left out of the reckoning, theists have no choice but to accept libertarianism. For, although theistic philosophers for the past fifty years or so may have been inordinately confident about the plausibility of incompatibilism per se, there are nonetheless peculiar, and fatal, difficulties with theistic compatibilism.

I do not wish to slight these difficulties: they are formidable. However, I do not believe that they are fatal, or even more troublesome than the problems which are peculiar to theistic incompatibilism. That is an opinion which would require a lengthy book to elaborate and defend. But in this chapter I shall attempt to show that there is much to be said for this opinion. To keep the discussion manageable, I shall sometimes have to restrict it to Christian theism – though much of what I say will apply equally to other forms of traditional theism. I shall also have to ignore the pertinent and pressing objection that the *tu quoque* arguments I will sometimes employ to defend theistic compatibilism simply strengthen the case against theism – though some of what I say will suggest ways of dealing with this objection. To sum up the conclusion of this section: when we bear in mind that a Christian theory of divine providence must respect the central doctrines of Christianity, and when we probe into the libertarian alternatives in sufficient depth and with sufficient rigour, it is scarcely obvious that Christian libertarians are in a position to cast aspersions on theistic compatibilism without casting equally serious aspersions on their own view. I shall try to lay the groundwork for a substantial argument toward this conclusion by considering what I take to be the three most serious objections that the theistic compatibilist must confront.

God the Great Manipulator

The first of these objections is that the all-determining God would seem to be, in the felicitous words of Antony Flew, the 'Great Manipulator'.[5] That is, if all our acts are ultimately determined by God, then our lives are manipulated, or managed, or contrived, or controlled, to a degree that negates our freedom – or at least to a degree incompatible with the kind and extent of autonomy or independence necessary for responding to God in genuine faith, trust and love.[6]

Arguments for this claim invariably contend that if determinism is true, then God's relationship to human creatures is relevantly similar to cases in which one human being controls the behaviour of another in a way that clearly eliminates or drastically reduces the latter's freedom or autonomy. Indeed, such arguments almost always appeal sooner or later to one or both of two analogies – a puppeteer who manipulates the puppet's every movement, or a hypnotist planting a post-hypnotic suggestion in the mind of an unwitting human subject. But, as a good many theistic compatibilists have noted,[7] these analogies are irremediably flawed, because theistic determinists do not have to believe that God causes us to do what we do by circumventing our own personalities. However precisely God causes human actions, that causality can operate through our own psychological make-up, in such a way that our actions proceed from our own beliefs, desires, feelings, processes of practical reasoning, etc. And divine causality can allow us to develop our personalities gradually over time, largely via the normal varieties of social interaction in human communities. An omnipotent being is not limited to the purely mechanistic causation of a puppeteer, or the direct implantation of desires in the minds of unwitting creatures.

There is, however, a more sophisticated version of this objection which must be addressed.[8] If God ultimately determines our behaviour, no matter at how many removes, we are ultimately controlled by a being who so arranges our circumstances that we want, intend and do only what that being has foreordained for us. Like the citizens of B. F. Skinner's Walden Two, even if we can do what we want to do and choose to do, we are nonetheless conditioned to want and to choose only what God intends us to. To be sure, divine social programming is benevolent, rather than sinister. But so is the social programming of Walden Two. In both cases, that programming robs us of much, if not all, of our freedom and dignity. It is just that the God of theistic determinism is a good little girl who always intends the best for her dolls, rather than a malicious mad scientist who intends nothing but the worst for his hapless victims.

The classical compatibilists, of course, in effect maintained that all of the varieties of freedom worth wanting could be enjoyed even under the sort of control exercised by the planners of Walden Two. But most compatibilists at present, including me, would accept this claim only with the greatest reluctance, if they would accept it at all.[9] And I do not think that theistic compatibilists have to accept it. For once again, there is a crucial difference between the human controller who takes away our freedom and the all-determining God. Human social engineers can be as benevolent, or for that matter as self-sacrificing, as you please; but the imagination, let alone the knowledge and power, of even the most impressive committee of human social planners is painfully limited, and therefore even they would foreclose on a great many possibilities that the world might otherwise afford us. But the infinite God can ensure that our lives will be filled with inexpressible delights for all eternity – 'Eye hath not seen, nor ear heard, neither have entered into the heart of man, the things which God hath prepared for them that love him.'[10] Not only will the blessed delight in the discovery of ever new aspects of God for evermore; they will endlessly delight in the discovery of new aspects of themselves which union with God will disclose to them. Divine 'control', far from taking away our freedom and dignity, can deliver us into 'the glorious liberty of the children of God'.[11]

God the author of sin

The second objection is that an all-determining God would be the 'author of sin', because such a God would intend creaturely moral evil – God would plan, purpose and foreordain our sin. I shall try to blunt this complaint by considering two wholly unpalatable consequences which are alleged to follow from the fact that God intends moral evil: I shall argue that the first does not follow from theistic determinism, while the second follows from theistic determinism only if it also follows from theistic libertarianism.

1. The first of these alleged consequences is that the God of deterministic theism violates a fundamental moral principle not only of Christianity, but also of Judaism

and Islam, which is encapsulated in the well-known expression, 'One must not do evil that good may come of it.'[12] More precisely, one must not visit harm on the morally innocent for the sake of the good produced. Now while strictly speaking, a God who determines every detail of the macroscopic world does not commit our sins, such a God nevertheless deliberately arranges the world so that human beings wilfully wreak evil, much of it abominably horrendous, on the innocent. And the distinction between an agent who freely commits such an evil, and someone who freely uses that agent as a means for the commission of that evil, is a distinction without a moral difference. Granted, theistic compatibilists are not so foolish as to believe that God intends morally evil acts as evil – God does not intend sin because God delights in it, but for the sake of the good that will result. And it must be admitted that an omnipotent and omniscient deity might somehow contrive to bring about a good great enough to outweigh the evil involved in sinful acts and their consequences. Nevertheless the good so produced, even if omnipotence itself could not obtain it without that evil, cannot justify that evil.

Nor can the theistic compatibilist retort that libertarians are in the same predicament. Libertarians can protect themselves from this objection by employing the doctrine of double effect, while compatibilists cannot. Briefly put, the doctrine of double effect states that an act which is reasonably foreseen to cause harm to innocent persons is nonetheless morally permissible if the good intended by the act is sufficient to outweigh the evil of the foreseen effects, there is no better way to achieve this good, and the evil is not pursued as either an objective (an immediate purpose) or an end (a broader purpose) of the act. The God of theistic determinism pursues moral evil as an objective: like a bomber who aims to end a war by deliberately dropping bombs on innocent enemy civilians and thus destroying enemy morale, and who will shift his target if he discovers that civilians have been evacuated from the town he was intending to bomb, God's plans crucially rely on the commission of creaturely moral evil. On the other hand, the plans of the libertarian God do not. While the libertarian God may have infallibly foreseen that human beings would misuse, or would very probably misuse, their libertarian freedom against the innocent, the divine purposes in granting us freedom would not in the least have been frustrated if we had never sinned.[13]

But the theistic compatibilist can offer at least two reasonable replies to this objection. First, it puts paid to any greater-good theodicy, however modest its apologetic aims, in which the evil to be justified is regarded as integral, rather than incidental, to the greater good. And a lot of greater-good justifications for evil fall into precisely this category. For instance, 'soul-making' theodicies often maintain that the actual occurrence of natural evil is a logically necessary condition for the shaping of human beings into creatures fit for the vision of God, so that God's chief purpose in creating us would have gone unfulfilled if, by some extraordinary coincidence, no natural evil had ever occurred.[14] Hence, anyone who urges this objection had better be prepared to reject a great deal of theodicy – which means that this objection is too controversial to be of much polemical worth.

Furthermore, the theistic compatibilist can argue that, even if creatures are bound by the principle of double effect,[15] God is not – and not for the usual ghastly theo-logical reasons beloved of runaway piety, such as those to be found in especially virulent strains of the divine command theory or of apophatic theology, but on account of God's infinite power, knowledge and benevolence. For the theistic com-patibilist can maintain that in visiting moral evil upon us, God resolutely respects the moral boundaries between persons – God never permits moral evil to be inflicted on a creature made in the divine image without providentially arranging that this evil eventually produces, in some appropriate way, some suitable benefit for that creature which could not have been obtained without that evil.[16] A number of prominent philosophical theologians, libertarians as well as compatibilists, have at least sug-gested that such a claim is true, if not that it is indispensable to theism.[17] If some such claim is true, then it is scarcely evident that an all-determining God would be morally blameworthy even for purposing, planning and bringing about moral evil. For unlike the 'terror bomber' of the last-but-one paragraph, God does not inflict evil on a created person to achieve goods none of which the sufferer can enjoy. Perhaps theistic compatibilists owe their critics some plausible examples of 'suitable benefits' which might justify God in deliberately bringing about moral evil – but that is another question.

2. However, though theistic determinism might not shift the blame for our sins to God alone, it has often been alleged that it does wholly take the blame away from sinners – if God determines all that we do, moral evildoers must be wholly excused for their sins. For when we sin, we are, to put it starkly, doing what God wants us to do – God foreordains, strictly determines and desires that we sin, in order to realise greater goods that would not otherwise have come about. So what justification can there be for punishing malefactors – apart from the feeble utilitarian evasion that without punishment, evildoing would run hopelessly out of control? Theistic liber-tarians, on the other hand, while they might agree with theistic determinists that God foresees our sins, can deny that God wants us to commit them: those sins are foreseen but unintended consequences of God's decision to grant us libertarian freedom – the only creaturely freedom worthy of the name.

But, while this is a problem that theistic compatibilists cannot ignore, libertarians who are Christians, at least, cannot ignore it either. Why was it that educated Chris-tians who visited the Faith Zone at the Millennium Dome in London, and who noticed its description of Christ Jesus as 'having died tragically young', did not know whether to laugh or weep? Because Christians have always believed that God fully intended Jesus Christ to suffer an unmerited death on the cross at the hands of sinners: 'For of a truth against thy [God's] holy child Jesus, whom thou hast anointed, both Herod, and Pontius Pilate, with the Gentiles, and the people of Israel, were gathered together, For to do whatsoever thy hand and thy counsel deter-mined before to be done.'[18] That is, the heinous moral evils done to Christ were indispensable means to the inestimable good of the redemption of the world, because the doctrine of the Atonement, however precisely it is to be understood, would be pointless if Christ had not been the victim of *moral* evil. Since God's holiest purposes for fallen creation would have been frustrated if Christ had not been unjustly put to death, why should his killers be blamed for it?

God the lover of gratuitous moral evil

Finally, it is almost universally believed these days that theistic compatibilism easily succumbs to atheistic arguments from moral evil. In fact, almost everyone believes that theistic compatibilism, but not theistic libertarianism, easily succumbs to the most ambitious version of this argument imaginable, whose conclusion is that the existence of God is logically incompatible with the occurrence of any moral evil whatsoever. That is, if complete causal determinism is compatible with human freedom or moral responsibility, then, in the bracing and frequently quoted words of J. L. Mackie, 'God was not [. . .] faced with a choice between making innocent automata and making beings who, in acting freely, would sometimes go wrong: there was open to him the obviously better possibility of making beings who would act freely but always go right. Clearly, his failure to avail himself of this possibility is inconsistent with his being both omnipotent and wholly good.'[19]

But is this possibility obviously better, all things considered? The first thing that ought to be noted is that within this argument is concealed an assumption which theists, including theistic compatibilists, could perhaps justifiably deny: that theism needs a theodicy, or at any rate a theodicy for moral evil. Many theists have argued that, while God must of course have exonerating reasons for creating a world with moral evil, belief in God can nonetheless be rational, at least for some theists, even if no human being has any inkling of what those reasons might be.[20] One strategy commonly employed to this end, a strategy which has become especially widespread over the past twenty years in Anglophone philosophy of religion, is to argue that because our intellectual capacities are woefully unequal to the task of imagining the range of exonerating reasons available to God for permitting evil – how much do we really know, for example, about the range of possible goods that an omnipotent, omniscient God could realise? – the fact (if it is a fact) that we cannot think of a plausible reason why God permits moral evil will have very little force against theism.

And if theism has no need of a theodicy for moral evil, then neither does compatibilistic theism. Granted, as we have seen, the theistic compatibilist will have to acknowledge that God must arrange that the benefits which result from suffering moral evil fittingly accrue to the sufferer. Still, if our cognitive limitations are as severe as many philosophers have suggested, we cannot argue very persuasively from our inability to see how God can satisfy this principle to the conclusion that God cannot.

But what if more is required? What if, in order to reply adequately to atheistic arguments from moral evil, theists must offer a plausible reason why God permits such evil? Again, I believe that, though the theistic compatibilist has to confront some imposing difficulties in responding to this challenge, the difficulties are no less severe for the theistic libertarian.

We can begin to see this, I think, once we observe that libertarians, as well as compatibilists, have to face up to the objection that God could have created free agents and given them, on the whole, much stronger dispositions to do what is morally right than those of typical free agents in our world. Libertarianism, after all, would be highly unattractive if it maintained that freedom and moral responsibility are incompatible with moral dispositions that strongly incline without necessitating. And a world in which agents are far more likely to do what is right seems a better option than our own world, especially as the consequences of moral evil in our world are often so appalling. But neither of the only two forms of theistic libertarianism which survive initial scrutiny can easily surmount this objection.[21]

One response to this objection is available only to modern Molinists, who, though libertarians, also believe that divine foreknowledge, even of free human acts, is exhaustive. According to this response, God was unable to create a world with morally better-disposed creatures than ours on the whole, not because God is incapable of foreseeing in complete detail the consequences of divine creative choices, but, to put it bluntly, because God is unlucky. Prior to any creative decisions on God's part, there is, for each free agent God could create, and for each morally significant decision that creature might make, a fact about which alternative that creature would choose. For instance, prior to God's decision to create our world, it was already true that, should God create this world and Judas Iscariot find himself in precisely the same situation on Maundy Thursday as described in the New Testament, Judas would betray his Lord. For the sake of convenience, let us call these facts 'conditionals of freedom'. To be sure, conditionals of freedom are logically contingent; but they are also firmly fixed prior to anything that God can do. And it is just an unfortunate fact that the conditionals of freedom with which God was confronted made it impossible for God to create a world with a better balance than ours of moral good over moral evil. So, even if God had created a world with free agents having stronger inclinations than ours to act in accordance with God's will, they would have behaved less admirably than we do. Nonetheless, the world God in fact decided to create has such a favourable balance of moral good over moral evil that God was justified in creating it rather than a world with no free creatures at all.

But, while this reply has often been presented to the philosophical public as a bare logical possibility,[22] Molinists have made no serious attempt to defend it as a live possibility. And it is not difficult to understand why. Even if God cannot create just any possible world, and even if we limit God to mere deistic providence, so that God cannot supply grace to free creatures to influence them to do good, God must still be able to choose from an infinitely vast panoply of worlds containing free creatures. To suggest that God could only create worlds very like ours, with so very much sin, seems to limit God's power far too drastically: like the Demiurge of Plato's *Timaeus*, God has to put up with an enormous reservoir of surd evil, about which nothing can be done. And this suggestion does not increase in plausibility when we bear in mind that orthodox Christianity believes in divine grace – which amounts to believing that God has an enormous repertoire of supernatural ways of working on the creaturely heart without violating creaturely freedom – and in the sinlessness of Christ qua human (if not also the sinlessness of the Virgin Mary): if the human nature of Jesus was preserved from sin throughout his life on Earth by divine grace, what could prevent God doing the same for others – or at least improving the overall balance of moral good over moral evil?[23]

According to the other libertarian theory of divine providence, God cannot prevent all moral evil, not because God's hands are tied by conditionals of freedom, but because God cannot foresee with certainty how free creatures will behave. Let us, more or less following Paul Helm,[24] call this the 'risky providence' theory. Again, however, even if God cannot make an initial creative choice in full knowledge of how the world will unfold thereafter, he still has a vast range of initial creative choices, and an impressive variety of means to exercise grace on the creaturely soul. So it seems highly probable that God could have created a world with appreciably better-behaved creatures than this one, and that the risk God would run of creating a world with much less well-behaved creatures was vanishingly small. And if God decided to go ahead and create such a world, what greater good would that have forgone – of a kind not available to a compatibilist theodicy?[25]

Hence, it is not clear that libertarian theists can deal more comfortably than theistic compatibilists with the problem of evil. And it seems to me that there is an important moral to be drawn from the preceding discussion – Christians, if not also other theists, should not blithely accept the principle that a perfect being always eliminates moral evil as far as it can.

III. THE ALL-DETERMINING GOD: DEVOUTLY TO BE WISHED?

The preceding discussion has, I trust, demonstrated that theistic compatibilism is decidedly better than its reputation. But, unlike the vast majority of theistic compatibilists, I am not a 'hard compatibilist' – I do not believe that we are free and morally responsible if and *only if* our acts are determined.[26] True, libertarians frequently underestimate the difficulty of accounting for free will and moral responsibility under indeterminism; but I am not convinced by arguments against the very possibility of doing so. Perhaps we shall some day discover that the process of human choice is never determined, and yet frequently conforms to some credible libertarian account of the positive conditions of freedom and responsibility. If we ever do discover this, then the arguments against theistic compatibilism might have much more force than at present.

Nonetheless, it must be asked how intellectually comfortable a theist could reasonably be if the empirical facts do turn out to favour libertarianism. Obviously this question is too complex for more than a cursory examination here. But in the space remaining, I can at least observe that, from the point of view of Christian theism if not theism in general, both of the defensible libertarian alternatives face at least one monumental problem that theistic compatibilism can wholly avoid. If the defence of theistic compatibilism in section II of this chapter is sound, then it may well be that Christian theists, if not theists in general, ought to hope with all their hearts that God is an omni-determining deity.[27]

Consider first the risky providence view. It has often been objected to this view that, contrary to the traditions of the various theistic religions, God could not be sure that any specific plan God might formulate for the world would come to pass.[28] And this difficulty seems especially acute for the Christian religion. Few doctrines can be more central to Christianity than the sinlessness of Jesus Christ. But according to the proponents of risky providence, it cannot be foreknown with certainty what a free creature will do when faced with a morally significant decision. Since Christ's death and resurrection have no salvific power unless his human nature is morally free, it follows that not even God could foreknow with certainty whether Christ's human nature would remain sinless throughout his life on Earth. But of course the sinlessness of Christ was essential to the plan of salvation which God envisaged for fallen humanity. Since God not only repeatedly announced this plan in advance, but also repeatedly predicted that it would be fulfilled, the God of the risky providence theory seems far too reckless to count as a wise creator.[29] And not only compatibilists, but also Molinists, can evade this difficulty.

On the other hand, the Molinist doctrine of conditionals of freedom seems to saddle Molinism with at least two major disadvantages vis-à-vis theistic compatibilism, not just from the Christian point of view, but from the perspective of theism itself.

First, since true conditionals of freedom are both logically contingent and true prior to God's creative decisions, Molinism is not easy to reconcile with anything resembling the traditional doctrine of divine sovereignty. Of course, libertarianism without true conditionals of freedom can loosely be said to impose limitations on the power of God to obtain what God desires, since God cannot ever ensure on a given occasion that a free agent chooses the good. But these limitations do not vary from possible world to possible world – that is to say, they are logical limitations, and are therefore consistent with divine omnipotence. There may be a possible world in which I always freely do what is right; but there is no possible world in which God can ensure that this comes about. God can only influence my will up to a point; after that, even God can only hope. But according to Molinism, the set of true conditionals of freedom about me could have been radically different – God could have had the happy choice of creating a world in which I never sin at all. So the facts which prevent God from doing this are only contingently true. And how can a God whose desires are frustrated by contingent facts antecedent to all creative decisions be the omnipotent God of traditional theism?[30] Moreover, nothing that God does can afford even a partial explanation of the truth of a conditional of freedom: divine activity cannot even be a causally necessary condition of such truths. Not only does this jar with the doctrine of divine sovereignty; it also subverts a large family of respectable arguments for the existence of God – namely, all arguments which ground a logically contingent truth in the will of God. If a conditional of freedom about what Judas will do on Maundy Thursday need not – indeed, cannot – have a divine explanation of its truth, why should any other contingent fact need such an explanation?

Second, the Molinist doctrine of conditionals of freedom seems to undermine libertarian freedom. Suppose the following conditional of freedom is true:

(C) If Keith Ward offered me £100,000 to cease and desist from publicly criticising his opinions, I would freely accept his offer.

Now suppose Ward actually makes the offer and I freely accept it. Can the truth of (C) depend on my actually accepting the offer? No. Here is one reason why not.[31] My acceptance of the offer depends on, among other things, Ward's making it; and that, in turn, depends on God's decision to create a world in which it comes about that Ward does so. And according to Molinism, God's decision to create such a world depends on the truth of (C), for God decides which world to create on the basis of God's knowledge of which conditionals of freedom are true. So if the truth of (C) depended on my acceptance of Ward's offer, a circle of relations of dependence would result; and that is impossible. Therefore, the truth of (C) does not depend on anything I actually do; and so it seems that I cannot be responsible for its truth. But, we may reasonably suppose, I cannot be responsible for Ward making his offer, either. Yet (C), combined with Ward's offer, entails that I accept it; which means that my choice – and for that matter, all other creaturely choices – is entailed by circumstances for which I am not responsible. And thus there is no such thing as libertarian freedom.[32]

IV. THEISTIC COMPATIBILISM AND COMPARATIVE THEOLOGY

Keith Ward has issued a magisterial summons to join him in the project of 'comparative theology', in which 'scholars holding different world-views share together in the investigation of concepts of ultimate reality, the final human goal, and the way to achieve it', but in which the particular view of each scholar, while likely to develop and deepen as the investigation proceeds, is also likely to remain largely the same in its basic elements.[33] In this chapter I have responded to that summons, and have argued that, despite widespread belief to the contrary, one particular world-view, theistic compatibilism, is worthy to participate in the project of comparative theology. Furthermore, while the form of theistic compatibilism I favour clearly diverges in a number of notable respects from traditional forms of that doctrine – for example, in its rejection of 'hard compatibilism' – I have also given reasons to believe that theistic compatibilism can survive the most searching investigations of comparative theology with its fundamental features intact. Whether it can in fact survive such investigations depends on whether theistic compatibilists can match the standards which Keith Ward has maintained throughout his illustrious career as both a philosopher and a theologian.[34]

NOTES

1 At one point, however, he briefly resorts to compatibilism: see n. 29 below.
2 I know of only two significant exceptions: Robert Young – see *Freedom, Responsibility and God* (London: Macmillan, 1975), ch. 14 – and Paul Helm – see *Eternal God* (Oxford: Clarendon Press, 1988), ch. 9, and *The Providence of God* (Leicester: Inter-Varsity Press, 1993), esp. chs 7–8.
3 An especially valuable anthology of important essays on these issues is Robert Kane (ed.), *Free Will* (Oxford: Blackwell, 2002).
4 For an exceptionally lucid and subtle statement of this problem, see Robert Kane, *The Significance of Free Will* (New York: Oxford University Press, 1996), 107–11.

5   Antony G. N. Flew, *The Presumption of Atheism* (London: Elek/Pemberton, 1976), 96.

6   Noteworthy statements of this objection may be found, among other places, in John Hick, *Evil and the God of Love* (1st publ. London: Macmillan, 1966), ch. 14, §4; Richard Gale, *On the Nature and Existence of God* (Cambridge: Cambridge University Press, 1991), 120–2 and 152–68; and Kane, *The Significance of Free Will*, 64–9.

7   For a modern example, see Helm, *The Providence of God*, 175.

8   This objection is taken from Kane: see n. 6 above.

9   Though it is still defended – see, for instance, David Blumenfeld, 'Freedom and Mind Control', *American Philosophical Quarterly*, 25 (1988), 215–27, and Bruce Waller, 'A Response to Kane and Hocutt', *Behaviour and Philosophy*, 20 (1992), 83–8.

10 1 Cor. 2.9, Authorised Version; all further biblical quotations in the chapter are from this translation.

11 Rom. 8.21.

12 The *locus classicus* of this principle in Christian thought is Rom. 3.8.

13 For my statement of this argument, I have relied on Peter Byrne's stimulating discussion in 'Helm's God and the Authorship of Sin', in Martin Stone (ed.), *Reason, Faith and History: Essays in Honour of Paul Helm* (Aldershot: Ashgate Publishing, forthcoming). I am grateful to Professor Byrne for sending me a copy of his paper prior to publication.

14 See, among others, Hick, *Evil and the God of Love*, ch. 15, §4, and Richard Swinburne, *Providence and the Problem of Evil* (Oxford: Clarendon Press, 1998), 161–7. Swinburne further claims that the actual occurrence of a particular form of natural evil – bad desires – is logically necessary for creaturely freedom of choice: ibid., 135.

15 But the doctrine of double effect has been much criticised, and some of this criticism could be put to good use by defenders of theistic compatibilism. For a brief summary of the more notable objections, with references, see F. M. Kamm, 'Nonconsequentialism', in Hugh LaFollette (ed.), *Blackwell Guide to Ethical Theory* (Oxford: Blackwell, 2000), 211–12.

16 Paul Helm has suggested as much, in response to the very objection that God permits evil that good may come: see *The Providence of God*, 208.

17 Note, for instance, this passage by the libertarian philosopher Eleonore Stump, which clearly suggests that such a claim is indispensable to theism: 'It seems to me nonetheless that a perfectly good entity who was also omniscient and omnipotent must govern the evil resulting from the misuse of [the] significant freedom [of created persons] in such a way that the sufferings of any particular person are outweighed by the good which the suffering produces *for that person*': 'The Problem of Evil', *Faith and Philosophy*, 2 (1985), 411, italics hers.

18 Acts 4.27–8; see also Acts 2.23; Luke 22.22.

19 J. L. Mackie, 'Evil and Omnipotence', *Mind*, n.s., 64 (1955), 209.

20 See, for example, the papers by William Alston, Daniel Howard-Snyder, Alvin Plantinga, Peter van Inwagen and Stephen Wykstra in Daniel Howard-Snyder (ed.), *The Evidential Argument from Evil* (Bloomington, Ind. and Indianapolis: Indiana University Press, 1996).

21 Space does not allow me to explain why the two versions of theistic libertarianism I am about to consider are the only ones worthy of serious examination, but see William Hasker, *God, Time and Knowledge* (Ithaca, NY: Cornell University Press, 1989), 53–63.

22 See esp. Alvin Plantinga, *The Nature of Necessity* (Oxford: Clarendon Press, 1974), ch. 9.

23 This paragraph is heavily indebted to Robert M. Adams, 'Middle Knowledge and the Problem of Evil', *American Philosophical Quarterly*, 14 (1977), §V. Note also that I have granted the Molinist an assumption which is rather contestable: namely, that for any morally evil creaturely act in our world, God could not have forestalled it by withholding the creature's freedom, because that would have resulted in an even greater amount of moral evil.

    Discussion of the all but innumerable difficulties of the orthodox Christian doctrine of grace must be deferred to another occasion.

24 Helm, *The Providence of God*, 39 *et passim*.

25 Richard Swinburne gives an interesting answer to this question, most recently in *Providence*

and the Problem of Evil: it is fairly obvious that when an agent does what is morally right, then the stronger the agent's inclination to do a morally wrong alternative, the more intrinsic goodness the right action has (87); so if God had created the world I have described in the text, God would have risked the loss of much of this sort of value (134–7). I should think that, far from being fairly obvious, Swinburne's principle is at best highly controversial. When, for example, I make progress in subduing a temptation to commit a particular kind of wrong act, why should that diminish (even *ceteris paribus*) the intrinsic goodness of my choosing a right alternative? It should be noted, however, that Swinburne does offer an argument for his principle (87), which for reasons of space I cannot consider here.

26 I have borrowed this convenient term from Thomas Flint: see his 'Two Accounts of Providence', in Thomas V. Morris (ed.), *Divine and Human Action* (Ithaca, NY: Cornell University Press, 1988), 172. It is not surprising that most of the influential theistic compatibilists have been hard compatibilists, since influential compatibilists well into the twentieth century have generally been hard compatibilists. As the reader will gather from the remainder of the paragraph in the text, I am not a 'soft compatibilist' either. Perhaps I am best labelled an 'agnostic for the time being', as I believe that, in the absence of the relevant empirical facts, we are not entitled to hold that freedom or responsibility are compatible with determinism – nor, as I argued in §I, are we entitled to hold that they are not.

27 There are other meritorious reasons for hoping this. One is that theistic compatibilism cuts the Gordian knot that libertarians inevitably seem to tie when attempting to reconcile divine foreknowledge and human freedom. For the details, see William Alston, 'Divine Foreknowledge and Alternative Conceptions of Human Freedom', *International Journal for Philosophy of Religion*, 18 (1985), §§I and II.

28 For a thorough presentation of this objection, see Thomas Flint, *Divine Providence: The Molinist Account* (Ithaca, NY: Cornell University Press, 1998), 101–7. Ward, who endorses the risky providence view, attempts to dispel this objection in *Religion and Creation* (Oxford: Clarendon Press, 1996), 259–61, claiming that 'even precise events far in the future can be predicted with certainty' (260). But a number of facts militate against this claim, not least the marked sensitivity of large-scale natural and social systems to minor variations in initial conditions and to small external fluctuations. To take just one example, if we have more or less as much freedom of choice as we think we do, how could even an omniscient being have predicted with certainty in 1900 that Hitler would become the leader of Germany in 1933?

29 Thomas Flint develops a similar argument in '"A Death He Freely Accepted": Molinist Reflections on the Incarnation', *Faith and Philosophy*, 18 (2001), 16–17. Ward confronts this problem head on in *Religion and Revelation* (Oxford: Clarendon Press, 1994), 261–5. But in the course of attempting a solution he abandons his incompatibilism, since he allows that a human will can be 'morally free' as long as it is 'able to decide in full knowledge of the facts and in accordance with [its] innermost desires, without external constraint' (264).

   Note that the risky providence view also has trouble accounting for Old Testament passages which traditional Christians have regarded as predictions of another key element of God's plan of salvation, mentioned earlier in the text – that the Christ would suffer moral evil for the sake of the world's redemption. See for example the Fourth Servant Song (Isa. 52.13–53.12).

30 This is a familiar modern objection to Molinism, which philosophers have raised ever since Molinism was revived in the mid-1960s: ever since, at least, William Wainwright's 'Freedom and Omnipotence', *Nous*, 2 (1968), 293–8.

31 For other reasons, see Flint, *Divine Providence*, 124.

32 This argument can be assembled from elements of standard objections to Molinism, and is developed at greater length in Hugh Rice, *God and Goodness* (Oxford: Oxford University Press, 2000), 98–100.

33 Keith Ward, *Religion and Community* (Oxford: Clarendon Press, 2000), 339.

34 I would like to express my thanks to Mark Wynn for his many incisive comments on a previous draft of this chapter.

10

All Things Considered: Providence and Divine Purpose

PAUL HELM

In his book *Religion and Creation* Keith Ward asks whether it follows from the willing permission of evil that 'the universe is exactly, in every detail, as God intends it to be'.[1] He claims that the answer is 'No'. Since I first read it, Ward's question has prompted me to reflect on the senses in which the universe is in every detail as God intends it to be.

Ward believes that this belief (let us call it 'AGI') is a common assumption in traditional theological thinking. He says, however, that since the universe is not at all the sort of universe which a perfect God could be expected to create, one is forced to deny AGI.[2] Ward does not cite any evidence for the belief that AGI is a common assumption in traditional theological thinking. One might have thought the reverse; that any thinking which has a place for a Fall must deny AGI. Or so at least it may seem. Nevertheless, I shall sympathetically discuss versions of AGI in what follows.

As part of this tribute to Keith Ward, this chapter is a rumination on his question by way of some observations on providence. I shall discuss features of a debate between those who were each committed to a version of AGI. This debate is approached in the spirit of what Marilyn McCord Adams calls sceptical realism: that there are facts of the matter independently of what we believe or think, but that the defence of any well-formulated philosophical position proceeds from premises which may be fundamentally controversial and therefore not universal in their convincingness or their appeal. Such a project is undertaken in the spirit of trying to formulate a particular philosophical position as clearly and fully as possible.[3] So while I do not believe for one moment that Ward shares many of the premises from which this discussion proceeds, I nevertheless hope that he will find points of interest in it, and even of partial agreement.

I. GOD'S INTENTION AND GOVERNANCE

We may first approach Ward's question by considering what Thomas Aquinas's answer to it might be. He says, 'God, and nature, and indeed every causal agent, does what is best overall, but not what is best in every part, except when the part is regarded in its relationship to the whole.'[4] It would be fallacious to suppose that God's attitude is the same overall and in every part. Those events which are not best in every part God brings about in furtherance of some wider consideration which is best overall. Thomas reminds us that it is a fallacy to think that because some arrangement is wise, every detail of that arrangement, considered in isolation, must be wise. (Let us call this 'Aquinas's point'; we shall return to it.) This is in fact an instance of Aquinas avoiding the fallacy of division, the fallacy of thinking that if the bag of sand is heavy then every grain of sand in the bag must be heavy. This claim is consistent with AGI, though obviously it needs other premisses in order to entail AGI.

Gerard Hughes has emphasised that in making moral judgements about an action, including moral judgements about the action of God, we need to be able to assess the action under a description – not just any description, but one that includes all and only those features which are relevant to making a moral assessment.[5] And as he says, settling on such a description is a tall order. What in effect Aquinas is proposing is that one feature which is morally relevant to assessing the goodness of what God intends is what God intends 'overall'. What God does is not best for the human race, or for the animate world, or for some individual person or thing, but best all things considered. Further – though considering this falls beyond the scope of this chapter – what God does overall must meet the objection that in so acting God is flouting some moral rule.

The objection that I shall consider in what follows might be called the *globalism objection*. God, for Aquinas, and for all proponents of AGI, must (it seems) think and act in global terms. God's care or concern for the particular or for the individual is subsumed under his concern for some greater global good and perhaps, ultimately, with a concern for himself, for his own glory. In response to this objection we shall now consider other aspects of AGI which might permit us to construct a less global version of AGI than that which Aquinas's point can be used to express.

II. INFRA- AND SUPRALAPSARIANISM

In the discussions that followed the establishment of Reformed theology attention was paid to the ordering of the divine decrees, or of the component parts of the divine decree, particularly with respect to the divine permission of the Fall. All parties to these discussions agreed that everything is efficaciously decreed by God (and so each subscribed to a strong version of AGI), but they differed over the logical arrangement of the decrees in the divine mind.

According to the infralapsarian way of thinking, the divine decree to redeem the elect followed in order (though not of course in time, this being an eternal decree) the decree to create and the decree to permit the Fall. The unfolding of these decrees in time – creation, then the Fall and then redemption through Christ – mirrors the logical sequence of their eternal ordering in the divine mind. The significance of this is that, on the assumption that divine providence is an exclusively and exhaustively teleological arrangement having one end, creation is first in the divine mind, the Fall as spoiling the good creation is second, and redemption as the restoration of creation is third.

By contrast, according to supralapsarianism in its textbook version, the decree to redeem the elect precedes in logical order the decree to create and to permit the Fall, so that creation and the Fall are for the sake of the redemptive end. Unlike infralapsarianism this view offers one clear, linear, means–end structure to the decrees. It may be thought that supralapsarianism is the harsher doctrine in that it embeds the Fall more deeply into the divine decree. In infralapsarianism the Fall, though necessary for redemption, is not a means to redemption, whereas for supralapsarianism creation and the Fall appear to be for the sake of redemption, as a means to an end: 'What is last in execution is first in intention.' We shall reflect further on this shortly.

I don't want to enter the vexed question of which of the two views (if either) is the more plausible. The Reformed churches have always recognised infralapsarianism to be the majority or received view while regarding supralapsarianism as a permitted alternative, as is evident from the confessions of faith of that period. As the supralapsarian William Twisse quaintly put it, the difference 'is meerly *Apex Logicus*, a poynt of Logick. And were it not a meer madnesse, to make a breach of unity or charity in the Church of God, merely upon a poynt of Logick?'[6] His point is that what the two positions hold in common vastly outweighs their differences. Nevertheless, mere points of logic can have significant consequences, a fact which Twisse himself would not have denied.

There is one apparently insuperable objection to supralapsarianism. How, it might be argued, can God decree to redeem certain people before (logically) he decrees to create them? The objection is (in the words of Twisse):

> God cannot worke upon a subject, unless the subject first be, and that occasion also whereupon he works; therefore, God cannot intend to work upon a subject unlesse first he intend to produce that subject, and permit (at least) the occasion whereupon he intends to work.[7]

Surely God cannot identify any of those individuals he decrees to redeem before (logically) he decrees to create them? The answer of the supralapsarians is that he can, in that those he decrees to redeem (prior to decreeing to create them) he regards as 'creatable'. Twisse again:

> As much as to say, because I cannot ride to London without a horse, therefore I cannot intend to ride to London, unless first I intend to get me a horse. Whence it manifestly followeth, that in execution I must first ride to London, and afterward get me an horse to that purpose.[8]

Just as one can first intend to ride to London without first intending to get a horse, so (Twisse reasons) God can first intend to redeem the elect without first intending to create them. From among all possible people God decrees to redeem some of them and then (in the next logical moment of his decree) decrees to actualise, to create them and all other members of the human race, then (in the next logical moment) he decrees to permit the Fall of the race.[9]

The question at issue is, what in this exclusively means–end arrangement is (or are) the end (or ends), and what are the means? According to supralapsarianism there is one divine end, namely the glory of God in the redemption of the elect, and all else is the means to that end – creation, the Fall, and whatever is encompassed by these events. On the other hand, according to infralapsarianism God's first end is creation, and his second end, given the Fall, is redemption. There is a sense, therefore, in which supralapsarianism offers a one-track, infralapsarianism a two-track, version of the divine decree. The 'poynt of Logick' appears to have interesting and significant consequences.

A common starting point in the debate was a commitment to particularism, the view that some people are not saved – not on a priori grounds, of course, but on the grounds that Scripture teaches it, and that experience confirms it.[10] And so besides the decree of God to redeem, consideration had also to be given to the non-redeemed, to the decree of reprobation.[11] Here further subtleties emerged, in order to protect the doctrine of the decrees from the inference that certain people were created in order to be damned. One subtlety was the clear enunciation of the distinction between the inscrutable divine decree to pass by some, not electing them to salutation, an act of pure sovereignty, and the decree to condemn those inscrutably passed by, the grounds for which lay not in the pure decision of God, but in the permitted, foreseen sin of those who were passed by.

Another subtlety is a further application of what we earlier called Aquinas's point, an avoidance of the fallacy of division in reflecting on God's decrees. It is possible to view these decrees, whether in the infralapsarian or supralapsarian order, as one decree. God's will to create, to permit the Fall, to redeem some and to harden others is not a series of separate decrees, but parts of one decree of the means, the end being the manifestation or display of God's love and justice. Both infralapsarians and supralapsarians claim that it is a fallacy to argue that because God wills (A, B and C) as a means to a given end D he therefore separately wills A as a means to D, B as a means to D, and so on. And so creation is not decreed as a means to salvation and damnation, nor is the Fall a mere means to the giving of grace. In other words, an atomistic, divisive understanding of the decrees is to be avoided, an organic understanding is to be preferred. As Twisse remarked, 'I make the decrees of creation, permission of sin, and raysing out of sin, not *subordinata*, but *coordinata* and *conjuncta*',[12] and 'So I say in like manner, God doth joyntly decree to give both grace and glory; I do not say God doth decree joyntly to give them, but he joyntly decreeth to give both grace and glory.'[13] Let us call this 'Twisse's point'.

Twisse offers a further subtlety. It is frequently said that the decrees, being eternal, do not have a temporal priority the one over the other, but a 'natural' priority. Twisse understands this in the following way:

> Alwaies the nature of the end duely considered, doth bespeak what shall be the condition of the means, so that this makes no priority of existence at all, neither in duration nor in nature properly so called, but only such a subordination between them, that the reason of the one, that is, the

nature or condition of the one, depends upon the nature and condition of the other. [. . .] They commonly call it priority of nature. But take heed you doe not apply it to any of these two kinds of priority of nature mentioned by Aristotle. For try as you please, and you shall find that none of them can possibly save the turne: What then is this priority of nature so called? I answer, it is only *prioritas rationis*.[14]

This further point concerns the way in which the divine decrees are considered to be 'co-ordinate'. Twisse argues that the sort of priority in the ordering of the decrees is neither temporal (it can't be that, since the decrees are all eternal) nor logical but *prioritas rationis*. That is, the co-ordination appears to be a structural connection (*ratio* is best thought of here not as 'reason' but as 'structure') between the various discernible elements in the decree, the nature and condition of the means depending upon (i.e. logically depending upon) the nature and condition of the end. It is not simply that there is a timeless ordering of separate decrees, each being co-ordinated by the one divine decree respecting them all, but that a full specification of the end entails the means.

Perhaps this means something like the following. The decree to redeem the elect logically implies their creation and likewise the decree to redeem them logically implies their need of redemption. The decrees to create and to redeem are thus not separate or separable decrees, though there may be no formal logical connection between them. The decree to redeem may imply fallenness.

This view appears to contain at least some of the elements of Leibniz's view of possible worlds. Leibniz referred to Twisse on more than one occasion. We may surmise that it may have been a point such as this that gained his interest.[15] We shall return to the possible significance of this later.

III. SOME CONSEQUENCES

I want now to explore some of the consequences that follow from these respective positions, these different versions of AGI, and having Ward's question in mind, to make some suggestions. The supralapsarian must hold AGI in a very strong form, for everything is either a means to the final end, or is that end itself. Or if he is Twissian on this, he will hold that the end and the means are part of the same intellectual structure in the divine mind. The supralapsarian would make Aquinas's point perhaps more emphatically than Thomas himself. Everything is as God intends it, because everything is subordinate, in a strong, logically structural sense, to God's end. But it does not and cannot follow from this (if we bear in mind Twisse's point, and his further subtlety) that every particular aspect of that decree, viewed in isolation from every other aspect, is as God decreed it. This would be false, and perhaps unintelligible; it would at once raise questions about counterfactuals the truth of which one could only speculate about. And so the only sense in which one can speak of the decree of the means and the end is in the *sensus compositus*, not the *sensus divisus*, because the means and end are structurally indivisible.

However, to the extent that it is intelligible for us to consider some matters in isolation, then it is possible for us to think of God taking up a variety of affectional stances with respect to these separately identifiable matters. Although given that God intended the Holocaust by willingly permitting it, or intended the death of a baby from cancer by willingly permitting that, we may surmise that he takes no pleasure in such events when viewed in isolation from the other features of the one eternal decree, features so numerous and interlaced that our present failure to grasp them leaves us baffled and perplexed by our experience of the incidence of goods and evils, horrendous and other. We may even surmise that *in sensu diviso* God's attitude to particular evils is as akin to that of a modern western liberal as you wish. This provides some mitigation, therefore, of the globalism objection, albeit of a rather hypothetical or speculative kind.

For the infralapsarian, however, though his scheme does not have the same tidiness as that of the supralapsarian, he is nevertheless able to impute to the creator much more emphatically than is the supralapsarian a valuing of the creation independently and separately from the value God places on redemption, however highly he may value that. For there is a separability to the divine decrees for the infralapsarian that the supralapsarian cannot countenance. Nevertheless, bearing in mind the infralapsarian's commitment to AGI, what is permitted, namely the Fall, is also divinely decreed. There is no scope even in the infralapsarian scheme for attributing independent value to the creation apart from considerations of salvation and perdition, despite the fears expressed by Karl Barth.[16]

In a recent discussion, Richard Mouw sees in infralapsarianism an avenue opening down which one can appreciate humanness for its own sake, whereas supralapsarianism is unable to address matters of generic human concern.[17] Mouw says:

> If we ask a supralapsarian a question about anything that happens in the universe, the full and correct answer must always be articulated in terms of the eternal destinies of these two classes of human beings. Why did Plato write *The Republic*? So that the decrees of election and reprobation might be actualised. Why did Babe Ruth hit sixty home runs in one season? Why did President Kennedy approve the plans for the Bay of Pigs invasion? Why did the Tokyo stock exchange experience serious declines during 1998? In every case the answer is that the final point of these events is that they promote the realisation of God's decision regarding elect and reprobate human beings.[18]

By contrast, Mouw thinks that infralapsarians are better placed than are supralapsarians to give independent value to creation:

> There is no reason why, for example, an infralapsarian could not view God as taking delight in a display of athletic prowess because of ultimate purposes that stand alongside of, rather than being subservient to, the goal of actualising the decrees of election and reprobation.[19]

Mouw claims support for this view from the Reformed dogmatician Herman Bavinck and from the passage from William Twisse most recently quoted. But as will be clear, I think that both Mouw and Bavinck misunderstand Twisse, who (as we have seen) if anything wishes to bind in together even more tightly all the means that subserve the one end rather than envisage separate ends.

If we are to do what Mouw wants to do, to give independent value to createdness, and so partly meet the globalism objection within the framework of a doctrine of the all-encompassing nature of the divine decree that is common to both supra- and infralapsarians, then I believe that we need to take a step or two back from the vital assumption about divine wisdom, or divine rationality, which is common to both positions. This vital assumption is that the divine mind works in a means–end manner, the end having an eternal, abiding significance; divine wisdom, or rationality, or both, is displayed simply in having one worthy eternal end, or several eternal ends, and in the ordaining of suitable means. This assumption operates whether we think of one end ('There is only one eternal end, and every event/state of affairs that is not that end is a means to it') or of many ends ('Every event/state of affairs is a means to some eternal end or other'). So long as we think of the decree (or decrees) of God regarding his own glory as following one or other such pattern, and especially if we think of the decree of God following the first pattern, then this version of AGI will be open to the full force of the globalism objection.

Let us assume that divine rationality has a means–end structure. Why should we think that the teleology of divine rationality is exclusively and exhaustively eternal? Perhaps we could surmise that because of an understandable exclusive pre-occupation with soteriology, with what Geerhardus Vos inelegantly called 'hypersoteriological onesidedness',[20] the infralapsarians allowed themselves to be sucked into making the assumption that all divine ends have to do with matters which find their fulfilment in eternity, an assumption certainly held by the supralapsarians, and one which may seem to be essential to their position, but which is certainly not essential to infralapsarianism as such, and perhaps not essential to supralapsarianism either.

Bavinck, I think, adopts a position similar to that of Mouw. He says, 'The history of the universe is not a mere means which loses its value as soon as the end of the age is reached, but it has influence and leaves fruits, for eternity.'[21] So Plato's *Republic*, and the stock market movements in Tokyo, for example, do not lose their value at the end of the age, but for Bavinck they have eternal value, fruits for eternity. Though what these fruits are is somewhat obscure. Maybe we can throw a little light on them.

If God were able to place a separate and distinct value on the creation from that which he places on redemption, then what stops him placing a different value, indeed different values, upon the various particularities of the creation? There is no saying a priori what these values might be, and we must be careful lest in speculating we create a God in our own image. But we might suppose that he may value certain things, for as long as these things last, for their own sake. So not only are some things willable as means to the one end of the eternal divine glory, they are willable for their own sake for as long as they last, and the divine glory which is the end of willing these states of affairs will last as long as they last, excluding complications about memory and divine eternality. Certain states of affairs have intrinsic temporal worth. There are things for which the question 'What good is this for?' can be answered by 'For its own sake' but for which the answer to 'What eternal good is this for?' is 'None'.

So we might make a distinction between a last or chief or eternal end, an end which is the most valued and which is not subordinate to some greater end, and temporal ends. For even if one allows that the chief end of creation is God's eternal glory, it does not follow that because the chief end is the eternal glory of God every other end is subordinate to the chief end in a linear fashion, for may there not be many temporal ends which glorify God? Why should not God be glorified in his creatures' enjoyment of temporal things for their own sake, and in his own enjoyment of them, for as long as they last? Such temporal (and temporary) states may each independently contribute to the chief end, or they may not. Things which considered in themselves are not 'for' anything, whether they are intrinsically valuable or disvaluable, may nevertheless be woven by omnipotent wisdom into a wider and broader means–end pattern. Or, standing alone, they may not.

When the Westminster divines famously stated that the chief end of man is to glorify God and to enjoy him for ever, they implicitly drew our attention to lesser ends that are other than glorifying God and enjoying him for ever. Maybe there are activities which are glorifying to God now, but not for ever. Maybe God gains temporary glory from the temporary, from states of affairs which bear no eternal fruits. Maybe there are states of affairs which are intrinsically valuable, but not for ever. If the Westminster divines allow this latitude to human beings made in the image of God, why may not God permit himself such latitude? God may delight in the particular and the temporary for its own sake, on account of its temporal intrinsic value.

Thus what is needed for AGI to parry the globalism objection more effectively is not only a two-track approach to the values embedded in the divine decree, but also a two-value or multi-value approach. On this version of AGI, God decrees everything, some things as part of a set of means to an end, and other things to be the objects of divine and human engagement for their own sake. It then may be necessary to state unambiguously that God has decrees, plural. But won't such a plurality of decrees jeopardise the divine simplicity? The short answer is that if the multiplicity of means in the decree of God as envisaged by both the traditional infralapsarian and the traditional supralapsarian does not jeopardise divine simplicity, why should this further proposal?

Of more importance is the question of whether postulating a two- or many-value track in divine providence is inherently inconsistent. It is not obvious that it is. A person may value or disvalue something for its own sake, delighting in its beauty, or shunning it because of its ugliness. All the same he may want to surrender what is inherently valuable, or admirable for its intrinsic worth, for something he wants more; the family silver may have to pay for the people carrier as there come to be more people in the family to carry. Alternatively, he may need what is inherently disvaluable, for example the infliction of pain, for some further end. God may not do evil that good may come, but he may willingly permit evil that good may come. Of course God does not have to give up the intrinsic beauty of the creation for anything else, or curtail examples of human grace or skill as time and space run out for him. The beauty remains for as long as it remains, even when another, longer track runs beside it. God may disvalue the particular occasions of pain and sin, even as their willing permission is necessary for some greater good.

Many human moral dilemmas are generated by scarcity; but there are no opportunity costs in divine operations. Not feeling the pinch of scarcity, the Almighty is not caught on the horns of any moral dilemma. And even if he were, recasting the problem of evil as involving a dilemma for God might be an advance on thinking of it as a putatively inconsistent set of propositions.

Must we then bid farewell to supralapsarianism, as suggested earlier? Not necessarily. According to the supralapsarian the decree to elect and to reprobate is logically prior to the decree to create (or, following Twisse, is part of the same rational structure). But this does not imply that the significance of creation is exhausted by the significance of redemption. Nevertheless, the supralapsarian will find it harder to avoid the globalism objection, because any two possible worlds in which precisely the same creatures are saved, and precisely the same creatures damned, must be very similar to each other. So while there are some features of our world, perhaps many such features, which are not bound up with the redemption of the elect and the damnation of the reprobate, these features will be comparatively few. The interests of redemption will dominate the interests of creation.

IV. CONCLUSION

So possible answers to Ward's question, 'Is the universe in every detail as God intends it to be?', are 'Yes', in so far as any detail is intended as a means to the divinely decreed end, but 'No' in so far as any such detail is judged in abstraction from its place as such a means; and 'Yes' in so far as any detail is intended for its intrinsic worth, or because it produces something temporal but valuable, and for God's glory displayed in it.[22]

NOTES

1   Keith Ward, *Religion and Creation* (Oxford: Clarendon Press, 1996), 219.
2   Ibid., 220.
3   Marilyn McCord Adams, *Horrendous Evils and the Goodness of God* (Ithaca, NY: Cornell University Press, 1999), 179–80.
4   Aquinas, *Summa Theologiae*, Ia, 48, 2 ad 3; translation from Gerard J. Hughes, *The Nature of God* (London: Routledge, 1995), 160.
5   Hughes, *The Nature of God*, 154–5.
6   William Twisse, *The Riches of God's Love unto the Vessells of Mercy consistent with His Absolute Hatred or Reprobation of the Vessells of Wrath* (Oxford, 1653), pt i, p. 35. Twisse was Prolocutor of the Westminster Assembly. There is a brief discussion of his Aristotelianism by Sarah Hutton, 'Thomas Jackson, Oxford Platonist, and William Twisse, Aristotelian', *Journal of the History of Ideas*, 39 (1978), 649–51, and by Carl R. Trueman, 'Puritan Theology as Historical Event: A Linguistic Approach to the Ecumenical Context', in W. J. van Asselt and E. Dekker (eds), *Reformation and Scholasticism* (Grand Rapids: Baker, 2001), 256–8.

7   Twisse, *The Riches of God's Love*, pt ii, p. 181. This and all subsequent references to pt ii of *The Riches of God's Love* are in fact from 'An Answer to a Letter of D.H. concerning God's Decrees Definite or Indefinite', paginated together with pt ii of *The Riches of God's Love*.

8   Twisse, *The Riches of God's Love*, pt ii, p. 181.

9   Ibid.

10 There is no logical connection between these versions of AGI and particularism: cf. William Hastie's supralapsarian universalism in *The Theology of the Reformed Church* (Edinburgh: T. & T. Clark, 1904).

11 This of course is not an invention of the Reformed churches but goes back to Augustine's Anti-Pelagian controversies and is to be found in equal measure in Thomas Aquinas (for example). Thus Thomas holds that God elects some and reprobates others (see for example *Providence and Predestination: Truth, Questions 5 and 6*, tr. R. J. Mulligan, SJ (Chicago: Henry Regnery, 1953), 12), though the medievals do not seem to have discussed the decrees with the same thoroughness as they were discussed in the seventeenth century in the Reformed church, a discussion prompted by the onset of Arminianism and to a lesser extent of Molinism.

12 Twisse, *The Riches of God's Love*, pt ii, p. 181.

13 Ibid.

14 Twisse, *The Riches of God's Love*, pt i, p. 67.

15 G. W. F. Leibniz, *Textes inédits*, vol. i, ed. Gaston Grua (Paris: Presses Universitaires Françaises, 1948), 344, 347, 433.

16 Karl Barth sees a tendency to 'anthropologism' in infralapsarianism in the separate value that it gives to createdness, and even to the encouragement that it provides for the cleavage between natural and revealed theology. He also sees the same tendency to an even greater degree in supralapsarianism, since it has as its end the redemption of individuals. See *Church Dogmatics*, vol. II, pt 2, tr. G. W. Bromiley *et al.* (Edinburgh: T. & T. Clark, 1957), 137. But this is surely based on a misunderstanding, for both schemes have God's glory as their chief end. It is this opposite 'tendency', an unblinking theocentrism, that makes the idea of an all-encompassing divine decree so unpalatable to many at present. Barth's own view is of course a distinctive kind of supralapsarianism.

17 Richard J. Mouw, 'Another Look at the Infra/Supralapsarian Debate', *Calvin Theological Journal*, Apr. 2000, 147. I am greatly indebted to Mouw for the stimulus of the ideas expressed in this article, as well as for points of information about Reformed theology that it contains.

18 Ibid., 142.

19 Ibid.

20 In his review of vol. 2 of Bavinck's *Reformed Dogmatics*, reprinted in *Redemptive History and Biblical Interpretation: The Shorter Writings of Geerhardus Vos*, ed. Richard B. Gaffin (Philipsburg, NJ: Presbyterian and Reformed Publishing Co., 1980), 490. I owe this reference to Steve Hays.

21 Herman Bavinck, *The Doctrine of God*, tr. W. Hendriksen (Grand Rapids: Eerdmans, 1951), 392.

22 I am grateful to Peter Byrne, Martin Stone and the Editor for comments on an earlier version and especially to Richard Mouw for helping me to correct misunderstandings.

11

God, Science and Philosophy

JOHN POLKINGHORNE

Reading Keith Ward is always a pleasure. One encounters a bright and lively mind, addressing issues of significance in a style that is clear and bracing. Here is someone who uses his philosophical training to clarify matters rather than to complicate them through undue intellectual fastidiousness. At times, reading a Ward book is rather like taking a cold shower – it stimulates the system, leaving one ready for vigorous mental exercise. Of course, all callings have their snare, as the hymn reminds us, and for the philosophical theologian this may lie in too great a reliance at times on the deliverances of the analytical method. In consequence, philosophical discussions of the problems of theodicy can sometimes seem to take too little account of the power and problematic of the tragic. I do not think that Ward is totally exempt from this tendency. He writes concerning an evolutionary world,

> On the newer, more holistic, picture, suffering and death are inevitable parts of a development that involves improvement through conflict and generation of the new. But suffering and death are not the predominating features of nature. They are rather necessary consequences or conditions of a process of emergent harmonisation which inevitably discards the old as it moves on to the new.[1]

To say this is to say something important, with which I would agree, but it scarcely seems sufficient to leave it at that.

One impressive feature of Ward's writing is the wide range of his knowledge and interests. This has included an engagement with questions arising from the interaction between science and theology, perhaps most notably discussed in his vigorous paperback *God, Chance and Necessity*. The participation of a leading theologian in this kind of interdisciplinary exchange is greatly to be welcomed, since too much of the initiative in this area has had to come from those of us whose initial intellectual formation has been in one of the sciences. We are very much in need of the help of our theological colleagues in this common endeavour. Ward's book has the typical merits of much of his writing: lively engagement with the works of well-chosen conversation partners and a hard-hitting discussion of the points at issue. In the case of *God, Chance and Necessity*, the selected interlocutors include two of his Oxford colleagues, the staunchly atheistic and scientistic writers Peter Atkins and Richard Dawkins. At times the virtuosity of Ward's philosophical approach seems almost to allow him to pull logical rabbits out of his philosophical top hat. Consider the following argument. Ward writes that, since only God can grasp all truths in one intuitive, non-discursive act of knowing, 'it seems, after all, that if everything can be understood [an assertion that Atkins makes], only a God could understand it, and so Atkins is committed to theism. In fact, I am rather puzzled by the fact that he does not seem to realise it.'[2] One admires the cleverness of the comment, but rather fears that one outrageous claim has been countered by another almost as excessive, as it would be possible to believe that a total understanding might be the asymptotically attainable goal of the community of finite beings. The further comment, made in the same paragraph, that there might be infinitely other universes beyond this one, which God would know but we cannot, seems something of a debating point.

At other times, Ward's critiques are rather more sober, as when he follows many others in pointing out that the assertion that speculative theories of quantum cosmology allow science to appropriate to itself the hitherto divine prerogative of creation out of nothing is based simply on a crude abuse of language. It is clear that the quantum vacuum, if it is indeed the matrix from which our universe spontaneously arose, is a highly structured and active medium, very different from anything that could properly be called *nihil*.

A good deal of *God, Chance and Necessity* is devoted to the exploration of themes that are common currency in the exchange between science and theology. What gives the book its novelty and freshness is the style of its approach, rather than its detailed content. A kind of cosmological argument for God's existence is presented. It is based on the idea of God as the ground for that deep intelligibility of the universe that science has discovered and exploited in the course of its investigations. Commenting on the alternative proposition that the physical world is simply a brute fact to be accepted without further question, Ward justly remarks that 'It seems odd to think that there is a reason for everything, except for that most important item of all – that is, the existence of *everything*, the universe itself.'[3] Of course, if science were our only source of reliable knowledge, that would be the case and we should just have to make the best of it. Yet those who are imbued with the thirst for understanding through and through – a desire so natural to the scientist – should not be content to accept without a struggle so limited an account of our experience of reality.

Ward is particularly vigorous in his rebuttal of scientistic reductionism. He says of Dawkins's somewhat strident assertions of materialism, 'he has to confuse science with metaphysics, and deceive the reader into thinking that all respectable scientists are really materialists – which is as false a belief as most that one can think of.'[4] Ward robustly denies reductionist claims such as the assertion that elementary particle physics is a 'Theory of Everything', from which all other levels of experience might be derived as admittedly complex corollaries. On the contrary, his stance is that of direct realism:

We simply operate in a world that we assume gives us reliable knowledge of an objective environment and of the thoughts and feelings of other persons. The commonsense world is a world of experiences. It is the scientific world of molecules and brain-states that is the result of very sophisticated observation and theory, and we believe in it because we trust the reliability of science. [. . .] The place we all start from, in thinking about the nature of reality, is a world of colours, shapes, smells and feels, of thoughts and feelings, of experiences which we naturally and unthinkingly interpret as conveying meanings and purposes that come to us from outside ourselves. [. . .] It is because of this that theism, of some sort, is an entirely natural and unforced belief for human beings.[5]

It is a common, and I believe correct, strategy to point out that theories based on extreme reductionism always prove eventually to be suicidal since, by denying the independent reality of reason, those who defend them saw off the metaphysical branch on which they are seeking to perch. Ward takes this line too: 'Materialist theories end up by denying the very realities of conscious experience they set out to explain, and in that sense they are not true explanations at all.'[6]

Ward's somewhat bantering style of critique is employed to good effect when he comments on Dawkins's notion that in biology it is only genes that really count, so that organisms are simply convenient survival machines for the propagation of the selfish replicators: 'It is like saying that the important goal of cookery is recipes. The cakes themselves are unintended by-products of the recipes. Something has gone seriously wrong.'[7] It has indeed.

There are two aspects of Ward's discussion in *God, Chance and Necessity*, however, with which I would like to take issue. One is his consideration of the role of mathematics in physical science.[8] Many of us who have worked in the trade regard this as a very striking and significant aspect of theoretical science. It is an actual technique of discovery in fundamental physics to search for equations that are characterised by the unmistakeable property of mathematical beauty. This quest is no mere indulgence in mathematical aestheticism, for it has proved to be the case time and again in the history of physics that it is just such equations that, by their long-term fruitfulness, persuade us that the theories based upon them are actually verisimilitudinous accounts of the structure of the universe. The great British theoretical physicist Paul Dirac was once asked what was his fundamental belief. He strode to a blackboard and wrote on it, 'The laws of physics are expressed in beautiful equations.' Dirac made his many and remarkable discoveries by a lifelong and highly successful search for mathematically beautiful theories. Einstein before him had done the same, formulating general relativity (his most profound scientific achievement) precisely by following this heuristic strategy. Dirac's brother-in-law, Eugene Wigner, himself also a Nobel laureate, called this phenomenon 'the unreasonable effectiveness of mathematics'. It is possible, and I believe intellectually attractive, to see the potency of mathematics in physical thinking as a pale but true reflection of the mind of the creator behind the order of creation.[9]

Ward thinks that taking this role of mathematics too seriously would place us in danger of embracing what Alfred North Whitehead would have called 'the fallacy of misplaced concreteness': 'one is so impressed by the mathematical elegance and predictive power of one's own construction that one comes to see *it* as the true reality, while the phenomenal experience from which the scheme began is relegated to the realm of mere subjective illusion.'[10] Here is the direct realist in full cry. I think that it is unfair to impute a judgement of 'mere subjective illusion' to theoretical physicists as being their attitude to raw experience, and mistaken to use the words 'one's own *construction*' to refer to the *discoveries* of theoretical science. No doubt quantum field theories are at some remove from the plenitude of ordinary experience but, as far as the subatomic world is concerned, they are remarkably isomorphic with the structure of our experience of that world. Not all of reality can be encapsulated in such formulations, but certainly some significant aspects of physical reality are thereby exhibited and made intelligible. In fact, it is in terms of these close relationships of the underlying mathematical structures to the forms of empirical experience that it is possible best to defend a realist understanding of scientific knowledge, even when the superficial pictorial account seems to change discontinuously – as when Newtonian action-at-a-distance was replaced by the Einsteinian geometry of curved space-time.[11] We need to take the unreasonable effectiveness of mathematics very seriously, in both our philosophical and our theological thinking.

My second problem arises from a brief discussion Ward gives of 'the goal of creation'. I would not dissent from the broad statement that

> All physical states come to be and pass away. The purpose is to realise a specific set of values, through an emergent creative and relatively autonomous process. When that purpose is achieved, the cosmos can pass away. The values it realised will be conserved for ever in the mind of God, and the conscious agents it has generated can pass beyond its confines to new forms of creative and communal life.[12]

However, it seems to me that much more needs to be said in response to the problems posed to theology by science's prediction of final cosmic collapse or decay. In the passage quoted, I think that one is once more seeing the philosopher's tendency to feel that when a logical possibility has been identified that responds to a problem, then it becomes an option for the discourse to pass on to other matters with a certain degree of blithe cheerfulness. Recently, in the science and theology community there has been a good deal of concern with the eschatological issues raised by cosmological prognostications of the eventual futility of this universe, which have been seen to merit fairly extensive consideration. A wide range of resources has been deployed in the effort to begin formulating some credible and considered theological response.[13] This is not the place in which to pursue the topic in further detail, but one may remark that among the questions that must be addressed are how the nature of the soul relates to human psychosomatic unity, and how one is to resolve the tension between continuity and discontinuity in thinking about the relationship of the new creation to the old. In response to these issues more needs to be said than simply identifying general theological possibilities.

Perhaps the most important of Keith Ward's contributions to the dialogue between science and theology – and certainly one that has been of enormous help to me in my own attempts to think about these matters – has lain on the theological side of the border, rather more than in the actual frontier exchanges between the two disciplines. In particular, his revision of many of classical theology's conceptual attitudes to the nature of deity has given us scientist-theologians a much more flexible resource to use in our discussions.[14]

One of the big transformations in scientific thinking in the last two centuries has been the recognition of the constitutive significance of time. Geology was the first scientific discipline to make this discovery when, at the end of the eighteenth century, it realised that the contemporary structure of the Earth's landscapes could not properly be understood without taking into account the history of their past formation. Biology followed this trend in the mid-nineteenth century, with its insight into the evolutionary character of the history of life. Physics was the science that held out longest against acknowledging the irreducible importance of temporality. As late as 1917, when Einstein used his new discovery of general relativity to formulate the first truly scientific cosmology, he supposed that it was necessary to find a solution to his equations that represented an unchanging state of the universe overall. Only the subsequent observational discovery by Edwin Hubble of the recession of the galaxies liberated physical thinking from its enthralment to a purely static picture of the cosmos.

A further transformation in scientific attitudes has resulted from the recognition of the role of contingency in the unfolding coming-to-be of the world. In the aftermath of Newton's great discoveries in mechanics, it seemed to his successors that science was committed to the necessitarian picture of tightly deterministic physical process. Such a view culminated in Laplace's image of the calculating demon who, possessed of complete knowledge of the dispositions and motions of matter in the present, could fully predict the future and retrodict the past. This merely mechanical view of the universe crumbled in the course of the twentieth century. The discovery of quantum mechanics, and subsequently of chaotic dynamics, showed that there are widespread intrinsic unpredictabilities present both at the microscopic level of subatomic phenomena and also at the everyday level of macroscopic processes. At the same time, understanding of biological evolution had drawn attention to the fruitful way in which 'chance and necessity' (that is to say, historical contingency and lawful regularity) interacted over billions of years to produce the fertile development of carbon-based life on planet Earth. This latter insight proved to be a particular, if extremely significant, case of a more general principle. Scientists have come to recognise that the origin of novelty occurs in regimes that they have learnt to characterise as lying 'at the edge of chaos'. Too far on the rigid side of this border, and the emergence of fruitful novelty is extinguished, to be replaced by the mere rearrangement of already existing entities. Too far on the haphazard side of the border, and nothing new persists. If novelties come into being, they do so fleetingly, only to fall apart and dissolve away. It is only in the region where order and disorder interlace each other that real novelty can emerge and continue.

In these ways, modern science discerns a world of intrinsic temporality and creative contingency, a universe characterised by both being and becoming. If God is indeed the creator of this world, one might surely expect that these properties of creation would prove to be some kind of resultant reflection of analogous properties present in the being of the creator. Moreover, the theologically underwritten belief in the freedom granted by the God of love to creatures[15] implies that the universe is indeed a world of true becoming in which the future is not there awaiting our arrival, but is something that humans play a part in bringing about through their free actions in the course of history.

In his writing on philosophical theology, and particularly in *Rational Theology and the Creativity of God*, Ward addresses these issues in a most helpful way. He argues that a purely necessary being could only give rise to a purely necessary world. Consequently, the contingency of creation must be interpreted as reflecting a degree of contingency present in its creator. Similar considerations relate to temporality and freedom: 'if the world is contingent and man really free, contingency and mutability must exist within God himself'.[16]

Such ideas are extremely congenial to the thinking of scientist-theologians.[17] We have always tended to have difficulties with classical theology's insistence on divine simplicity and total divine atemporality. It is very reassuring to find a theologian saying that 'the whole doctrine of Divine simplicity arises from a misinterpretation of the truth that God is not divisible into parts, that all his properties are interconnected. [. . .] I can see no a priori reason why the Divine should not be internally complex, each part depending essentially on the unity of the whole.'[18] This sort of theological thinking comes as a great relief. It is liberating for the scientist-theologian to receive philosophical sanction to countenance the divine polarities of eternity–time and necessity–contingency that seem so naturally suggested by what we know of God's creation. I am not suggesting that 'Ward has spoken' totally settles the issue for us, but those of us who lack a training in philosophy are encouraged to learn that the polarities that we instinctively espouse are ones that command a measure of support among the philosophically sophisticated. Given the nature of the philosophical community, one could not ask for more than that by way of endorsement.

Lest I should seem to be in danger of being too gushingly enthusiastic, let me record that, as in the case of Ward's contributions to the science and theology exchange itself, there are some matters on which I feel a degree of reserve. Quite often he says words to the effect that God is either logically necessary or logically impossible.[19] I am afraid that scientists approach arguments about logically necessary beings, whether originating from Anselm or from Ward, with a degree of suspicion. If, as Kurt Gödel showed us, we cannot demonstrate the consistency of arithmetic, our logical powers in relation to the existence of God might be expected to be less than fully adequate. The sorts of argument that philosophical theologians employ are certainly clever, but are they too clever by half? This is ground on which one can only tread with extreme caution.

My second reservation relates once again to the issue of theodicy. Ward argues that God must know our feelings by direct acquaintance: 'Is the one who really knows us not one who feels our sorrows and grieves with us? Rejoices in our happiness and knows the unformulable secrets of our hearts?'[20] Given the amount of suffering in creation, God's experiences cannot be those of unmitigated happiness. Nevertheless, Ward summarises his conclusions by saying,

> God is supremely blissful, since the being of God itself contains infinite actualized perfections, and since all created evil will be turned to good or eliminated. Sorrow will exist in God, but it is redeemed by its integration into a wider experience of goodness and beauty. There is an immutable and transtemporal divine perfection and bliss.[21]

Earlier Ward had endorsed a number of Paul Fiddes's arguments against divine impassibility,[22] but it seems to me that Ward does not fully take into account the divine embrace of the tragic that one finds so powerfully expressed in Fiddes's writing, or the full extent of divine participation in suffering that we find expounded by Jürgen Moltmann in his Trinitarian account of the cross.[23] Once more it may seem that philosophical argument is a little too detached from existential anguish.

The final area of Keith Ward's thinking that has been particularly helpful to those engaged in the dialogue between science and religion is his extended discussion of the ecumenical encounter between the world faith traditions. I greatly admire the breadth of learning and the sympathetic insight that he has brought to the four volumes of his major project in comparative theology. For me, as a scientist-theologian, it is *Religion and Creation* that has been of particular importance.

Despite the fact that there has been comparatively little writing in the science and theology community about world faith issues,[24] some of the problems greatly trouble those of us with a scientific background. Although science in a recognisably modern form arose in the specific setting of seventeenth-century Europe, building on medieval insights that had been particularly fruitfully developed in the Islamic community, scientific understanding has subsequently spread worldwide. Stop suitably qualified people in the street in London or Tokyo, Delhi or Islamabad, and ask them what matter is made of, and they will all tell you 'quarks and gluons'. Yet were one to ask four people in these four cities what is the nature of ultimate reality, one would be likely to receive four very different-seeming answers. The contrast between the universality of science and the largely regional character of religion is very unnerving. Might it not, after all, imply that science is real knowledge and religion is no more than culturally influenced opinion? I think that the proper understanding of the relationships of the world faiths is a major issue on the theological agenda for the twenty-first century, and probably for the third millennium.

The matter is perplexing because of the intertwined strands of similarity and dissimilarity present in it. When one meets adherents of other faith traditions, one is properly impressed by the seriousness and authenticity of their spiritual lives. It seems clear that all major traditions preserve and propagate true experience of encounter with the sacred. Yet the accounts they give of that encounter are very diverse and they do not seem at all easily reconcilable with each other. It seems extremely difficult to treat them simply as culturally conditioned perspectives on the same reality, for the cognitive clashes between the world faith traditions are severe. They do not relate only to obvious points of disagreement, such as the status of Jesus or of the Qur'an, but they extend to issues such as the nature of the human person. Is the individual human being of persistent and unique significance in the sight of God (as the Abrahamic faiths all affirm), or recycled through reincarnation, or ultimately an illusion from which to seek release?

Those of us who worry about these issues face the problem that, while we respect our brothers and sisters in other faiths when we meet them, we really understand so little of the inwardness of their traditions. Religions are deep and complex and they cannot properly be encountered simply by external inspection and by the cursory reading of some of their more important scriptures. We need assistance from those who have been able to devote much more time and effort to interfaith enquiry.

I find Ward particularly helpful in this respect. There are two main reasons for this. One is that he writes with great sympathy for the traditions that he is exploring, but at the same time he writes from an acknowledged Christian standpoint. I think that this approach is just right. I am suspicious of alternative approaches that claim to be able to stand on some common neutral ground beyond any specific tradition. Too often the latter strategy seems to lead to a 'lowest common denominator' account of religious belief, so bland that, in fact, no adherent of a world faith tradition would find it even half-adequate as a description of their own position. Difficult and painful as it is, I am certain that the world faith traditions have to meet each other in the integrity of their own specificities.

The second reason why I find Ward helpful lies in his technique of choosing interlocutors from the traditions and then using their thinking as the basis for the dialogue. In *Religion and Creation*, he first summarises the relevant scriptural deposits to be found in the Hebrew Bible, the New Testament, the Qur'an and the Upanishads, and then he engages with a quartet of twentieth-century thinkers: Abraham Heschel for Judaism, Karl Barth for Christianity, Muhammad Iqbal for Islam and Aurobindo Ghose for Hinduism. Ward's careful and respectful explorations lead him to discern a degree of commonality in the insights of the four traditions into the divine relationship to the world of our experience. He summarises his conclusions as follows:

> In the four traditions that have been considered, there is agreement that the heart of religious belief is commitment to a being of supreme power and value, whether described as *Sachchidananda* or as God the sole creator of all things in space and time. Some of the most eminent twentieth-century theologians from those traditions all stress that God is involved with the universe, that there is a sort of divine pathos (Heschel), a divine will for fellowship (Barth), a divine emergent creativity (Iqbal), or a self-manifestation of the Divine in the forms of space and time

(Aurobindo). In that respect, they all wish to modify their own classical traditions, which stressed the complete simplicity, eternity, and immutability of God. Yet they do not wish to reject the classical views. [. . .] They rather wish to complement the classical view by asserting that the same God who is infinite and incomprehensible, beyond all name and form, also manifests itself in real relation to the universe, in time, passion and creativity.[25]

If there is indeed this degree of commonality between the faiths, that is a very important and hopeful conclusion. However, it is difficult for the ordinary reader not to feel some reservations. The four interlocutors were not randomly chosen and might it not be that their positions are not wholly typical of the traditions they were chosen to represent? (Yet, in fairness, a Christian commentator must acknowledge that Barth would not have been the twentieth-century theologian expected to be most accommodating to interfaith agreement.) Are we seeing again the philosophical tendency to value intellectual parallelism in the abstract and to underestimate the differences resulting from contrasting practices and ways of life? (It is notable that in intra-Christian ecumenical discussions it has often seemed easier for commissions of theologians to achieve a measure of convergence than it has for the ecclesial communities from which they are drawn, particularly when issues of authority are on the agenda.) I do not know the answers to these questions, but I am grateful to Keith Ward for his insightful writings on these matters. At the very least, he has delineated a kind of interfaith understanding that can serve as what a mathematician would call a 'zero-order approximation', a valuable starting point from which to attempt further and even more precise treatments of the problem. And that puts us greatly in his debt.

NOTES

1   Keith Ward, *God, Chance and Necessity* (Oxford: Oneworld Publications, 1996), 87.
2   Ibid., 33.
3   Ibid., 23, emphasis his.
4   Ibid., 101.
5   Ibid., 152.
6   Ibid., 153.
7   Ibid., 137.
8   Ibid., 26–31.
9   See John Polkinghorne, *Belief in God in an Age of Science* (New Haven: Yale University Press, 1998), 2–4.
10 Ward, *God, Chance and Necessity*, 28, emphasis his.
11 See John Polkinghorne, *Faith, Science and Understanding* (London: SPCK, 2000), 78–84.
12 Ward, *God, Chance and Necessity*, 164.
13 See John Polkinghorne and Michael Welker (eds), *The End of the World and the Ends of God* (Harrisburg, Pa.: Trinity Press International, 2000); John Polkinghorne, *The God of Hope and the End of the World* (London: SPCK, 2002).
14 See esp. Keith Ward, *Rational Theology and the Creativity of God* (Oxford: Blackwell, 1982).

15 See the essays in John Polkinghorne (ed.), *The Work of Love: Creation as Kenosis* (London: SPCK, 2001).
16 Ward, *Rational Theology*, 80–1.
17 See John Polkinghorne, *Scientists as Theologians* (London: SPCK, 1996), chs 3 and 4.
18 Ward, *Rational Theology*, 64.
19 See, for example, Ward, *God, Chance and Necessity*, 115; *Rational Theology*, 19.
20 Ward, *Rational Theology*, 132.
21 Keith Ward, *Religion and Creation* (Oxford: Clarendon Press, 1996), 344.
22 Ibid., 253–5.
23 Paul Fiddes, *The Creative Suffering of God* (Oxford: Oxford University Press, 1988); Jürgen Moltmann, *The Crucified God* (London: SCM Press, 1974).
24 See, however, Polkinghorne, *Scientists as Theologians*, ch. 5; also John Polkinghorne, *Science and Christian Belief* (London: SPCK, 1994), published in the US as *The Faith of a Physicist* (Princeton: Princeton University Press, 1994), ch. 10.
25 Ward, *Religion and Creation*, 109.

12

Creation and Cosmology

ROBERT CUMMINGS NEVILLE

I. ON THE USEFULNESS OF METAPHYSICS

Alfred North Whitehead said, 'The useful function of philosophy is to promote the most general systematization of civilized thought', and that philosophy 'attains its chief importance by fusing the two, namely, religion and science, into one rational scheme of thought'.[1] Keith Ward is one of the few English philosophers to carry on Whitehead's programme, though without adopting Whitehead's own metaphysics as his 'rational scheme of thought'. To that programme Ward has added the acknowledgement of serious differences among the world's religions and the attempt to fuse them, along with science, into a rational scheme of thought.[2] Ward knows that a sympathetic but empirical approach to religions requires careful comparative study in order to generate the generalisations that would fit into a 'systematization of civilized thought'. He has pursued this programme in an intellectual environment hostile to both comparative theology and metaphysics (the development of rational schemes of thought).

I share his programme as so described. In this chapter I want to propose and defend the following thesis that bears upon the programme's plausibility: a metaphysical hypothesis, including an ontology about God and the world, should be vague enough to tolerate further specification by anything science might plausibly hypothesise. The double reference to *hypothesis* displays a commitment to a pragmatic approach both to science and to metaphysics, an approach Whitehead shared.[3] That science is hypothetical is not much contested these days, although different interpretations of the nature of hypothesis abound. That metaphysics is hypothetical is counterintuitive to those who believe that metaphysics is what Kant refuted, namely, an a priori foundational form of knowledge. Understanding metaphysics to be foundational, many thinkers of the last century rejected its possibility. Nevertheless, metaphysics as hypothetical in the forms practised so brilliantly by Peirce and Whitehead, among others, is indeed possible, being actual. So for us the question is not whether metaphysics in the hypothetical mode is possible but whether a given metaphysical claim is right, the best hypothesis so far as we can tell. Some postmodern thinkers would deny that it is useful or important to develop a rational metaphysical 'scheme of thought', arguing that this can only be logocentric and therefore arbitrary in ruling out or marginalising points of view that do not register within the scheme. But part of good form in a metaphysical hypothesis is the conscious identification of points that are marginalised or that fail to register, and the amendment of the hypothesis to accommodate and assess them.[4]

The thesis proposed obviously calls for a parallel thesis regarding vagueness and differences among religions.[5] One difference between metaphysical vagueness relative to science and that relative to religions is this. Science as developed in the West seeks a consistent, universal and univocal language. Although this has not been achieved, even in those sciences that can formulate both the constants and variables of their main findings mathematically, it is an ideal. Even when there are heuristic reasons for not attempting to combine the languages of two sciences into a common expression, metaphysical fairness to them does not necessitate admitting more than temporary incommensurability. In the case of comprehending the many world religions into one view, both their singularity and their potentially differing truth values are matters to be investigated. They are not necessarily commensurable, and they are not necessarily equally true in the same respects. Finding a fair metaphysics, vague enough to allow all religions to make their cases, is more complicated than finding a metaphysics that allows for scientific tolerance of different theories. This chapter deals only with metaphysical hypotheses about God and the sciences. It will sketch a particular metaphysical hypothesis whose strengths include a proper degree of vagueness and non-arbitrariness. My thesis about vagueness is more complicated than might be thought.

II. ON ARBITRARINESS, SYMMETRY AND ASYMMETRY

Whitehead listed four formal criteria of a philosophical 'scheme of thought': consistency, coherence, adequacy and applicability.[6] To this should be added non-arbitrariness. A metaphysical system should not have arbitrary elements immune to criticism. That said, several preliminary limitations, to be justified later, should be noted to non-arbitrariness as a metaphysical criterion.

First, all thought is historically situated and thus arbitrary to the extent that its history is particular. This is as true of science as it is of metaphysics; more is likely to be of lasting value in the philosophies of Plato and Descartes than in the sciences of their days.[7] History shapes the questions asked in both the sciences and metaphysics. The best remedy against historical arbitrariness is self-awareness of history, critical analyses of its particularities and the assumptions hidden within them, and repeated attempts to identify and limit the biases that come from history. Perhaps the most signal contribution of post-modernism is to make people aware of this. No historically neutral platform exists from which to discern historical particularity and bias. So the task is to expand the sense of history with a critical eye. Any particular historical arbitrariness that is identified can then be measured in metaphysical and scientific expressions that contain it. Because all hypotheses are fallible, mistakes when identified can be corrected.

Second, arbitrariness is inevitable with regard to the idiosyncrasies of individual thinkers and collaborative communities. These have to do with tastes, talents, schooling and the accidents of friendships and societies; most of all they have to do with choices concerning what to study and think about, what ideas to pursue further. Like the historical situations that condition the shape of scientific and philosophical discussions, personal and interpersonal situations have an arbitrary edge. As with historical particularity, the best remedy is to identify and control for personal and interpersonal arbitrariness as much as possible. When I speak in this chapter about God and creation, this way of putting a deeper issue reflects my historical situation as a westerner and the personal situation of being a Christian to whom that language is native; Keith Ward shares the same particularities, and would be among the first to say that, by rights, we should talk about 'the Ultimate' or something like that in view of the traditions of the Tao and Brahman, Emptiness, and the like, which provide different rhetorical and conceptual systems for dealing with the metaphysical problems of the one and the many, contingency and so forth.

A third and more complicated kind of arbitrariness is possible though not inevitable on certain metaphysical hypotheses. Perhaps 'metaphysical hypotheses' is too determinate an expression. I have in mind a fundamental distinction, difficult to formulate, between two intuitions or instincts about what makes sense – the symmetrical instinct versus the asymmetrical instinct.[8] The notions of symmetry and asymmetry in this context are extremely vague, specifiable only via examples of symmetrical and asymmetrical metaphysical hypotheses. The symmetrical instinct, beloved of mathematicians, is that the base of things is equilibrium and that explanation is tracing things back to equilibrium. In metaphysics, the great systems of the fullness of being, for instance Plotinus's theory of the One or Thomas Aquinas's theory of *actus esse*, reflect the symmetrical instinct, and so do the great Buddhist systems of absolute non-being and the Advaita Vedanta non-dualist theory of Brahman. Equilibrium seems to be the very model of non-arbitrariness. The great difficulty for all these theories is explaining the particular tilts of the cosmos: why the Big Bang differentiated itself into unevenly distributed galaxies instead of wholly homogeneous soup, why some people are rich and others poor, why an earthquake kills some but not others. Once a system of diverse particular, singular causes is established, laws of equilibrium can show how that has particular results; but why is there ever a singular non-equilibrium anywhere?

The asymmetrical instinct supposes that an arbitrary ontological condition or act is at the base of things, and ultimate rationality is identifying and pointing to that arbitrary foundation. The great metaphysical systems with an asymmetrical base are the various creation *ex nihilo* theories which say that the character of the creator comes from what is created, which is always particular. The asymmetrical views deny that there is an antecedent divine nature, purely full or purely empty, that expresses itself, and affirm instead that the arbitrary particularity of the cosmos is one with the particularity of its foundation. On the asymmetrical views, particular, singular act 'precedes' the nature of the actor. The difficulty for the asymmetrical views is to explain the equilibrium that is indeed found in the cosmos. I myself incline to the asymmetrical view, and look to evolution to explain equilibria: those things without enough equilibrium to give balance to, and receive reinforcement from, the environment do not last beyond moments after the Big Bang or in organic life and human society; this applies to regularities as well as actual individuals. Things seem to me to be a tumble of achieved and failing harmonies or equilibria, at root arbitrary, and ordered only in so far as they harmonise with internal and external environments. Moreover, I think the asymmetrical impulse, formulated as a hypothesis, can explain near-fundamental equilibrium as one possible outcome of the asymmetrical base condition, though not one for which there is much empirical evidence.

If the asymmetrical sense of rationality with its ontological suspicions is true, then a fundamental arbitrariness does exist in cosmic events and all conditions contained within them, such as human life and history. Enquiry aims to locate and understand the fundamental particular conditions of things, both the particular regularities and the arbitrary decisive givens: why the cosmos has the natural laws it does when it might have had others, why some people are rich and others poor, why some are natural victims and others victors. At some point, for instance an act of creation of all space-time and things, the 'why' question will be answered by the identification of an arbitrary act with the singular character of making the singular world. An asymmetrical metaphysics can recognise and account for whatever regularities – a form of equilibrium – can be discovered by science, philosophy or any other arts of enquiry that lie within the singular world.

Unacceptable arbitrariness in the asymmetrical view is to stop short of identifying the antecedent conditions and the exact decisive acts that determine the outcomes we observe, and has two forms. One is the unacceptable assumption that anything to be explained necessarily has some mechanical, statistical or other 'universalisable' regular principle that explains it: the cosmos might not have evolved regularity to govern that situation, and enquiry must look empirically to see what is the case. The other is that a complex state of affairs can simply be left unexplained as given. Any complex needs to be understood in terms of the conditions, regularities and decisive creative acts that account for it. Where the conditions and regularities are insufficient, decisive creative acts need to be located and understood in terms of their limitations and what they produce.[9] To put this second point differently, given a complex state of affairs, phenomenological description is not enough to satisfy rational enquiry. An asymmetrical metaphysics, at least of the sort I promote, is thoroughly empirical: no uncriticisable assumptions about regularities, even a base equilibrium, are allowed except as working hypotheses to be tested against the evidence, and no assumptions that given complexities are just there and cannot be explained by creative acts are to be allowed to thwart enquiry into decisive makings.

III. NON-ARBITRARINESS

The criterion of non-arbitrariness, whether applied to symmetrical or asymmetrical fundamental hypotheses, rules out resistance to further critical enquiry on any point. In fact, the criterion requires pursuing every plausible angle of possible correction. In practice this is nearly impossible. Good enquirers follow the leads of critical correction their community offers. Yet communities in their historicity are arbitrary too, and so deliberately moving outside the standard conditions of a community's sense of enquiry is crucial. In religion this means looking at how other religions would see the problem. In science it means deliberately hunting for alternative scientific paradigms. In metaphysics the implication is that good argument funds the opposition, as Dewey was reported to have said, which in our time means exploring the perspectives and rhetorical powers of East and South Asian philosophical traditions as well as those of Islam, a point Ward has made often. To correct a hypothesis, especially one that has been tested in standard ways and reformulated and amended through the critical discourse of the community within which it arises, usually requires attaining to a critical perspective outside the hypothesis. This cannot be done by methodical doubt in Descartes's sense. Peirce called that 'paper doubt', doubting on paper what no one could concretely imagine doubting. Non-arbitrariness requires systematic construction in metaphysics in order to look critically from all imaginable angles.[10] Such a task can never be finished.

Within a metaphysical or scientific hypothesis are certain elements that can be recognised as conditionally non-arbitrary. Deductive arguments, for instance, seem non-arbitrary. Yet a larger context is assumed for the sake of deductive arguments, and that context surely contains many arbitrary elements. Even the rules of logic might be revealed to be arbitrary by a subsequent logical theory with greater generality; Aristotelian logic, for example, does not allow for the logic of vagueness. In the case of science, Thomas Kuhn's distinction between normal and revolutionary science has some explanatory power here. Hypotheses and arguments that are non-arbitrary within a normal paradigm are revealed to be arbitrary within the context of a paradigm change; they might be shown to be plain wrong, but more likely are insufficiently generalised, that is, arbitrary in their limitations. In one sense Newton's laws of motion are mistaken in the context of twenty-first-century physics; in another sense they are just a special case, arbitrarily represented as universal. In philosophy, less of a distinction can be observed between normal and revolutionary thought. Dedicated Thomists, Kantians or Whiteheadians can be motivated by the conviction that their master's thought just has to be made to work somehow. Yet this is transparently arbitrary to a wider philosophic community.

In recent paragraphs I have written as if the criterion of non-arbitrariness applies only to the building of metaphysical and scientific systems. It applies as well to assessing debates and intellectual disagreements. The next section will illustrate this.

IV. METAPHYSICAL VAGUENESS AND PHILOSOPHICAL THEOLOGY

In my graduate studies I was deeply concerned to develop a metaphysical theory of divine creation that was compatible with contemporary scientific understanding. At that time, the early 1960s, the steady state theory of Fred Hoyle was in great favour, and what came to be known as the Big Bang theory was regarded by the scientific literature I read as a somewhat daffy speculation. Nevertheless, I endeavoured to frame a hypothesis that would tolerate either theory turning out to be true. I proposed that anything determinate in any way is created, using the argument that the problem of the one and the many requires such a claim.[11] If anything determinate is created, then science and the other arts of enquiry can determine just what determinate things there are, and thus what the character of the created world is.[12] If the steady state theory turned out to be true, with its view of an infinite stretch of time and constant small creative novelties, then that could be a way of making specific the claim that everything determinate is created. And if the Big Bang theory wins the upper hand as it seems to be doing, with its conception of a beginning of time, this can be a specification of the ontological claim as well. A somewhat technical way of saying this is that the hypothesis that the created world consists of everything which is determinate is *vague* with respect to whether those determinations are of the steady state or Big Bang sort.

What kind of conception of God goes with the hypothesis that everything determinate is created? It cannot be that God is a determinate being alongside other beings, and determinate with respect to them. In fact, my analysis of the problem of the one and the many argued that if God be one of the many, a deeper context of unity is required (which we then would call 'God', or 'the Godhead', or 'the God beyond God', or the Tao, Brahman, the Ultimate, etc.). So God in the crucial sense cannot be determinate. On the other hand, the many determinate things of the world, including space-time and its relations, require a deeper ontological context in which they can be mutually relevant, which we call God (or the Ultimate by some name). What can this 'context' be, indeterminate in itself but functioning as the ground of such diversity and unity as the determinate things of the world possess? I argued that it is God as creator *ex nihilo*, whose act of creation has no character in itself but acquires the character of being the creative act from creating the creatures. Thus God's 'nature' as God the creator is a product of the creative act and there is no other more general or antecedent divine nature. To find out about the divine nature within this metaphysical frame requires finding out what has been created, for instance a Big Bang or steady state world. This part of the hypothesis about God illustrates the non-arbitrariness of an asymmetrical view, acknowledging the singularity of the world (to be discerned by science and other disciplines) without presupposing an arbitrary antecedent divine nature to account for it. If we arbitrarily assume that every creative act proceeds according to antecedently established principles (as Whitehead does[13]) or from the antecedent nature of a creative agent, we would not be able to acknowledge the pure making involved in creating the determinate principles.

What is gained by saying that a divine creative act without an antecedent nature creates the world of determinate things? Does that not reduce to saying that the created world just is? What is added by saying it is created by an ontological creator *ex nihilo*? These queries have force, however, only if nothing counts as an explanation except an antecedently natured agent and/or antecedent principles. And the hypothesis proposed is that decisive, creative *making* is explanatory. Moreover, such making is familiar throughout experience. Even with a deeply determinate actual nature, and all the principles in the world, an agent cannot do or make anything without producing something new over and above the antecedents. Even if the principles are of a heavy-duty equilibrium sort so that each act produces something just like the thing before, perhaps a replication of the agent itself, nevertheless at least the novelty of the repetition, the new instance, is made. Human agents of course have the characters of heredity and learning, and the conditions of their environment. In most areas of life action is by habit, with little significant novelty beyond repetition. But in some areas of life, action is by decision, shaped by semiotic engagements with the possibilities and often conscious, or partly so. Decision is, among other things, the spontaneous selection of possibilities to actualise, and the actualising of them. Probably few areas of life are totally devoid of decision. We likely think we are on automatic pilot far more than we are, just because we are unconscious of our decisions, or of many dimensions of them. So long as we are aware of actually making and doing things, we are aware of causal factors, making factors, other than antecedent conditions and principles of regularity.

Moreover, although all people have their given natures and conditions, and operate within a causal world with many strict regularities, over time what we identify most as their unique moral character is the cumulative achievements of their free decisions, deeds and makings. The interesting part of human agency is what people do with the nature, conditions and regularities they share with one another. This point should not be taken to slight conjoint action, the elements of moral character that derive from belonging to a community, or the real differences in historical circumstances among people. But what is unique to human dignity is the ability to make a life whose outcomes are somewhat free.

V. DIVINE NATURE AND FREEDOM

On the hypothesis of creation *ex nihilo* in my sense, in the case of God no antecedent divine nature, no antecedent environing conditions such as winds beating upon the deep, and no antecedent regularities of causation are involved. The divine creative act is completely unconditioned. Its making is entirely free, not partially free in the Tao's subtle loopholes like our freedom. The whole of the divine nature is the result of the creative agency producing the world. As even Karl Barth might be astonished to admit, God is wholly revealed in creation because there is nothing more to God than the creating with its outcome, if we but know how to read it. God is wholly self-caused in agency and nature. This part of the hypothesis answers to the element of non-arbitrariness that says we cannot rest just with a given complexity – the world of determinations – but must move on to the conditions and acts that explain it. In a cosmological sense, antecedent agents, regularities, and bits of spontaneous, sometimes humanly significant, creativity explain subsequent complexities. In an ontological sense, the existence of space-time and the other determinate things of our world is explained as produced by the divine creative act. That act is infinite in the sense of having no constraints of antecedents or principles, though it is finite and singular in the sense of producing a singular world.

What more can be said about such a creator God? Two sides put pressure on that conception. On one side the sciences want to keep the conception vague so as to tolerate further specification by any theory that might plausibly turn out to be true. On the other hand, the religions want the conception to be tailored immediately to the conceptions of the Ultimate symbolised in their scriptures, liturgies, practices and confessional theologies. Before I respond to these pressures, however, permit me a partial metaphysical answer to this question.

Part of metaphysics, perhaps better called philosophical cosmology (Whitehead's term in the subtitle of *Process and Reality*), enquires into the generic traits of existence (Dewey's term) or the transcendentals (the medieval term). From the beginning of my analysis of the one and the many, I have found it useful to analyse the traits of determinateness per se. The best hypothesis about this, I argue, is that to be determinate is to be a harmony of conditional and essential features. Conditional features are constituted by relations with other harmonies so as to make the harmony determinately different; essential features are those by which the conditional features are integrated so as to give the harmony existential reality of whatever sort it has. Things are mutually determined by their conditional features. These mutual determinings make up the web of cosmological causal factors. Because harmonies cannot exist with conditional features except by virtue of their essential ones, harmonies need to be together on a deeper ontological level than the cosmological one of mutual conditioning. The need for ontological conditioning, in which the essential features of different things can be together as well as their cosmologically conditioning conditional features, points to the creator that supplies the ontological context of mutual relevance by creating the harmonies. Because many if not all harmonies are spatio-temporal in extension, or aspects of spatio-temporal harmonies, the process of harmonisation involves the coming together of components into harmonies that have at least temporary patterns, existentially located in space and time, and achieving whatever value accrues from having those components together that way in that place relative to the other harmonies. The temporal process that brings harmonies together also blows them apart, sometimes in the rhythm of larger harmonies of creation and destruction. So cumulatively we have the notions of harmony, essential and conditional features, components to be harmonised, forms of harmony, existential location, and value achieved in harmony, all interpreted in terms of spatio-temporal rhythms. These are transcendental traits of all determinate things, at least on my metaphysical and cosmological hypothesis. Hence we can say that God is the creator of a world with these transcendental traits. The traits describing harmony can be specified by Christian notions of the Logos, and those describing harmony's pulses of creation and destruction can be specified by aspects of the Christian notion of the Holy Spirit.[14]

The pressure science puts on the vague hypothesis about God is to make sure it is vague enough to tolerate anything science might plausibly believe to be true. Although the Big Bang hypothesis seems to be winning its debate with the steady state theory, within the Big Bang hypothesis many variants of cosmic history remain open. If the vague hypothesis about God as creator is taken to include the metaphysical transcendentals just sketched, then the conception of harmonies in space-time arising and ceasing needs to be vague enough to tolerate quantum-mechanical phenomena, a point on which Whitehead's theory of actual occasions can be faulted.

Special relativity theory rules out a privileged axis of time defining simultaneity for temporal events in space, and hence there can be no singular continuous divine mind or creative activity; the conception of God as creator of all determinate things, including four-dimensional space-time, is properly vague in this respect.

But the pressure from religions to make the vague hypothesis about God honour their specific symbols of God is not so happy. Monotheisms have symbol systems that represent God as a being, a person (though they also have symbol systems representing God in non-personal ways as beyond being). If God creates all determinate things, then God cannot be a being except in so far as that results from creating. The implication of special relativity is that God cannot have a continuous identity to which all things are related in a univocal space-time frame. Thus when we use personal language about God, as we do in the monotheisms if not in Buddhism, Confucianism or Taoism, we have to be clear that this is a matter of personifying something we know to be not personal in the sense of having unique temporal continuity. Persons are ineluctably temporal, responding as subjects to objects and objectifying responses for other subjects. Theologies such as process theologies and personalisms count it a virtue that God is finite in the sense of being over against the world and its events, responding to them. Petitionary prayer, if taken literally, requires God to wait to hear our pleas. Yet in serious metaphysical analysis, the past, present and future are not together temporally; they allow temporal things to be together temporally precisely because the togetherness of the modes of time is temporal. Relative to time, all the modes of which are created, the creator is eternal.[15] Augustine's attempt to include the past and future in a divine present failed to give them a reality equal to the present, which is ever relative and changing. Not only is God so non-personal as to be eternal rather than temporal, God has no absolute position in space-time that would allow univocal relations with all things. To use Calvin's phrase, God is 'immense', not measurable. To be immense is to have no possible personal relations with anything because the distinction between self and other drops away. God creates a world in which all relations are matters of relative frames of reference, as special relativity says.

VI. ANALOGY AND SPECULATIVE METAPHYSICS

Keith Ward is a late representative of a long, noble tradition that responds to difficulties like this with a doctrine of analogy. For Thomas Aquinas, heir to Aristotle as well as the Neo-Platonic tradition, philosophy alone showed him that a simple personalism is impossible. To be perfect God has to be simple and pure, eternal, and unaffected by the world. Pure simplicity is as religiously vacuous as total indeterminacy, so Thomas had to say something more. The doctrine of analogy supposes that finite beings within the world are mixtures of excellence and finite failing, and that the perfection of God is the purity of excellence with none of the drawbacks of the finite. Thus God is wise, but infinitely so; knowing, but omniscient; powerful, but omnipotent. Ward has brought this argument up to date by exploiting his background in comparative religions and his deep appreciation of the implications of

contemporary science. In *Religion and Creation*, parts III and IV, he develops a mas-
terful analogy for God as a perfect being, treating the topics of power, creativity,
wisdom, love, goodness, divine awareness and happiness, and eternity.

The problem with building conceptions of God from analogy is to know what
parts of the analogue to affirm and what to deny. Ward, for instance, working with
the analogy of finite creators, says that the fact that finite creators start with an
antecedent nature is to be affirmed, while chanciness of action is to be denied. I
argued otherwise above – the best part of finite creators is their own contribution on
top of their inherited antecedents. Ward concludes that it is nonsense to think that
God creates the divine nature, because agents act out of their natures. I argued to the
contrary that God's freedom is total precisely because it is not affected by any
antecedent nature or material, and that this is analogous to the best thing in finite
creators. It is the freedom of those finite creators, however otherwise constrained.[16]
Duns Scotus's worry about the doctrine of analogy was that it is necessary to have at
least one positive univocal affirmation about God in order to control for the
measured affirmations and negations of the analogue. Because Thomas made
the 'analogy of being' go all the way down, he had difficulty with the positive
univocal affirmation. Ward, I believe, treats the notion of perfection as the
positive univocal affirmation, though it is vacuous unless it is filled in by analogy.

The metaphysical approach I have urged for a cosmology of creation is not an
argument to a creator by analogy but the speculative construction of a hypothesis
about creation and why it requires a creator. The constraints on this hypothesis are
many and include tolerance in a vague sense of what science might plausibly assert
and the ability to give a responsible contemporary expression to the basic symbols,
doctrines and texts of the faith (or of all faiths), in such a way that the question of
truth might be raised.

It remains to say a bit more formally what is involved in tolerance in a vague sense.
A vague claim is one that does not by itself determine an object but requires further
specification, and tolerates specifications that might be contradictory to each other.
'God creates everything determinate' is vague because it needs to specify some determinate things. A steady state world is one set of determinate things, and a Big Bang
world contradicts that. The claim tolerates both although both cannot jointly be
true without reformulation. Yet in itself the claim is definite in excluding the claims
(1) that God creates only some determinate things, being determinate in the divine
nature a priori, and (2) that God does not create determinate things (perhaps
because they do not need creating). A metaphysics of creation will be falsified if
science in the long run accepts something it cannot tolerate. A metaphysics is not
interesting if there are no plausible scientific theories that specify it in relevant
respects; for example, a metaphysics that gives a large cosmological role to angels
would not be of much interest these days, especially to people who are tuned in to
science. The vagueness proper to metaphysics should tolerate alternative specifications of its categories by science, but should not tolerate specifications universally
thought to be absurd, although the historicity of such 'universal judgements' means
that conditions of interest and vagueness are fallible hypotheses.

Some of the recent debate concerning religion and science has been motivated by the intent to find some role for God in natural processes to complement the causal powers invoked by science. The 'God of the gaps' argument goes further, saying that without the hypothesis of God, science cannot explain something it ought to be able to explain. This motive is misguided. With regard to the created order, a metaphysical hypothesis about God should have no positive content about what science might discover: no theological premiss should introduce an arbitrary commitment that would prevent the study of the world from being entirely empirical. A hypothesis about God which includes transcendental categories describing creation should explain why there is a world, and it too is empirical in a very broad sense. That broad sense includes not only dialectical arguments, such as those dealing with the one and the many, but also a happy tolerance of anything science might plausibly put forward, and a healthy respect for what is known through the arts, through practical disciplines such as ethics, and so on. Also, a proper metaphysical hypothesis about creation and cosmology ought to be able to give helpful opinions on what is worthy and what is not in the major religions of the world. Charles Sanders Peirce said that an argument should not be conceived like a chain, which is only as strong as its weakest link, but like a rope with many strands, each perhaps slight in itself, but which when twisted together form a sturdy hypothesis that passes the tests it is put through.

VII. CONCLUDING SUMMARY

This chapter has discussed the thesis that a metaphysical hypothesis, including an ontology about God and the world, should be vague enough to tolerate specification by anything science might plausibly hypothesise. I have taken the thesis as an opportunity to weave together considerations, not only about the nature of metaphysics, but also about fundamental ontological symmetry and asymmetry, the relative priority of the divine nature and the act of creation, creation and freedom, transcendental categories for knowing the fundamental characters of the world, and similar topics. These topics are not disconnected, because any metaphysics of creation concerning the cosmos as known by science (and other forms of enquiry) must deal with them. Keith Ward is one of the few thinkers of our time with an intellect capacious enough to deal with these classic problems and sharp enough to do so with analytical control. To engage him in dialogue is an education, a rare privilege and an honour.

NOTES

1   A. N. Whitehead, *Process and Reality: An Essay in Cosmology*, ed. David Ray Griffin and Donald W. Sherburne (New York: Free Press, 1978; 1st publ. 1929), 17, 15.

2   See, for instance, his comparative work in *Images of Eternity: Concepts of God in Five Religious Traditions* (London: Darton, Longman and Todd, 1987) and his magnificent tetralogy in comparative theology (all Oxford: Clarendon Press): *Religion and Revelation* (1994), *Religion and Creation* (1996), *Religion and Human Nature* (1998) and *Religion and Community* (2000).

3   The pragmatic approach to hypothesis in metaphysics and science was first developed by Charles Sanders Peirce. See, for instance, his essay 'A Neglected Argument for the Reality of

God', in *The Collected Papers of Charles Sanders Peirce*, vol. vi, ed. Charles Hartshorne and Paul Weiss (Cambridge, Mass.: Harvard University Press, 1935), 311ff., reprinted in many anthologies. For Whitehead's discussion of metaphysics as hypothetical, as of course he thought science is, see *Process and Reality*, ch. 1.

4 I have dealt with this problem at length in *Normative Cultures* (Albany, NY: SUNY Press, 1995), chs 1–4. A shorter discussion is in *The Highroad around Modernism* (Albany, NY: SUNY Press, 1992), ch. 6.

5 I have indeed defended such a thesis in an essay with Wesley J. Wildman, 'On Comparing Religious Ideas', in Robert C. Neville (ed.), *Ultimate Realities* (Albany, NY: SUNY Press, 2001), ch. 8. That volume, along with Robert C. Neville (ed.), *The Human Condition and Religious Truth* (Albany, NY: SUNY Press, 2001), resulted from the Comparative Religious Ideas Project at Boston University, a collaborative effort involving many scholars from a variety of religious traditions, as well as generalists.

6 In Whitehead, *Process and Reality*, ch. 1.

7 Thomas Kuhn's *The Structure of Scientific Revolutions* (Chicago: University of Chicago Press, 1962) is the classic statement of the historicity of scientific theories. Stephen Toulmin's *Human Understanding: The Collective Use and Evolution of Concepts* (Princeton: Princeton University Press, 1972) makes out the historical details of this in far more convincing fashion.

8 I owe this distinction to Wesley J. Wildman.

9 This point is similar to Whitehead's 'ontological principle': see *Process and Reality*, 18, 24 *et passim*. The ontological principle is that determinate things are made out of antecedents (objects prehended, in Whitehead's language) plus the process of creativity or making. He cites Locke's notion of 'power' as the source of this idea of sheer making. For Whitehead, every event is a combination of prehended antecedents plus the subjective process of making a new thing out of them. Every complex state of affairs requires an ontological analysis. He applied this principle rigorously in explaining temporal things within the process of the world. He failed to apply it in asking how there could be the complex state of affairs of a world with certain metaphysical properties and actual realisations. Had he done so, he would have noted that no antecedent conditions would be possible, and so sheer subjective creativity must have established the primordial arbitrary conditions of the cosmos. That would have been a version of creation *ex nihilo*.

10 See Peirce, *Collected Papers*, vol. vi, pp. 342ff.

11 The outcome of those graduate school speculations was published as *God the Creator: On the Transcendence and Presence of God* (Chicago: University of Chicago Press, 1968; new edn Albany, NY: SUNY Press, 1992).

12 See my 'A Metaphysical Argument for Wholly Empirical Theology', in Robert J. Roth (ed.), *God Knowable and Unknowable* (New York: Fordham University Press, 1973), 215–40.

13 For Whitehead, the metaphysical principles apply to every creative act except perhaps the primordial creative act that some claim establishes the metaphysical principles themselves.

14 This hypothesis is spelled out in more systematic form in ch. 1 of my *Symbols of Jesus* (Cambridge: Cambridge University Press, 2001). The philosophical cosmology is detailed at great length in my *Recovery of the Measure* (Albany, NY: SUNY Press, 1989), which, along with *Normative Cultures* and *Reconstruction of Thinking* (both Albany, NY: SUNY Press, 1981), constitutes a systematic project I call an Axiology of Thinking that cumulatively defends the philosophical conception of value briefly mentioned in the text. All of this furnishes material for cumulative arguments for the hypothesis about God.

15 I have developed a hypothesis about conditions for personifying God in *Religion in Late Modernity* (Albany, NY: SUNY Press, 2002), ch. 4. On time and eternity within God, see my *Eternity and Time's Flow* (Albany, NY: SUNY Press, 1993), pts 3 and 4.

16 I argue this point at some length with reference to Ward's texts in *Symbols of Jesus*, ch. 1.

Part III
HUMAN NATURE

13

What is So Good about Having a Body?

RICHARD SWINBURNE

In *Religion and Human Nature*,[1] the third volume of his impressive comparison of the beliefs of major religious traditions, Keith Ward draws our attention to the different attitudes of western religions (Christianity, Judaism and Islam) and eastern religions (Hindu and Buddhist traditions) to embodiment here and hereafter. For western religions the human body is a good thing – in need of discipline certainly to keep bodily desires under control (e.g. fasting for temporary periods), but something which makes for the fullness of our humanity, and something with which we shall be re-endowed after death in the general resurrection. (On most Christian views there is a temporary period between death and resurrection when most humans will have only their essential part, their soul.) For most eastern religious traditions the body is a prison in which we are shut in this life, but from which eventually (maybe after many re-embodiments) we may hope to be liberated. This eastern view is not always expressed as the view that we shall survive without our bodies as individual persons – for some eastern thinkers, we shall be merged into some greater spiritual whole – but when it is expressed in the former way, it does entail the view that on Earth humans have two separable parts – body and soul – and the soul is the essential part of the human person.

I believe that the western view also entails this. For even if there is no intermediate period between death and resurrection, the issue arises as to what will constitute some future person being me rather than someone else. The new body being made of reassembled atoms of the old body? But many of these may have come to form some other body[2] or have been turned into energy; and there is no difference between the energy formed from one chunk of matter and the energy formed from another.[3] The future person having my apparent memories[4] and character? But innumerable future persons could have my apparent memories and character. You may think that God will ensure that only one future person will have my apparent memories and character. But such an act of God cannot *make* a future person me – preventing similar people from existing cannot make any difference to who *I* am. So in my view a future person will only be me if he has as his essential part my immaterial soul which was linked previously to my former body. And if that soul is linked to a new body, that body will be my body in virtue of that link (irrespective of whether or not the new body is made largely of bits of the old body). In my view substance dualism – that humans on Earth have these two parts, of which the soul is the essential part (whose continuing makes for my continuing) – is unavoidable for purely philosophical reasons having nothing to do with the demands of theology. I do not, however, seek to re-argue here this highly controversial view.[5] Rather, I presuppose it and ask whether, if it is correct – if we need only souls in order to exist – and if it is a good thing that we should survive death as individual persons, God is doing us a favour if he gives us bodies as well, on Earth and in another life. What is the point of embodiment?

To have a body in the way that we humans on Earth have bodies seems to me to involve four things – it is to have: (1) a (normally moveable) public region of basic control, (2) a (normally moveable) public region of basic action and perception – regions through which we are tied down to acting and perceiving – (3) a public 'machine room' necessary for our actions and perceptions, which (4) is also the source of our desires. By a public region I mean a region whose condition is in principle equally accessible to others as well as to ourselves. My heart and my brain are public regions, because if I know about their states better than others, that is only a contingent matter. Others can devise ways of finding out the state of my brain just as well as I can.

By the public region of my basic control I mean that region whose goings-on I can and do affect just by choosing to do so, by my causally basic actions. Moving parts of our bodies are the causally most basic public actions which we can do. When I do A intentionally and intend thereby to cause some effect whose bringing about constitutes doing B, doing A is causally more basic than doing B.[6] I take the book off the shelf by grasping it and pulling it towards me; grasping and pulling it cause it to come off the shelf. The latter, like the former, is a public intentional action in the sense that (although it includes a private part – my intending) it consists in bringing about a public state of affairs. But I do not grasp the book or pull it towards me by intentionally doing anything else public. Things have to happen in my body if I am to do the public actions – various neural impulses have to travel from my brain to my arms, mouth, etc. But though my intending may cause these neural impulses, I do not intentionally bring them about (they are not what I am seeking to bring about), nor will I normally know much about them. What I do as a basic intentional action is to move a part of my body. Thereby I often seek to produce and succeed in producing more distant effects. By the sentence I utter I change your beliefs; by the motion of my arm I push the door open. Whether my efforts to produce more distant effects succeed depends on nature, the world beyond my body. The most I can do is to move my body. My intentional bringing about of the distant effect is a non-basic or mediated action, which I do by doing the basic action – moving my hand or saying the words.

My body is that region which I control most immediately and by which I seek to control other things. My body is also the public region containing the sense organs by whose operation I learn about the world; because of their operation I have a region of basic perception surrounding my body. Only through light from distant objects impinging on my eyes, sound waves impinging on my ears, etc. do I learn about the world. After the waves impinge, various things about which I am not likely to know very much have to happen in my body if I am to acquire beliefs about the world. I call the public region about which I acquire knowledge by the use of my sense organs, but not by inference from other knowledge provided by my sense organs, my region of basic perception. When children first come to acquire knowledge by means of their sense organs, the region of their basic perception is the region of a few metres surrounding their bodies, in so far as their line of vision is unimpeded by solid objects. The region of basic perception being larger than the region of basic control, we can learn about distant effects of our actions within the former region and thus learn to do this rather than that non-basic action.

Since among the basic intentional actions we can perform (unless we are paralysed) is moving our bodies, we can readily change the region of our basic perception, and thus learn about yet more distant effects of our actions and causes of our perceptions. Seeing people and other things damaged by falling stones in different places, I can infer that if I throw a stone over a wall it will hurt anyone on the other side of the wall, even though the other side of the wall is outside my region of basic perception. And having seen furniture arranged in a room in a certain way, I find that when I look through a telescope at the room from a long distance away, I observe an image of the furniture arranged in just that way; and so I learn to infer from an image in a telescope to what is happening, even when the latter lies outside my region of basic perception. What starts as an inference becomes so natural as to become an intentional action (to hurt anyone there may be on the other side of the wall) or a perception (of the arrangement of furniture in a distant room). My perception is a non-basic or mediated perception, because I perceive the distant event by perceiving the nearer event, in the sense that my perception of the distant event has the same sensory content (patterns of colour in my visual field, or noises heard) as my perception of the nearer event. Telescopes, radio and e-mail are means by which we have learnt to extend the range of our non-basic actions and perceptions by a large degree.

Thirdly, my body is the 'machine room' which translates my intentions into bodily actions, and turns the incoming light, sound, etc. waves into sensations and beliefs about the external world. I need to look after my body (by providing it with food, drink, sleep and exercise) in order that it may provide effective control and perception. And fourthly my body is the source of desires (continuing over time, or stimulated by circumstances) to do and avoid various things. Many of our desires are for things conducive to our survival or that of our species – desires to eat, have sexual intercourse or avoid dangerous heights, for example. The satisfaction of desire gives pleasure, and its frustration pain (in a wide sense). Prominent among the desires which may be frustrated are desires not to have certain sensations, e.g. those caused by bodily damage, and their frustration involves pain in a narrow sense.

Desires get reinforced by the memory of past pleasures and pains associated with various actions, and awareness thereof encourages us to do or avoid such actions in future – to drink wine again, or not to put our hand into the fire in future. My body is also so programmed genetically as to be susceptible to environmental influences leading to more sophisticated desires – for love and fame, power and fortune. Even if

all our desires have good effects on some occasions, they operate when their fulfilment would not be a good thing – we desire to eat when we need food but also when
we don't and others need the food instead, and so on. We have considerable natural
proneness to wrongdoing, caused in part by our bodies.

Now what is the point of having a body of this kind on Earth? It is a great good
that there should be beings with a free choice between good and evil, able to influence through their actions themselves, each other, lesser conscious beings, and the
inanimate world. Given that to recognise some possible action as good involves
having some minimal desire to do it, in the absence of bad desires we will inevitably
do what we believe to be good. We can only have a free choice between good and evil
if we also have desires to do what (in the circumstances) is bad.[7] A proneness to
wrongdoing is a necessary condition of a free choice between good and evil. It is
good that we should have serious responsibility for others, and so for how it goes
with others for good or ill to be up to us, and so that we should have the choice of
harming as well as benefiting them (all of this within limits – there needs to be a limit
to the amount of harm we can do to others). But doing bad is bad and so it is good
that we should have the choice of making ourselves persons so naturally inclined to
the good that we have no temptation to do evil; or alternatively, to make ourselves so
that we are subject to no desires and cease to be moral beings. (Only with the latter
possibility available to us will our final destiny be really in our own hands, and not
depend on the prior choice of some superior power.)

All of this requires us to have bodies in the sense of public regions of basic control
and perception, and a machine room necessary for our actions and perceptions and
the source of our desires. To have a choice at all I need some power over and knowledge of a region. My region of basic control will have to be different from that of
other people if I am to control it, unless their wills coincide with mine. If many other
people made my arms move when I did not wish them to, I would not have control
over my arms. And my regions of basic control and perception will need to be
limited if I am to have the choice of whether or not to extend them. To have the
opportunity to extend my power and knowledge, there must be something I can do
with them to extend their range. To choose to gain new knowledge, I must choose to
exercise my basic powers – especially of motion (to get new bits of information from
other places), and also of inference. New knowledge by discovery and/or inference of
what follows what enables me to extend my powers by producing an event of the
former kind in order to produce an event of the latter kind. With a region of basic
control and perception, so long as it is placed in a world of natural laws sufficiently
simple for us to discover and manipulate, we can choose whether or not to extend
our knowledge and control.

Each of us could have his or her own regions of control and perception, not
located in a common public world. But we could not have serious responsibility for
others unless their regions belonged to the same world as ours; above all we could not
co-operate with others to help someone achieve extension of knowledge and
control, or to hinder such extensions. All this requires belonging to a common world
– requires that our regions of control and perception should be public. And public

communication also requires this. If I am to communicate with you (or have the choice of not doing so), there has to be something which I can do which will show you what I believe and desire. If we produce public effects (movements or noises), that allows others to interpret them as having certain meanings. Others seek the simplest system of beliefs and desires which will explain why we produce these movements in these circumstances, beliefs and desires as similar to their own as can be postulated. A natural, very simple such assumption is that we are seeking by our movements and noises to say something which we believe to be true; and by supposing that, others can come to understand what we are saying – if they so choose. But if others are to have some choice of understanding or not, there must be the possibility of their refusing to hear what I have to say (e.g. by moving away) and of different languages or amending old languages so as to convey new ideas. Then others can choose whether or not to work out what we are getting at – or not to bother.

In order for me or others to have the choice of causing pleasure or pain to me, curing or maiming me, we must all have access to my machine room. By taking drugs I can give myself pleasure; by sticking a needle into me you can cause me pain. You can limit my powers by cutting off my arm; but if I get ill or am maimed, surgeons and other doctors can intervene to repair me. You can help me extend my powers to perform basic actions by helping me to run faster; or give me drugs to improve my vision or memory. The ability to hurt others requires that their machine rooms are not too easily moveable by them, at any rate in unpredictable ways. I cannot hurt a poltergeist if I cannot hold it down. And again, the possibility of collaboration in benefiting or harming each other requires that the machine room be public.

Although the desires, good and bad, which we need for significant choice need not arise from our bodies, if they do, there is again the possibility of others in collaboration influencing them for good or ill. Others can give us drugs to help control our cravings (for nicotine or heroin), or allow us to be educated in circumstances which will stimulate our latent desires for fame and fortune.

For all of these reasons it is good for us to have some sort of embodiment. There can be different degrees and ways of embodiment. We could be embodied in some of these respects and not others – we might have a region of basic control but be able to perceive what is happening everywhere; or our machine room could be located somewhere quite other than within our region of basic perception.[8] Our familiar three-dimensional physical space is a suitable space for our embodiment, but other kinds of 'space' might suit.[9] The bodies we have are spatially extended (occupy a volume of space) and not merely spatially located (at a point); and the powers which our machine rooms give us result from the machine room containing many separate and sometimes replaceable bits. To have that sort of machine room is an obvious way in which we can be publicly tampered with. But our machine room could consist of a simple particle, so long as there were different things we could do to it which would make different differences to our mechanisms of control, perception and desire production.

So we need a body on Earth if we are to have the sorts of choices between good and evil which it is good that we should have. But suppose, as a result of our choosing the good with such determination on Earth, that we make ourselves so naturally good that we no longer have the choice of evil, and God takes us to his 'nearer presence' where we are always fully conscious of his loving care. Would we need bodies then?[10] Not if heaven consists solely of the 'flight of the alone to the Alone'. But surely it is good that people should co-operate in doing good; and the heaven of the blessed as depicted in the last book of the New Testament and in much Christian liturgy and piety is a place where the saints do things together – above all worship God and help to forward his purposes. That minimally requires a public presence. And while the blessed have no temptation to do evil, there is no reason to suppose that they lack free will (any more than God does) to choose between innumerable alternative good things – and these good things may include giving each other pleasure and helping each other to extend their powers and knowledge in various ways. And for these purposes they need a public presence – a place from which they can extend their power and knowledge, speak, and hear, and a machine room which can be stimulated to provide different kinds of pleasure and good desire. No doubt the blessed love all the other blessed (and all humans on Earth as well), but the expression of love requires recognition of particular individuals and their particular characteristics. A can express his or her love and affection for B only by singling out B from the rest of the blessed, and that requires there to be a place at which A's action (e.g. of hugging or kissing or kind words) will affect B alone, an action which must involve a recognition of the way in which B differs from the rest of the blessed – by her past and her interests – and so one which involves words and actions appropriate to that difference. And again the heaven of the blessed as depicted in much Christian liturgy and piety is not one in which the blessed forget their past or lose their interests – it is represented as full of 'patron saints' interacting with humans on Earth having particular interests and concerns. But cannot all this be achieved if the saints have telepathic access to each other? One might imagine each saint having a large mental screen in which he could reach another saint by concentrating on a particular point on that screen, and be reached by another saint through (for example) that point getting much bigger on his visual screen. But such points taken together would constitute a public space; and once we fill out the details of how the blessed access each other and what they can do to each other and to us, this system of powers and liabilities associated with each individual will constitute a system of bodies. For to have a body is, as we have seen, in the main just to have a system of powers and liabilities (including the ability to communicate) accessible to others and alterable gradually (but not immediately) by ourselves and others. Only through bodies can finite beings have meaningful personal relations with each other. But such relations do not require having bodies which are a source of desires to do bad as well. So we might expect the blessed to have bodies, but ones somewhat different from our present bodies.

That the blessed in heaven will have bodies after the general resurrection, but bodies freed from many earthly limitations, especially by way of causing pain or mal-functioning, has been the universal Christian view. St Paul wrote of the resurrected human body as a 'spiritual body'.[11] But if the above arguments are correct, and the blessed in heaven are already able to co-operate in worship and so on (as is normally supposed in Christian liturgy and piety), it follows that they must already be embodied – which is contrary to the normal Christian view that (with the occasional possible exception, such as Mary) the blessed are only re-endowed with their bodies at the general resurrection. Some qualification is therefore required to the latter, normal Christian view. We will need to say that they are embodied, but not fully (they don't have all of what is involved in having a body) or not with any of the matter of their original bodies until the general resurrection.

God, however, being essentially omnipotent in his control and omniscient in his perception, cannot be tied down to a region in which he operates and through which he acquires knowledge. Nor can he have a 'machine room', for his abilities depend on nothing. But just one of the reasons which make it good for us to have bodies makes it good that God should have a body in a very limited sense. While God will inevitably be aware of what we seek to say to him, we will only be aware of what he seeks to say to us publicly (that is, to many of us together) if there is a public region under his direct control, whose states and changes of state we can interpret. In this sense the world is God's body. It is by the way he controls it – both by the normal operation of natural laws and by his occasional intervention in their operation – that he reveals his purposes to us communally. But God is not tied down to operating through this world – he could reveal his purposes to others through another world, or not reveal them at all.

It is possible, however, for God voluntarily to acquire a smaller body in a much fuller sense, which he uses (for as long as he chooses) as a mode of action and know-ledge acquisition additional to his normal mode. That, the Council of Chalcedon taught, is what happened when God the Son became incarnate in Jesus Christ, acquiring a human body (and also a 'rational soul').[12] Thereby he could produce effects (e.g. make a door close) which he could also produce by bringing them about as a basic action, and learn things (e.g. by seeing them) which he would be learning anyway, just by their happening. And this human body had a machine room, as a result of which others could cause pain to God Incarnate or give him food which would keep that body alive. And plausibly Christ's body was the source of many of the desires to do less than the best, that is temptations, to which Christ was subject – for example, the temptation to turn stones into bread.[13] Lesser councils have implied that this union of God the Son with human nature, body and soul, is a permanent one.[14] This could be a way in which after this life God continues to express his solidarity with his human creation.

It has also been a Christian doctrine, emphasised by St Paul, that the Church is 'the body of Christ';[15] the Church's 'members' are the parts of this body. This body is naturally thought of as an extension of Christ's human post-resurrection body. This means, at least perhaps, that Christ moves the members of the Church to move their bodies as his basic actions. What I do with my body does not normally coincide with what God wants me to do with my body. But if I voluntarily choose to do with my body what Christ (that is, God) wants me to do with it in the continuation of

Christ's earthly work, it becomes part of his body as well as being my body. The Church being the body of Christ also perhaps involves Christ learning things through the members of the Church learning them (as well as perceiving them anyway), feeling pain when things go wrong with the members and pleasure when they go well. And it is because not merely our bodies, but our wills and feelings, are the vehicle of Christ, of his interaction with the world, that we – not merely our bodies – may be said to be 'the body of Christ', and this is a far fuller sense than that in which the inanimate world is God's body. Our human bodies do not always do what we try to make them do – our arms and legs may not work properly. But they remain parts of our body if they have a potentiality for working as we want them to work. So, too, with members of the Church only partly open to the influence of its head. And it is, of course, good that God in Christ should have a Church body, because that means that we are used by him as the vehicle by which he transforms the world; but good too that it is up to our free choice how well it works.

Whether for humans on Earth, or humans in heaven, or God himself, embodiment (of different degrees) makes possible co-operation in interaction.

NOTES

1   Keith Ward, *Religion and Human Nature* (Oxford: Clarendon Press, 1998).
2   Patristic and medieval theologians worried about the problem of the cannibal who eats only human flesh. How could both he and his victims rise again? In *Summa Contra Gentiles*, IV, 81, 13 Aquinas gives the answer that in this case the human flesh will constitute the risen body of him 'to whose perfection it belonged more intimately' and 'if something was present in both [of two humans], in the same degree of perfection, it will rise in him in whom it was the first time': *On the Truth of the Catholic Faith. Book 4: Salvation*, tr. Charles J. O'Neill (New York: Image Books, 1957). This idea that some parts of the body are more central than others to the essence of the person is espoused also by the many modern writers who claim that it is identity of brains which constitutes the identity of human persons. But this view, whether in the form espoused by Aquinas or that espoused by modern writers, has the consequence that if the cannibal's most 'central part' is made from the atoms of the 'central parts' of other humans, they cannot all reacquire bodies. Aquinas's view entails that it is the cannibal who cannot rise again.
3   It may be that fundamental particles (and so the atoms which they compose) have 'thisness', e.g. there is an intrinsic difference between two electrons which have all the same properties of mass, charge, etc. In that case I suppose that God could re-create the atoms constituting our previous bodies which had been turned into energy. However, in my view and perhaps in the view of the majority of philosophers and physicists who have given thought to this issue, fundamental particles probably do not have thisness (see my 'Thisness', *Australasian Journal of Philosophy*, 73 (1995), 389–400). In that case there would be no intrinsic difference between qualitatively similar bodies composed of the same number of the same kinds of fundamental particles arranged in the same way. But a body could not be mine just because God omitted to create a qualitatively similar one.
4   By someone having my 'apparent memories' I mean it seeming to them that they did and experienced the things which I did and experienced. Only if they really did and experienced these things would they be me.
5   See my *The Evolution of the Soul*, revd edn (Oxford: Clarendon Press, 1997), esp. pt 2.
6   The distinction between basic and non-basic actions is due (under that name) to A. C. Danto (see his 'Basic Actions', *American Philosophical Quarterly*, 2 (1965), 141–8). The more precise

definition of causally basic action is due to Annette Baier – see her 'The Search for Basic Actions', *American Philosophical Quarterly*, 8 (1971), 161–70.

7   I have argued this more fully in many places; see for example my *Responsibility and Atonement* (Oxford: Clarendon Press, 1989), 43–8.

8   As in Daniel Dennett's amusing paper 'Where Am I?', in his *Brainstorms* (Hassocks, Sussex: Harvester Press, 1979), 310–23.

9   P. F. Strawson brought out the inadequacies of a purely auditory space in his *Individuals* (London: Methuen, 1959), ch. 2.

10 For reasons of space, I shall not discuss the issue of whether the damned in hell, if there are any, need bodies. For my general view on the fates of different groups in the after-life, see my *Responsibility and Atonement*, esp. ch. 12.

11 1 Cor. 15.44–6.

12 H. Denzinger (ed.), *Enchiridion Symbolorum*, 33rd edn (Barcelona *et al.*: Herder, 1965), §301 (p. 108).

13 Matt. 4.3; Luke 4.3.

14 For example, the Lateran Council of AD 649 implies this in stating that at the Last Judgment Christ will come to judge 'the living and the dead', 'in the flesh and rational soul which were assumed by him': Denzinger (ed.), *Enchiridion Symbolorum*, §502 (pp. 171–2), translation mine.

15 See, for example, 1 Cor. 12.12–27.

14

Varieties of Uniqueness and the Person of Christ: Does Uniqueness Matter?

VERNON WHITE

The link between 'uniqueness' and 'mattering' has been well noted. Helen Oppenheimer, for example, provides useful reflection on the uniqueness of human persons as individuals and how that might matter.[1] She defines this uniqueness as the uniqueness of our *irreplaceability*. In what sense are we irreplaceable? Most would now say that this irreplaceability is primarily a relational concept. That is, our irreplaceability is not established only or necessarily because we have some quality which belongs uniquely to us in our intrinsic constitution (whether some supposed empirical uniqueness in our genetic make-up, or supposed metaphysical uniqueness such as the shape of our soul): rather, it is established by our unique *relationships* with others, and with God; we are made irreplaceable by the unique web of relations we have with others.

This seems to me an acceptable view, at least in general terms – and always provided we do not rush to define people so relationally that we dissolve the personal centre altogether and imply we are only a web of relations (a problem which Augustine seemed to have had with the Holy Spirit, and which more recent Christian theologians are now having with their anthropology[2]). In other words, we may want to say that our relations are unique because the individual him/herself is unique as well as vice versa. Nonetheless, the general point remains that irreplaceability is best experienced and perceived through the unique relations in which we are involved.

Irreplaceability – relationally understood – therefore lies at the heart of human uniqueness. And this is where we most immediately and incontrovertibly see that each person *matters*. It is precisely in the sense of their irreplaceability that their mattering claims us most forcefully (most poignantly when we lose someone by death, or by betrayal). There is a distinction here between personal mattering and other kinds of mattering. If a particular blade of grass or even a particular tree withers, it does not matter in the same way as the death of a person because they are replaceable in a sense that no human person is. A replanted tree from the same genetic stock eventually replaces the fallen tree. A friend, father or child cannot be replaced in the same way.

In short, when uniqueness is analysed as irreplaceability this is where we most clearly encounter 'mattering' in its most profound personal sense.

If we want to analyse further the meaning of mattering then at the very least it must be clear that it is a self-evidently *moral* notion. Someone mattering is an experience of their value, which then makes a moral claim on us. Mattering is therefore the experience of finding a fact (like someone's irreplaceability) to be of itself an experience of the person's value. As such it is the sort of experience which transcends Hume's logical divide between fact and value. Again, Oppenheimer is good on this, in a very common-sense sort of way – which is often the best way to deal with Hume's divide. There are certain kinds of facts which simply are value-laden, and the uniqueness of persons, understood as their irreplaceability, is one of them.

We now need to extend the context to theological matters. In particular, if it is true that the uniqueness of Jesus Christ makes him matter, what sort of uniqueness makes him matter in what sort of way? Does the notion of irreplaceability help here?

To begin with we simply have to say that he is unique in the same way that every human person is, because he has at least the same sort of irreplaceability which is true for us all. The historical man Jesus, qua man, is irreplaceable in at least the same sense that every other person is irreplaceable. That is as true of his relation to God as it is of his relation to other people. He has a unique relation to God in the same sense of uniqueness as all other people's relation to God. My relation both to God and to you can never be identical to anyone else's, and this will also be the case for Jesus of Nazareth. To be sure, there are formal characteristics of all our relations which we share with others: for example, in relation to God we are all as creature to creator or (analogously) as child to parent; in relation to others we may share the same roles as friend, neighbour, brother, sister, child, employer, employee. Nonetheless, the existential content and substance of the relationship, whether with God or others, is always unique – and that is the force of its irreplaceability. The key notion here is that this sort of uniqueness arises from our particularity. We are not just identical instances of some generic quality of human nature. We are individual and particular persons, therefore unrepeatable, and so we generate unrepeatable relationships with God and others. And all that is equally true of Jesus of Nazareth.

But of course that is not the kind of uniqueness which has generated the *theological* kind of mattering normally associated with Jesus Christ. In addition to the 'generic' uniqueness which belongs to us all, he has been ascribed a specific uniqueness in his relation with God that is different in kind to all other unique relations. This is the distinction which has been variously conceived in the Christological formulations of the centuries. There is no space here to embark on an extensive review of all these, not least because it has been done much better elsewhere (Sarah Coakley's book on Troeltsch, *Christ Without Absolutes*, is a good example[3]). But I do want to press the specific question about how the notion of uniqueness is operating in at least some of them, in order to highlight the different kinds of mattering associated with them. This needs a brief mapping exercise to begin with, to look at the range of options which theology has presented to us.

A simplified summary of the main formulations of uniqueness in Christology, and the questions they raise, might go like this. They can be divided broadly into two. First, in classic Chalcedonian definitions Christ is unique in his *being*. He alone is held to be divine in some aspect of his being: that is, he shares divine being in the way he is a person in a way that no other creature does. This is normally expressed through the notion of his 'hypostatic' union with God. Second, Christ is often conceived to be unique in his *function*, a refocusing of uniqueness which often arises when formulations of unique being come under pressure for being conceptually difficult or historically hard to justify. One function is that of conveying a unique *revelation* of God: providing the best picture of God and his purposes that could be given in historical, human form. Another function is being a unique *agent* of God's purposes: for instance, one who uniquely announces the Kingdom of God on Earth and advances it by example or inspiration. A more radical function is as a unique *constitutor* of this kingdom: one who actually makes salvation possible both on Earth and in heaven through some mystical or metaphysical act of redemption on the cross and in the resurrection, an act which fundamentally changes our relationship with God.

The questions which arise about uniqueness from this sort of typology go like this. First, can they be separated? In other words, to what extent do these unique functions depend on a unique kind of being? Which of them (if any) require the hypostatic union of classic Christology in order to be effective? In particular, is the claim of a mysterious metaphysical act of redemption which constitutes us in a new relationship with God only possible through one who was fully human and fully divine (as, for example, Gregory Nazianzen believed)? Alternatively, could some of the work be done (as the later Schleiermacher seemed to think) by a person who simply had a greater consciousness of God than the rest of us? Or do all these functions, whether of revelation or redemption, just depend for their effectiveness on the unique set of historical circumstances? In other words, did it really require a person of unique being or even just unique God-consciousness to be this effective revelation or agent – or was it simply that particular web of religious, social and political circumstances of first-century Palestine which enabled God to be uniquely revealed and/or effective in the person of Jesus? Even this last, fairly minimalist Christology could still permit a decisive revelation or action of God, precisely because the circumstances are unrepeatable, just as each particular person is unrepeatable.

There are further questions. If Christ's uniqueness is conceived to lie in his divine being, is it the sort of hypostatic union with God which will always and eternally be of a different kind to ours? Or is it the type of something into which we shall ourselves be drawn? That is, are we supposed to see deification not just in the reality of Jesus Christ, but as our destiny as well? Historically the East has been more comfortable with deification than the West, but the gap may now be lessening. A different kind of question, already trailed, surfaces more acutely when Christ's uniqueness is conceived in terms of function. To what extent is he merely showing us the possibilities of salvation, and to what extent is he actually making it possible? In other words, is the life and death of Jesus Christ merely revelatory of salvation, or is it also constitutive? Most modern soteriologies slide into the former view and evade the latter, more difficult one: that is, they fight shy of articulating clearly any view that Christ actually makes our salvation happen in some way, taking refuge instead in expounding what general principles of salvation Christ reveals. This is partly because the constitutive view is thought to be difficult to conceive, and also thought to imply an exclusivist doctrine of salvation, at odds with the moral scruples of a pluralist culture. In fact the conceptual difficulties are not insurmountable and exclusivism is not a necessary outcome.[4] Nonetheless, these are some of the questions often raised in contemporary Christologies and soteriologies which help map out something of the range of options about Christological uniqueness.

But what are the different sorts of mattering which arise from these different options? Classic formulations which stress Christ's unique divine being have mattered in various ways. Historically they have mattered as a litmus test of doctrinal orthodoxy. In particular they tend to have been used to bolster exclusivist views of Christian truth. This happens when the unique being of Christ is held to give unique being, identity and status to the Church as the repository for this truth. They have also mattered doxologically, because they invite unequivocal worship of Jesus Christ himself. When this sort of worship forms a people in a certain way this also means they have mattered ethically. For example, when Christ is worshipped as divine perfection beyond our own ethical reach it can inculcate humility (at best), or passivity and fatalism about our own capacities (at worst). Thus in one way or another we are likely to be made more lowly when Christ's uniqueness is construed as his divine being. All these are kinds of mattering which are associated naturally, though not necessarily or exclusively, with this kind of uniqueness.

The functional formulations of Christ's uniqueness have also mattered in different ways. As touchstones of orthodoxy they have generally been less fixed, but this is not always the case in the central question of salvation. If Christ is a necessary agent of true knowledge of God or true salvation, then the exclusivist strand of Christian self-understanding tends to be hardened, not relaxed. It means that other faiths and unfaith are more likely to be confronted rather than accepted or incorporated. On the other hand Christ's unique revealing or saving functions can be reconceived without that consequence. Christ may be conceived, Rahner-like, as an anonymous agent of salvation, operating effectively but without our knowledge through other faiths and unfaith: in this way he is still believed to be a unique and necessary agent of God, but does not need to be known as such, at least in the economy of this life. The doxological mattering of functional Christologies is also various. Overall it is best characterised as pneumatological: that is, a functional view of Christ as active in saving or bringing in the Kingdom is more likely to draw people into worship through the Spirit of Christ, because the Spirit is the more obviously dynamic form of God. This leaves the historical Jesus as the human example and companion rather than the object of worship: worship is in and of the Spirit of Christ. Such worship then forms people ethically with more sense of the possibilities of transformation (personal or social, depending on other theological and ecclesiological priorities). In other words, in functional definitions Christ's uniqueness matters more in what he can do for us and with us, rather than what status or identity he gives us as creatures before God or as the Church before other faiths.

Such mapping of the mattering associated with different Christologies is more impressionistic than the conceptual analysis of different senses of uniqueness. But at the very least it demonstrates how the relation between different kinds of uniqueness and mattering is so multi-stranded and flexible. That in turn raises the obvious question. Can we, should we, must we keep struggling with such a complex picture? Can we clarify and simplify the theological uniqueness which properly and necessarily belongs to Christ – or even abandon it altogether? Either way might make life easier and tidier. This is the sort of plea Maurice Wiles makes to Karl Rahner, at least implicitly.[5] Rahner's general theological method presupposes a universal human orientation towards God and a universal divine offer of self-communication towards us. Such a method provides an inclusive and coherent theological framework within which the particularities of any religious tradition could all find some safe home, and there is no apparent need for the sort of uniqueness which generates exclusive claims. But as Wiles points out, we then encounter some Christological convictions in Rahner which seem at odds with this. These are often based on traditional formulations. They portray the divine and human in Christ as coming together in 'a final and unrepeatable way'. The trouble is, as Wiles complains, there is no clarity about how the general theological method relates to these Christological convictions – so why do we have to cling to these Christological convictions at all?

It is here that I want to turn to Keith Ward for further perspectives. To begin with we simply need to say that he too exemplifies the problem qua problem. When trawling through his extensive corpus it is possible to find most of these positions. There is a roving Christological quest, arguably unresolved. In fact we might well complain, as Wiles did about Rahner, that the overall result needs tidying up. Ward seems to range across all the positions I have outlined, but without settling within any one of them.

For example, *A Vision to Pursue* appears to be both functional and limited in its Christology, seeing Christ's uniqueness largely in his capacity to reveal God uniquely at a particular time, rather than for all time.[6] But later, in *Religion and Revelation*, there are clear statements about Christ as a unique kind of enhypostatic union of Jesus with God the eternal Word.[7] Jesus Christ is not a human being whom God the Word indwelt in some temporary or contingent way, but a unique union which is 'original' and 'indissoluble'.[8] However, Ward then reverts to expounding Christ's uniqueness in relation to a unique historical context, though here he makes wider claims for its scope than in *A Vision to Pursue* because this historical particularity is the 'originative point' through which Christ creates 'absolute' and 'final' truth about God – not just a truth for one time but for all reality.[9] This appears to be a return to functional uniqueness, but with a wider scope of mattering than before. Later still, in *Religion and Human Nature*, Ward claims there is a unique purpose to explain God's action in Christ, which is to provide not just a limited example but an event of atonement which creates a vehicle of the transforming Spirit.[10] This is apparently a constitutive view of Christ's work. It is also, incidentally, an interesting confirmation of the kind of mattering produced by this kind of uniqueness: to believe Christ has this sort of unique function tends toward worship in the Spirit and thoughts of transformation. In short, here is a writer ranging through a number of modes of uniqueness, unwilling to be too constrained in his Christological definitions, whatever the risk of theological untidiness.

This becomes even more apparent in relation to some other theological concerns. For instance, Ward is generally concerned to expound the significance of Christ's suffering but he does not clarify its mode of uniqueness. Thus he does *not* seem to see it specifically as a kind of event through which God defines or constitutes a unique relation between himself and human suffering, for he sees that suffering must also be experienced by God everywhere else as well.[11] What is uniquely significant in Christ's suffering (if anything) therefore remains unclear. There is another kind of ambivalence in his essay 'Cosmos and Kenosis'.[12] There he first seems to demonstrate clearly that there can be no constitutive view of Christ's saving work after all, since God relates effectively to creation anyway, apart from the Christ event. All Christ does is reveal rather than constitute that wider relation. This is further reflected in his sustained interest in unfolding the action of God in other religions as well as Christianity. But then Ward claws back some sense of unique constitutive action and purpose when he claims there is a specific moment of kenosis in the Incarnation by which God makes this relation possible, not just visible.

If this means that we can only have untidy maps and unresolved patterns of thought, whether in theology in general or in Ward as a microcosm of it, this would hardly matter. It is just as likely to be a theological virtue as a vice. Yet this sort of agnosticism (or pluralism) should only have the last word if all further avenues of thought have been fully explored. And in fact there is just such an avenue in Ward's own work. It is another aspect of his overall theology which could shed more light on this question of uniqueness, and its significance. It lies, interestingly, in his general cosmology and metaphysics, rather than specifically within his Christology. Ultimately it lies within his doctrine of God.

In *Religion and Creation* Ward offers a general conception of the creator God specifically as the creator of new values: in other words, new *mattering*.[13] Such mattering comes about with every new particular state of being which emerges in the creative process. When each particular emerges within its ever-changing and irreplaceable world of other particulars it becomes itself a profound form of value and mattering, or at least a necessary condition for such mattering. Just becoming particular is, therefore, close to the heart of mattering. This is especially true for the experience of value which arises in particular personal relationships, most of all in interpersonal love. This sort of relational particularity is what creation is primarily *for*. It is also, incidentally, the ultimate rationale for the creation of a world of change. Change is to be understood through what Ward calls new 'dispositions and valued states', which are the new particularities of experience (thus change implies much more than simply the unfolding of properties already in existence).

In terms of our discussion the crucial point unfolds when this is seen as the specific context from which Christology takes its rationale: that is, a key component of the meaning and purpose of God's kenosis in Christ is that it realises some new particulars of experience in himself. In short, God in Christ becomes himself a new state of being by being particular, and this is an essential part of the doctrine of God. It is not hard to see why. This experience of particularity ought indeed to belong to God, otherwise something would be missing from God's mattering. If God is just universal, God would not matter in every way: we would have a kind of mattering denied to God. Thus God in Christ is *also* particular. I am now beginning to take the argument beyond Ward's own text, but it is surely susceptible to this way of developing it.

Yet is this any more than just another kind of 'trivial' uniqueness: a sense of particularity and mattering which is simply the sort of uniqueness we all bear? After all, although God in Christ may be particular, is there not *some* sense in which God is also particular in us? This would only return us to a sort of generic uniqueness, the point where we began. But this does not follow if God is particular in Christ by a unique hypostatic union: a union which is foundational or constitutive of his being particular elsewhere. That by definition would be a unique kind of particularity. It might, *ipso facto*, give greater value to all particularity but would itself remain *sui generis*.

Of course, any talk of the universal God being (uniquely) particular is vulnerable to the usual sorts of charges levelled against the old Christological formulas. It seems like a contradiction in terms, a categorial confusion. How could God be truly particular and experience the nature of particularity and remain the God of universal experience and omnipresence? The problem is sharply framed by Henry Simoni: 'Any particular human experience [. . .] has a quality that incorporates the very particularity of the experiencer'.[14] He calls this 'radical particularity'. It means that particularity by definition excludes the sort of universal being and experience that God must have to be God at all in distinction from all other, finite beings. So does this merely return us to the familiar conceptual difficulties of any real doctrine of incarnation, about which the literature is legion and the problems apparently insoluble?

Maybe. But not necessarily. Some of the most interesting moments of theological discussion are found in throwaway comments, phrases in parentheses, and there is just one such in Simoni's article. His comment actually reads, 'Any particular human experience (*perhaps excluding mystic oneness*) has a quality that incorporates the very particularity of the experiencer.'[15] In other words, there may be an experience ('mystic oneness', in his terminology) in which particularity and universality *can* both be radically present without diluting each other. This will be an experience where the sort of mattering which belongs by definition only to particularity and novelty is retained, but where it is nonetheless experienced as universal. The performance of great music or acts of personal love can point to this sort of experience, at least analogously. Moreover, if we ask whether there is any remotely rational way of articulating such apparent contradictions then there is at least one tradition which could support it. Apophatic theology has long claimed to be able to say and unsay things which appear to be contradictory without formal contradiction precisely because it is articulating different dimensions of experience and reality co-existing within the same event. Poetry is the more usual way, of course, as the medieval carol about incarnation suggests: 'in this rose containèd was | Heaven and earth in litel space'.

But whether we try to express it discursively or poetically, what we are wanting to say is clear enough. We are claiming that a general metaphysical concern for the value of particularity can fasten on Christ without simply reducing him to just one more novelty amongst others. His uniqueness can matter in other ways, with universal dimensions.

This immediately sets up interesting possibilities. For instance, as already hinted, his particularity could be (uniquely) a universal paradigm of the value of all particularity, rather than just one instance of it. As such I could believe in him, worship and be formed by him, as one who is unique in a sense beyond all other particulars, but without undervaluing them in their particularity. In fact I would value them all the more because of the significance that he has given to them. In short, there is an experience and concept of particularity which is unique in its mattering without being exclusive – and that is what we claim for Christ. This sets a clear Christian agenda for valuing other faiths, but does so on the basis of its own claims to incarnational uniqueness, rather than by compromising them. Such a view ought at least to commend itself widely within orthodox Christian faith, if not always beyond.

The grounds for believing that this sort of uniqueness is actually true of Jesus Christ can only be established in other ways. It requires a cumulative argument which draws on history, experience and faith (centred to a significant degree, in my view, on the resurrection). It will also depend on more general notions of moral and spiritual fruitfulness and congruity. Here I have been concerned only with the possible *meanings* of the claim, and how it might matter.

Nonetheless, although this is a very limited remit it might at least help us to take care with our language. For one thing is certain: language about uniqueness can easily be misunderstood and misused. Loose language has always cost lives, in religion as in other things. And so I trust that even this modest attempt to clarify meaning may have some value. This debate itself matters – not just within academic theological circles but in the world beyond, and perhaps in today's religious climate it is going to matter even more than in times past. Apparently arcane theological debate has a habit of resurfacing with new relevance in new contexts. A sign, perhaps, of some deep truth in its subject matter, whatever the limitations and untidiness of all our attempts to express it.

NOTES

1   Helen Oppenheimer, *The Hope of Happiness* (London: SCM Press, 1983).
2   For example, Alistair McFadyen, *The Call to Personhood* (Cambridge: Cambridge University Press, 1990). I point to the reductionist danger in radically relational definitions in *Paying Attention to People: An Essay on Individualism and Christian Belief* (London: SPCK, 1996), 103–4; see also Harriet Harris, 'Should We Say that Personhood is Relational?', *Scottish Journal of Theology*, 51 (1998), 214–34.
3   Sarah Coakley, *Christ Without Absolutes* (Oxford: Clarendon Press, 1988).
4   See Vernon White, *Atonement and Incarnation* (Cambridge: Cambridge University Press, 1991).

5   Maurice Wiles, *Christian Theology and Inter-religious Dialogue* (London: SCM Press, 1992), ch. 3.

6   Keith Ward, *A Vision to Pursue* (London: SCM Press, 1991), esp. ch. 6.

7   Keith Ward, *Religion and Revelation* (Oxford: Clarendon Press, 1994), 265–70.

8   Ibid., 269.

9   Ibid., 278–9.

10 Keith Ward, *Religion and Human Nature* (Oxford: Clarendon Press, 1998), 191; see also, for example, *God, Faith and the New Millennium* (Oxford: Oneworld Publications, 1998), 134–6.

11 See, for example, Ward, *Religion and Human Nature*, 193–4.

12 Keith Ward, 'Cosmos and Kenosis', in John Polkinghorne (ed.), *The Work of Love: Creation as Kenosis* (Grand Rapids/London: Eerdmans/SPCK, 2001), 152–66.

13 Keith Ward, *Religion and Creation* (Oxford: Clarendon Press, 1996); see esp. 311–15 ('The Idea of Creative Emergence').

14 Henri Simoni, 'Divine Passibility and the Problem of Radical Particularity: Does God Feel Your Pain?', *Religious Studies*, 33 (1997), 333.

15 Ibid., emphasis mine.

15

The Moral Status of the Early Embryo

RICHARD HARRIES

Keith Ward was F. D. Maurice Professor of Moral and Social Theology at King's College London from 1982 to 1985. During his time at King's he was closely connected with the Centre for Law, Medicine and Ethics (later the Centre of Medical Law and Ethics), which Ian Kennedy directed from 1978 to 1993. During the early period of his academic life his published work was primarily in ethics, for example *Ethics and Christianity*.[1] But when in 1985 he moved from the F. D. Maurice chair to become Professor of the History and Philosophy of Religion at King's and I asked him why he had made the switch, he replied that 'All the main philosophical moves have been made.' That may or may not be true but the issues remain as controversial as ever, notably the moral status of the early embryo, the subject of this chapter.

A committee chaired by Dame Mary Warnock reported to the Government on this issue at the end of 1984.[2] After extensive discussion the main recommendations of the Warnock Committee passed into legislation as The Human Fertilisation and Embryology Act 1990. This legislation was enacted primarily to regulate the practice of in vitro fertilisation and the creation, handling and destruction of embryos formed by this means. The Human Fertilisation and Embryology Authority (HFEA) was set up to issue licences, under strict conditions, for research on human embryos. Under the Act research on embryos older than fourteen days (or when the primitive streak has appeared, if earlier) is prohibited. For a licence to be issued the Authority has to be satisfied that the proposed use of embryos is necessary for the research, and the research has to be for one of five purposes, all connected with reproduction.

In January 2001, after the report of an expert group under the chairmanship of the Chief Medical Officer, Parliament drafted regulations adding three new purposes to the five in the original Act:

- increasing knowledge about the development of embryos;
- increasing knowledge about serious disease;
- enabling any such knowledge to be applied in developing treatments for serious disease.

Although these regulations were passed the House of Lords set up a Select Committee to look at the whole issue again.

The Committee had a range of questions to consider, legal and commercial as well as ethical and scientific. The key scientific question was whether research on stem cells derived from embryos was really necessary or whether all research, and subsequent treatment based on it, could be done on adult stem cells. Stem cells are present in a number of parts of the body, as well as in the umbilical cord and foetus, and recent research has shown that treatment based on the use of adult stem cells is increasingly promising. The question remained as to whether it was still necessary to do fundamental research on stem cells derived from embryos if subsequent benefits from work on adult stem cells were to be fully realised. The Committee concluded that such research was still necessary.[3] That issue is beyond the scope of this chapter but it is clearly related to two issues which will be considered: the moral status of the early embryo, and how the Christian tradition has understood that moral status.

The position of the Roman Catholic Church as stated in the Catholic Catechism is that 'Human life must be respected and protected absolutely from the moment of conception.'[4] The basis of this view is that either the early embryo is a person or it might be, and that even in the latter case it must be given the benefit of the doubt. In practical terms, even if it is not certain that the early embryo is a person, it must be treated as though it is. This view is not confined to Roman Catholics but is shared by a significant number of other Christians; I shall call it, for short, the conservative position.

Before considering some of the arguments that question this position, it is important to put out a health warning about language. Language can be used in this debate in such a way as to bludgeon people's emotions, as when some people refer to the developing foetus as 'a blob of jelly' and others draw attention to its baby-like features. More significantly from our point of view is the way language can be used in a stipulative manner to rule out certain possibilities. For example, all might agree that persons should be accorded absolute respect and never used merely as a means to an end. Persons are then defined in terms of certain mental capacities and characteristics: the ability to think, choose, react and so on. It is then just a short step to deny that the foetus, for example, is a person, because it lacks those capacities. The House of Lords Select Committee on Stem Cell Research used the term 'early embryo' to refer to the entity developing from fertilisation to the formation of the primitive streak after fourteen days or so. Others have preferred the terms 'pre-embryo' or 'proembryo'.

The arguments against the conservative position are as follows. First, there is no clear continuity of individual identity from fertilisation to the foetus in the womb. This is in contrast to the position later for although the mental capacity of a foetus or baby is undeveloped, there is a continuity between what they are then and the adult they will become. So we say, looking at a photograph, 'That was me as a baby' or, looking at the picture of a baby in the womb, 'That will be my child.' When it comes to the undifferentiated cells of the fertilised egg in its first fourteen days or so, before the formation of the primitive streak, which is the basis of the nervous system, such continuity of identity with the adult cannot be posited. For those cells also form the placenta and umbilical cord. Furthermore, and crucially, they can divide to form identical twins. Because there is no continuity of identity it would be more natural to refer to those undifferentiated cells as human life with the potential to become a person rather than a person.[5]

This argument has been criticised by Professor Michael Banner, who writes:

> The uncertainty about whether an early embryo will go on to become an individual human being or will become two or none is just that: an uncertainty. In the present state of scientific knowledge we do not know what the outcome of the development of a particular embryo will be. It is, however, odd to argue from our uncertainty about whether something is true (i.e., whether the early embryo will finally become an individual human being) to its being false (i.e., that the early embryo is not an individual human being) or to its being permissible for us to act as if it were false.[6]

It might be replied that this objection fails because when questions of identity are at stake certainty is required. In a police line-up of suspects the witness to a crime must be certain that the person they pick out really was the one they saw committing it. Any uncertainty at this point means that there is no case.

Some would argue that this ontological point about identity is in fact undergirded by scientific knowledge. Although the fertilised egg contains the same genetic make-up as the adult it will eventually develop into, that genetic make-up by itself is not enough to bring about such developments. No less essential are biochemical signals from the womb of the mother. This observation could perhaps be enlarged to make a further point: it is the relationship of the mother to the developing foetus in the womb that is also a crucial factor in the development of personhood. For mind is a social reality. We become persons in relation to other persons and even at that early stage of development the mother becomes conscious of what is in her womb and begins to develop a relationship towards what is there.

This reply, however, is not as strong as might appear. When questions of identity are unclear, as in the example of the police line-up, we act on the assumption that runs the least risk of injustice. Here as elsewhere in the criminal justice system there is a presumption of innocence. If this principle is applied to the early embryo, then even if we are uncertain that the fertilised egg is an actual individual, we should act on the presumption that it is, for the greatest injustice would be to destroy an actual individual. This is why someone like Norman Ford, although he regards the possibility of twinning before fourteen days as very significant, nevertheless supports the conservative position against embryo research.[7]

Secondly, the fact that a person has the potential to qualify as a member of some class in the future, if certain conditions are met, does not by itself confer the rights that belong to members of that class. For example, a medical student is a potential physician and if he or she qualifies may practise as such; but that potentiality alone does not confer a right to practise. We even recognise such a distinction in nature. We trample hundreds of acorns underfoot but put a preservation order on a grown oak. From this point of view it might be right to accord a great deal of respect to life with the potential to become a person, that is the human embryo less than fourteen days old. But it does not follow that because it has this potential it is to be accorded the absolute respect associated with personhood.

Thirdly, there is the extent of early embryo loss. The exact figure is much disputed but some have suggested that as many as two-thirds of fertilised eggs do not in fact implant, with many of these suffering from chromosomal abnormalities. From a theological point of view, if each of these fertilised eggs is a person, we have the strange picture of the human population of heaven consisting mainly of those who had never been born. But even leaving the theological dimension out of the picture, the prodigality of nature undermines the concept of absolute respect for every fertilised egg. If so many fertilised eggs are lost anyway it is difficult to prize each one as being absolutely precious. This argument has been much criticised by use of an analogy with the developing world. In some developing countries infant mortality is still very high and more than 50 per cent of children die before their first birthday. But the high level of infant mortality does not mean that we should treat those infants as less than human persons.

This point, however, suggests another argument against the conservative view, for when an infant dies, the parents grieve over the loss of the child and that child will be buried with public rites that mark the loss of a human person. So, fourthly, neither personally nor socially do we mark the loss of an early embryo as though this were the loss of a human person. Human parents grieve deeply over a stillborn child and can feel a very painful sense of loss over an aborted foetus. Sometimes they may indeed feel a sense of sadness at the loss of a newly implanted early embryo, particularly if they are striving desperately to have a child. But the loss is not marked by any ritual or public acknowledgement that this is the loss of a person.

Against this it might be argued that our moral judgements should not be based either on our human intuitions or on cultural practice. However, human intuition, over so many centuries and across so many cultures, is something that at least should be taken into account. Long-established moral intuitions and distinctions can be a helpful guide even before they are refined by philosophical analysis.

In recent decades the importance of the principle of embodiment, the fact that we are physical beings, psychosomatic unities, has emerged at various points in theological and philosophical discourse. Its relevance to the debate on the embryo is that it is the actual physical entity which we see, hear, touch, smell and even taste. It is the physical shape of what is before us which makes us reflect on whether it is or is not a person. The theme of embodiment has sometimes been coupled with criticism of stipulative definitions of what it is to be a person. As argued earlier we do indeed need to be aware of stipulative definitions that define a person in terms of their mental capacities and thereby rule out the possibility of regarding the early embryo as a person. In contrast to that approach the importance of taking seriously the actual physical entity, from fertilisation onwards, can be affirmed. But this can work two ways. The early embryo is not in any recognisable sense, i.e. to the eye or ear, a person. To the eye it is indeed a blob of jelly less than the size of a pinhead. Later, with the use of X-rays, we can see the actual shape of a baby, with limbs, beginning to form in the mother's womb. What is actually there in physical form can and does affect our understanding of the moral status of that entity. So we can and should take a principle of embodiment seriously, respecting the actual physical entity of the fertilised egg: but that same principle would suggest that the stage of development of that physical entity also needs to be taken into account.

None of these arguments are conclusive and they do not finally settle the question as to whether early embryos can legitimately be used for research purposes. The Warnock Committee urged that the early embryo, though not to be accorded absolute protection, 'ought to have a special status', one which 'should be afforded some protection in law'.[8] This is reflected in both the existence and the legislation of the Human Fertilisation and Embryology Authority. For the HFEA is only allowed to issue licences for research if the research cannot be done by any other means and it can be shown to be both necessary and desirable.

The report of the Select Committee, after considering some of these arguments, said:

> Burden of proof arguments are notoriously hard to resolve. If there were no morally serious reasons for undertaking research on human embryos, then the mere possibility that the early embryo is a person would be sufficient reason not to do such research. However, if there are morally weighty reasons for doing such research a decision must be reached on the basis of arguments that fall short of proof.[9]

It went on to argue that 'There are morally weighty reasons for doing research that may lead to therapies for many serious and common diseases [. . .]. Unless early embryos have an unconditional claim to protection, therefore, it would be wrong to rule out research involving them for such a purpose.'[10]

In addition to the arguments deployed above, the question arises as to what light the Christian tradition sheds on the problem of the moral status of the early embryo. For this tradition the Aristotelian concept of delayed ensoulment is of prime relevance. Aristotle taught that before developing a rational soul a human embryo first developed a vegetative soul and then an animal soul. The rational soul only came into being at forty days in the case of a man and ninety days in the case of a woman. This concept of delayed ensoulment is clearly closely related to the distinction between an unformed and a formed foetus. This distinction became very important in Christian ethics because of the translation of Exodus 21.22 in the Septuagint, which was the version most commonly used by the early Christian Fathers, as well as by the New Testament writers, and which was followed in the old Latin version, which became the language of the moral tradition of the West. According to the Septuagint, if anyone strikes a pregnant woman and she miscarries, then if the foetus is formed the penalty is death; if on the other hand the foetus is *me exeikonismenon*, not yet so formed as to be a copy of or portrayal of the human form, then the penalty is a fine. The questions at issue are how far such distinctions shaped the Christian tradition and if they did, how far they are relevant to the moral status of the early embryo. In an important essay, 'The Human Embryo in the Western Moral Tradition', Gordon Dunstan, Keith Ward's predecessor as F. D. Maurice Professor at King's, argues that these distinctions were fundamental to most of the western tradition and that it was only with the papal bull 'Apostolicae sedis' of Pius IX in 1869 that they were rejected. Pope Pius

> declared excommunicate all who procured abortion, without distinction either as to the method, direct or indirect, intentional or involuntary, or as to the gestational age of the fetus, whether it were formed or unformed, animate or inanimate.[11]

The Revd Fr Dr David Jones, until recently Director of the Linacre Centre for Healthcare Ethics, disputes Dunstan's reading of the tradition.[12] What follows is my own attempt to assess these respective readings in as fair and balanced a way as possible.

It is crucial when studying the Christian tradition on the moral status of the pre-implantation embryo to interpret the relevant texts in their context. We need to ask what readership the author has in mind and what he is trying to achieve by his argument. Simply plucking passages out of context to construct a catena of sayings can be very misleading. This point is particularly pertinent to the interpretation of the Apostolic Fathers. For although they condemn abortion per se and make no distinction between formed and unformed, animate and inanimate, an analysis of the context in which they made this condemnation reveals that such distinctions would have been totally beside the point. For example the *Epistle of Barnabas* (14.11 and 19.5) and the *Didache* (2.2) were criticising the sins of their society. Their condemnation of abortion occupies one line in a list of wrongs that they wish to condemn, such as adultery and infanticide. In this context, with such a purpose in mind, people simply do not make fine moral distinctions, even if they are moral theologians (which these two writers were not). Today we might condemn the lies, greed, violence and virtual abortion on demand in our society without getting into discussion about when, if ever, it might be right to tell a lie, steal, defend oneself or have an abortion. The purpose of such statements would be prophetic criticism of widespread wrongs. In pastoral discussion someone properly qualified might very well make distinctions which it would be inappropriate or misleading to make in a public condemnation. The fact that the Apostolic Fathers do not make distinctions which later moral theologians made sheds no light on whether they did or did not accept such distinctions.

The same point can be made in the immediate post-Apostolic writings. To take just one example, Hippolytus in *Refutation of All Heresies* fiercely criticises Callistus and his followers. He argues that Callistus allows people to have sex without getting married, to resort to drugs to produce sterility, and to have abortions 'on account of their not wishing to have a child either by a slave or by any paltry fellow, for the sake of their family and excessive wealth' (IX, 7).[13] This is not a context in which fine distinctions would have served the argument.

Gordon Dunstan suggests that Tertullian rejects the idea of a moral distinction between the animate and inanimate foetus and thereby regards him as a dissentient from the tradition. But Tertullian is difficult to interpret and his phrase 'we may not destroy even the foetus in the womb, while as yet the human being derives blood from other parts of the body for its sustenance [*dum adhuc sanguis in hominem delibatur*]' (*Apology*, 9)[14] applies to the foetus in all stages of the pregnancy, not just the early stage.

Gregory of Nyssa has two relevant passages which are difficult to reconcile with one another. In his letter against Macedonius, who denied the full divinity of the Holy Spirit, Gregory argues that such people cannot be called Christians. It is in this context that he says an unformed embryo cannot be called a person, only a potential one (*On the Holy Spirit against Macedonius*). It is quite true, as David Jones argues, that Gregory is not dealing directly here with the moral status of the foetus. He is using the unformed embryo as an analogy in relation to an argument on another subject altogether. We have therefore to be careful. However, sometimes it is in people's asides, the analogies they use, that they are most revealing about what they really believe. In this passage Gregory seems to take it for granted that not just he himself but everyone capable of reading his letter would agree that the unformed embryo is not a human being, only a potential one. On the other hand, in *On the Making of Man* (28–9) he clearly rejects the idea of delayed ensoulment. He argues against the notion of pre-existent souls and reincarnation. He also denies that the body comes first, followed by the soul, and that therefore the soul exists to serve the body. They are to be seen as a unity from the first. The soul is invisible but gradually manifests itself as the foetus develops, just as a grain of wheat gradually unfolds into the full-grown stalk of corn. This development does not depend upon any external cause but is inherent in the unfolding entity, whether seed or embryo, from the first. The same view is to be found in *On the Soul and the Resurrection*. In this work he is not discussing the relative gravity of early or late abortions. Nevertheless, an implication of what he is saying is that if the soul is present from the first then an abortion at an early stage would be as grave as one later. This is the obvious implication of what he is saying but it is not inescapable. If for example we take the analogy of heating a pot of water, heat is there from the moment a pot goes on the stove and molecules start to agitate. There is a gradual process of heating until a critical threshold is passed when the water begins to boil. So although the soul can be there from the first, gradually becoming more manifest as an entity develops physically, this does not rule out the possibility of critical thresholds which could be morally significant. In the case of abortion, quickening has always been considered a natural one. After quickening it is obvious to the mother that there is a living entity in her womb. But even if it is regarded as more likely on the basis of *On the Making of Man* that Gregory ruled out any distinction between a formed and an unformed foetus, there is still the question as to how this is to be reconciled with what clearly seems to be his position in his letter against Macedonius. Gregory of Nyssa is not a clear witness for either side of the debate.

In the light of this discussion it would seem that both Gordon Dunstan and David Jones claim too much in relation to the earliest period of Christian thinking on this subject. Dunstan argues that Basil of Caesarea, whose views are discussed below, and Tertullian are dissentients from a tradition that makes a distinction between the formed and the unformed foetus. Jones suggests that the early tradition did not acknowledge such a distinction. Analysing the texts in their contexts, as above, shows that whether or not such a distinction was acknowledged by these writers it would have been totally inappropriate and counterproductive for them to discuss it given the purpose of their writings. This means that the earliest writing on this subject has to be seen in the light of the fourth and fifth centuries. On the side of Dunstan, that there is a strong early tradition of making a distinction, we can point to the Septuagint translation of Exodus 21.22, whose importance to the early Church has already been noted. Then there is the view of Augustine:

> Therefore, if what is brought forth is unformed [*informe*] but at this stage some sort of living, shapeless thing [*informiter animatum*], [. . .] then the law of homicide would not apply, for it could not be said that there was a living soul in that body, for it lacks all sense, if it be such as is not yet formed [*nondum formata*] and therefore not yet endowed with its senses. (*Questions on the Heptateuch*, II, 80: PL 34, 626)[15]

On the other side of the argument is Basil's first letter to Bishop Amphilochius:

> The woman who purposely destroys her unborn child is guilty of murder. With us there is no nice enquiry as to its being formed or unformed [*ekmemorphomenou kai anexeikonistou*]. (Epistle 188, §II)[16]

Then there is the fact that Basil's letter, which itself was a commentary on the canons of the Church, was later included in those canons. It is true that the earliest Church legislation simply condemns abortion as such, although Canon 21 of the Council of Ancyra in 314, 'Concerning women who commit fornication, who destroy that which they have conceived', closely links abortion with the sin of fornication. The canon reduces the penalty from lifetime excommunication to ten years' penance. However, Basil's letter, which specifically mentions the distinction between the formed and unformed foetus, and condemns the abortion of both equally, was incorporated into the legislation of the Council of Trullo (692), the canons of which were formally confirmed at the seventh and last ecumenical council, at Nicaea in 787.

On the subsequent history of Christian attitudes to the embryo there is, I believe, more agreement. The Anglo-Saxon and Celtic Penitentials (from the seventh century) and the canon law of the Latin Church (from the eleventh century) made a distinction between the formed and the unformed foetus, with abortion of the former carrying more severe penalties than abortion of the latter. This was mirrored in the teaching of the Church, with the exception of Pope Sixtus V in 1588, and was, for example, reflected in English law. Again, although the point at which soul and body were joined was not agreed in the fourth and fifth century the dominant view in subsequent western tradition was for a later ensoulment. This for example is the teaching of St Thomas Aquinas.[17] This philosophical view ran in parallel with the dominant medical understanding of conception and quickening. All this said, the abortion of an unformed or inanimate foetus was never regarded as less than a very grave sin closely akin to homicide.

The situation changed in 1869 when Pius IX abolished the distinction in legal penalties between early and late abortions. A greater understanding of embryogenesis linked to changes in philosophical understanding led to a belief in conception as the point at which body was joined to soul, though it has been suggested that conception at that time meant not so much the moment of fertilisation as the implantation of the fertilised egg in the womb.

What are the implications of this tradition for Christian thinking today? Although, as stated above, abortion of the unformed foetus was always regarded as a very grave sin, nevertheless, for nearly 1,500 years, until 1869, the western tradition drew a distinction in the seriousness of the wrong depending upon whether the foetus was formed or unformed. It remains an open question, not susceptible to definitive resolution at the moment, whether that tradition goes back to the early centuries. It should be noted that the distinction is in the status of the foetus. In English law, as in the laws of other countries, there are greater and lesser penalties for an offence depending upon the culpability of the guilty person and the guilt is related to such matters as their motivation and their responsibility. However, the distinction in penalties and culpability for abortion in the Christian tradition has nothing to do with the degree of responsibility of the person who carries out the abortion or procures it for someone else. It has to do with whether the embryo is formed or unformed.

It is also to be noted that the concern of moralists was with something that everyone regarded as wrong, namely killing, and that this wrong, in the case of abortion, was always closely associated in people's minds with other wrongs such as fornication. There was no question of relating what in most circumstances would be regarded as wrong with a good. In the modern debate about the permissibility of research on embryos, the equation includes the enormous potential good that this research could lead to. Obviously, from the standpoint of the Christian tradition, if the pre-implantation embryo is a person with full rights then no prospective good from research could override the protection due to that person. However, until 1869 the dominant western view made a distinction between an embryo which was to be accorded the rights of a person and one whose rights were less than that. David Jones, in his evidence to the Select Committee, maintains that the first theologian to suggest explicitly that the embryo had a graded moral status, that is, a relative value which could be outweighed by other values, was Thomas Sanchez in the late sixteenth century, and that his view was rapidly condemned by others.[18] But implicit in the whole western tradition is the idea of a graded moral status. Furthermore the case that Thomas Sanchez had in mind was that a woman could legitimately abort an unformed foetus to avoid public shame of a kind which might endanger her life. The great benefit that could come from research on embryos would seem to be a more weighty consideration than that discussed by Sanchez. The whole concept of delayed ensoulment implies that what we have before forty days or so is not a rational soul. On the Aristotelian view of the matter we have first a vegetable soul and then an animal soul. It is only after that stage that the evolving entity develops a rational soul. The destruction of a vegetable or animal soul is obviously of less moral consequence than the destruction of a rational soul. That, surely, is why the penalties were less. Although the philosophy and science that lay behind the western moral tradition are different from our own they were, as Gordon Dunstan puts it, 'important to us as carriers of a moral tradition; they provided the forms in which moral judgments were expressed and degrees of culpability were decided'.[19]

Summing up the evidence we can conclude that:

- For the first three centuries of the Church's existence we cannot draw any conclusions about whether theologians recognised a distinction between the animate and inanimate, the formed and unformed, foetus.
- From the fourth century in the West, as reflected especially in the Anglo-Saxon and Celtic Penitentials from the seventh century and the canon law of the Latin Church from the eleventh century, such distinctions were both recognised and authorised. They were all rejected by Pope Pius IX in 1869.[20]
- From the fourth century in the East and subsequently in the eastern Church, such distinctions have not been recognised.

There remains the crucial question as to how this tradition is to be applied today. For many Christians, not just Roman Catholics, the papal position of 1869 is definitive because with the obsolescence of the Aristotelian concept of delayed ensoulment, fertilisation is the point at which human life emerges and, as vulnerable human life, it is particularly worthy of protection. As noted earlier, many Roman Catholic theologians take the view that because the early embryo may be a person, and because this is such a crucial matter, the embryo must be given the benefit of any doubt.

For other Christians, however, the fact that the Christian tradition, for so much of its history, made a distinction between the moral status of the unformed and formed embryo, and thought of the human person in the full sense only arriving with the rational soul, remains significant. The tradition carried a moral distinction which remains valid even though the Aristotelian philosophy on which it was once based is no longer defensible.

NOTES

1   Keith Ward, *Ethics and Christianity* (London: Allen and Unwin, 1970).
2   Mary Warnock, *A Question of Life: The Warnock Report on Human Fertilisation and Embryology* (Oxford: Blackwell, 1985, repr. 1993).
3   The Committee, which I chaired, reported on 13 Feb. 2002: *Stem Cell Research: Report from the Select Committee*, HL Paper 83 (i) (London: Stationery Office, 2002).

4   *Catechism of the Catholic Church* (London: Geoffrey Chapman, 1994), ¶2270.

5   The most sustained version of this argument is by Norman Ford, *When Did I Begin?* (Cambridge: Cambridge University Press, 1984), though he does not endorse its conclusion – see the article cited in n. 7 below.

6   Michael Banner, 'The Practice of Abortion: A Critique', in Michael Banner, *Christian Ethics and Contemporary Moral Problems* (Cambridge: Cambridge University Press, 1999), 112.

7   Norman Ford, 'We Don't Have to Clone', *The Tablet*, vol. ccliv, no. 8362 (9 Dec. 2000), 1672.

8   Warnock, *A Question of Life*, ¶11.17.

9   *Stem Cell Research: Report from the Select Committee*, ¶4.16.

10 Ibid., ¶4.17.

11 G. R. Dunstan, 'The Human Embryo in the Western Moral Tradition', in G. R. Dunstan and Mary J. Seller (eds), *The Status of the Human Embryo: Perspectives from Moral Tradition* (London: King Edward's Hospital Fund for London, 1988), 52.

12 His argument is set out in the evidence supplied to the Select Committee and reprinted in *Stem Cell Research: Report from the Select Committee. Evidence*, HL Paper 83 (ii) (London: Stationery Office, 2002), 78–80.

13 Translation from *Ante-Nicene Christian Library* (hereafter ANCL), ed. Alexander Roberts and James Donaldson (24 vols; Edinburgh: T. & T. Clark, 1867–72), vol. vi, p. 345.

14 Translation from ANCL, vol. xi, p. 71.

15 Translation based on Dunstan, 'The Human Embryo in the Western Moral Tradition', 45.

16 Translation from *A Select Library of Nicene and Post-Nicene Fathers of the Christian Church*, 2nd ser., ed. Henry Wace and Philip Schaff, vol. viii (Oxford/New York: James Parker and Co./The Christian Literature Co., 1895), 225.

17 See the passages cited in Dunstan, 'The Human Embryo in the Western Moral Tradition', 47–8.

18 *Stem Cell Research: Report from the Select Committee. Evidence*, 79–80.

19 Dunstan, 'The Human Embryo in the Western Moral Tradition', 50.

20 For one reading of the tradition see Germain Grisez, *Abortion: The Myths, the Realities, and the Arguments* (New York: Corpus Books, 1972), ch. 4. About the act of Pius IX of 1869 he writes: 'In effect his act endorsed the growing awareness that the old distinction between animated and non-animated foetuses was grounded in neither experimental evidence nor necessary reasons. While the distinction might still be maintained theoretically, the arguments of Fienus, Zacchaia, and others finally had their practical effect' (177).

Part IV
COMMUNITY

16

The Bishop as Theologian

PAUL AVIS

If theology is 'speaking of the things of God', the *logos* of *theos*, then every thoughtful Christian is a theologian. Baptism, with its confession of the Trinitarian faith, mandates us to know and to bear witness to the truth of God revealed in Jesus Christ. The *sensus fidei* is the Christian's homing instinct for 'the truth as it is in Jesus'. However, to engage actively in theology as a calling goes well beyond the intuitive reflection of the believer. To theologise is to reflect in a disciplined, informed and critical way on the knowledge of God.[1]

In his discussion of theological method in *Religion and Revelation*, the first volume of his *magnum opus*, Keith Ward endorses Aquinas's view of theology as 'a body of disciplined reasoning about Divine things based on revealed truths'. Ward goes on to gloss this definition to take account of the plurality of religions, the differentiated nature of revelation and the contributions of the sciences. This leads him to propose that theology is 'the discipline of reflection upon ideas of the ultimate reality and goal of human life, of God, and of revelation'. However, this view does not tip him into the non-realist abyss where the ultimate object of theology becomes merely human insights and experiences. Fundamentally, for Ward, theology remains 'disciplined enquiry into God'.[2] His definition supports the concept of theology deployed in this chapter.

Many lay Christians, without an academic training, aspire to do this and some distinguished theologians have been or are laypeople. However, all the Church's recognised ministers – not least the ordained – undergo a training that is intended to equip them for disciplined, informed and critical reflection on the faith of the Church. The calling to engage in theological reflection applies pre-eminently to those called to the episcopate. The Ordinal attached to the 1662 Book of Common Prayer urges the candidate: 'Give heed unto reading, exhortation, and doctrine. Think upon the things contained in this Book [the Bible]. Be diligent in them'. The Ordinal of The Alternative Service Book 1980 asks: 'Will you be diligent in prayer, in reading holy Scripture, and in all studies that will deepen your faith and fit you to uphold the truth of the Gospel against error?' Thus a bishop is charged, at his consecration, to study the Scriptures assiduously – to study them in the light of relevant learning and to interpret them in such a way as to refute error and to enlighten the faithful with the truth of God. The bishop is mandated not simply to proclaim, but also to interpret, the Gospel. A bishop is required to be a theological interpreter, and to be a theological interpreter is to be a maker of theology, not simply a defender of tradition.

I. IN SEARCH OF THE BISHOP AS THEOLOGIAN

The lines of theologian and bishop[3] – distinct in the early Church – converged by the fourth century into the figure of the scholar-bishop, whose supreme exemplar is St Augustine of Hippo. A millennium later, the problems of the late medieval western Church (the fragmentation of the papacy, the demand for the reform of abuses, and the need to deal with 'heresies') required the contribution of conciliar thinkers; three hundred scholars were present and voted at the Council of Constance in 1414. The Reformers were almost all pastor-theologians. Luther, Calvin, Cranmer and Bucer united the calling to govern the Church and the calling to be creative theologians. The Protestant tradition of scholarly leadership fed, three centuries later, into the early ecumenical movement. At the first assembly of the World Council of Churches in 1948 one delegate commented that he saw before him practically all the authors of the books in his library.

While some Protestant churches have ceded control over doctrine to the theologians (in the Evangelische Kirche in Deutschland (EKD) it seems to be the professors, not the bishops, who effectively have oversight of doctrine), the modern Roman Catholic Church has absorbed theological authority into the papacy, which has consistently ridden roughshod over theological advisers and conferences of bishops alike. The theological renaissance that both heralded and flowed from the Second Vatican Council was stifled. In 1969 a theological declaration signed by 1,360 Roman Catholic scholars in 53 countries rejoiced in the restoration of theological liberty by Vatican II. They were soon to be disillusioned. Over the past thirty years, virtually all of the most creative Roman Catholic theologians have come into conflict with the authorities and many have been formally disciplined.

Where is Anglicanism in this debate? The most seminal of all Anglican theologians, Richard Hooker, was not a bishop, though both his patrons, John Jewel and John Whitgift, were outstanding scholar-bishops. The Church of England can celebrate a line of episcopal divines that, if not yet quite extinct, is now rather precarious.[4] In this respect, Anglicanism stands between Protestantism and Roman Catholicism. Unlike most Protestant churches, Anglicanism is episcopal in its ecclesial constitution. But unlike the Roman Catholic Church, Anglicanism is not hierarchical. There is a striking difference between the Roman Catholic notion of the 'hierarchical communion' of bishops with each other and with the Pope, who is the head of the episcopal college and without whom it cannot act and in fact has a rather shadowy existence, and the Anglican understanding of episcopal collegiality, even granted the modest, though real, place given to primacy in Anglican polity.[5]

Every bishop is called to be a guardian and teacher of the faith by virtue of office. But in some cases deep theological exploring may require greater freedom than the office can sustain. In the 1980s the Church of England was shaken by 'the Durham affair'. David Jenkins, formerly a teacher of theology in the University of Oxford and a professor of theology at the University of Leeds, but by then the Bishop of Durham, the fourth most senior bishopric in the Church of England, publicly questioned the literal interpretation of two credal tenets: the virginal conception and the physical resurrection of Jesus. Half the nation became intensely agitated by the spectacle of a senior bishop seeming to undermine the faith. The finer points of theology were discussed wherever two or three were gathered together in local watering holes throughout the land. Jenkins had touched a nerve in the half-Christian psyche of the nation. On the one hand, he seemed to articulate the questions of many honest doubters. On the other, he seemed to be betraying his calling as a guardian of the faith. The ambivalence of his position was perfectly apparent to millions who were not regular churchgoers. Attention was focused on the role of a bishop. Is it compatible with being an academic? Is it right for a bishop to question traditional beliefs? Is theological exploration a form of unbelief? The affair led directly to the report of the House of Bishops on *The Nature of Christian Belief* in 1986 and indirectly to the report of a group set up by the two archbishops on *Episcopal Ministry* (1990).

Episcopal Ministry[6] gave due weight to the bishop's role as teacher and guardian of the faith but said little about the bishop as theologian. (A good many readers, I suspect, turned straight to Appendix III (a) on 'Women in the Episcopate', a personal contribution by the then little-known Bishop of Bath and Wells, George Carey.) The report set out a rather daunting ideal of a bishop:

> our bishops should be strong teachers of the faith who are both deeply engaged in the continuing education of the people of God [. . .] and powerful defenders of the faith and winners of souls in the world [. . .]. There must be well-balanced expository preaching of the Scriptures; [. . .] sensitive and hopeful response to the challenge of our society, and to human need in our time [. . .]; a steady endeavour to fill minds and souls with the greatness of a vision that looks to an eternal future. The diocesan bishop has rich opportunities of speaking and writing, in the media as well as directly to his people, on matters of both faith and morals[.] (288)

Teacher, preacher, apologist, defender of the faith, evangelist, inspirer, visionary, prophet – a catalogue of qualities that would make the most gifted candidate for the episcopate quail. Mercifully, the report noted that this picture 'involves a diversity of gifts, not all of which can be looked for in a bishop, but which we must seek to ensure are present in their fulness in the episcopate as a body' (ibid.). However, the report does not say that a bishop should be a theologian.

Disappointed by the neglect of the bishop as theologian in this Church of England report, I turned expectantly to the documents of the Second Vatican Council. Here I expected to find rich treasures on the theological vocation of a bishop. There are 119 entries in the index of the Abbott edition of the documents of Vatican II under 'Bishops', but no mention of theology in any of them. There is, however, a good deal on the preaching and teaching ministry of bishops. They have

Christ's authority to teach the faith and to ward off errors.[7] This preaching and teaching ministry should have an apologetic slant; it should commend the faith in the light of modern circumstances and problems.[8] Furthermore, it is the bishops' responsibility to ensure that there are theologians equipped to teach the faith to seminarians, clergy and laity.[9]

The emphasis in Vatican II is on the teaching, sanctifying and governing roles of the bishop – the standard prophetic, priestly and pastoral aspects of episcopal ministry. His responsibility is to see that the authentic, inerrant teaching of the Church is handed on, that error is refuted, and that the Church is preserved in purity and truth. But there is no explicit recognition that to theologise is part of the calling of every bishop. There is no sense that the bishop is bound to wrestle with truth, to explore mysteries, to launch out into the deeps of faith.

J. M. R. Tillard goes beyond the institutionalised role that Vatican II sees for the bishop's teaching ministry.[10] Tillard is clear that the bishop's task is not that of mere 'faithful repetition'. It involves 'a constant re-reading' of the content of the Church's memory (living tradition) in order to facilitate its reception in the constantly evolving context of local churches (dioceses) and its transmission to the next generation, which needs to hear it in its own way, 'For, the Word of God being offered to the whole of humanity, it has to be heard and understood by all people of all time and cultures'.[11] Tillard thus emphasises the place of theological interpretation in teaching.

When, however, Tillard comes to consider the role of theology more particularly, it is a tamed, controlled, somewhat instrumental understanding of theology that he proposes. Theology helps the Church to discover, to confront and to refute dangerous errors. It helps the Church to mediate the faith to diverse cultures. It serves spiritual contemplation of the truth of God. It enables discernment of new ideas to take place. And finally 'it guides it in the elaboration of its legislation by which rights are guarded and duties described with precision'.[12]

William Telfer's study *The Office of a Bishop* has a chapter on 'Bishops and Theologians'.[13] Telfer argues that 'being a theologian is not among the necessary qualifications' of a person chosen to be a bishop (156). There is even, he suggests, some reason for thinking that theological gifts may not always be an asset. Though a bishop is called to form a judgement on theological issues and will need to provide himself with expert advisers, 'The task of theologians is different from that of the hierarchy. Theological thinking is exploratory thinking' (157). That nicely sharpens the issue that we are considering: can a bishop be also a theological explorer, or must a bishop be simply an exponent and defender of received tradition?

II. THE THEOLOGIAN AS BISHOP: DAVID JENKINS

We return to David Jenkins, Bishop of Durham until 1994. Voluble and somewhat naïve, Jenkins was not gifted with tact and discretion. An academic, he was pitched unprepared into the bishop's role. He evidently assumed that he could continue the seminar approach to matters of Christian belief. Jenkins was not a theologian steeped in tradition. The worst insult that he could hurl at one of his lay critics who accused him of heresy in a radio phone-in programme – as I heard for myself at the time – was, 'You are medieval, madam.' He operated in a fairly shallow layer of modern theology. Nevertheless, some of his earlier work, especially *The Contradiction of Christianity*,[14] is on the whole cogent and incisive.

A man of staunch faith and strong courage, Jenkins was dismayed and distressed when his questioning of the virginal conception and the bodily resurrection of Jesus caused uproar, orchestrated by the tabloid press. Bloodied but unbowed by the experience, he remained adamant that he must speak the truth as he saw it. He refused to accept that he could speak only as a representative of the Church's tradition and not in a personal capacity. That view he dubbed 'plainly unreasonable, plainly faithless and plainly impracticable':

> It is plainly unreasonable because if a question is there it must be faced. 'The Tradition' cannot decide what are real questions [. . .]. But in any case the attitude is faithless because if we really believe in God then we can face any real challenge. It is also impracticable because the faithful cannot hide from real questions forever.[15]

Jenkins attracted a huge postbag. Some 4,000 of the letters he received between 1984 and 1986 have been analysed. Four broad perceptions on the part of his public emerge. First, a bishop is expected to be a guardian of the faith, an upholder of tradition. This gives him his authority as the representative of a Church that is defined by its loyalty to a body of received doctrine. Second, a bishop is a shepherd of his flock. His authority derives from the trust that he inspires in those who follow him. His flock expects to be 'gently led in uncontroversial consensus'. Third, a bishop is an ethical prophet and moral judge. His authority depends on his unquestioning loyalty to a narrowly defined morality (mainly personal and individual, rather than social and political). Fourth, a bishop is an explorer, who is engaged in adapting religion to a new age and fresh challenges. He brings out the relevance of the tradition, which is understood as a resource of wisdom.[16]

Clearly, Jenkins's relation to the first three was tenuous. He undoubtedly saw himself as a guardian of the faith, but not in any static sense. He certainly aspired to be a shepherd and wanted the trust of his people: but he wanted them to trust him to lead them further in their faith. And while Jenkins aspired to be something of a moral prophet, who clashed with leaders of industry and with the Thatcher government, he was not an upholder of conventional, middle-class values. He would have been most comfortable, I think, only with the fourth perception of a bishop's role, that of explorer of the faith. The other three, he would have maintained, reveal a disturbing understanding of the nature of authority in the Church as existing to protect the faithful from uncomfortable questions and to reinforce them in their unexamined prejudices.

As Jenkins himself commented, authority here is conceived only as providing assurance and security, and never as providing stimulus or challenge: 'Authority is thus a means to serving personal security in a very individualistic form and goes with a high degree of dependency.' Jenkins bluntly rejected this: 'Unless doctrines engage the responses of heart, soul and mind there is no point in speaking about them, and unless each believer can argue honestly for his or her beliefs in terms of present-day reality our faith is irrelevant.' The public, representative role of bishops places on them a responsibility to come clean, to be honest, to face reality.[17] Jenkins took encouragement from the fact that Jesus' own teaching was often provocative.

The Jenkins episode confirms that the role of the bishop as theologian is deeply ambiguous and paradoxical. It is paradoxical to affirm the Incarnation while at the same time questioning the virginal conception. It is paradoxical to preach the resurrection while in the same breath suggesting that it might not have been a physical event. Reflective Christians understand that the virginal conception was not the essential vehicle of the Incarnation. It is not the case that the only way in which the eternal Word could have been made flesh was through a virginal conception. They also know that it is Christ's victory over sin, suffering and death that constitutes the Easter faith and that the empty tomb is an eloquent and appropriate expression of this fact. But many lay Christians (and some clergy) seem unable to distinguish between the Incarnation and the virginal conception (some even confuse the latter with the immaculate conception of the Blessed Virgin Mary). By the same token, some Christians seem unable to distinguish between the resurrection and the empty tomb. They are not aware of the ambiguity of the biblical material on these two matters.[18]

Ambiguity seems to be inherent in the idea of representing a tradition, which a bishop undoubtedly does, whilst at the same time interpreting it afresh in every generation (as the Preface to the Declaration of Assent, made by clergy and others in the Church of England, puts it). There is ambiguity in offering biblical teaching, which a bishop is bound to do, when one is committed to a scholarly, critical method of interpretation that takes the human and historical element of the Bible seriously. Ambiguity of authority arises from the contingent nature of history (whether anything had to turn out the way it did). The truth of God is mediated to us through created, contingent, unstable forms. We walk by faith, not by sight. We have assurance but not certitude. As an impressive succession of Anglican theologians, from Hooker to Gladstone, taking in Locke, Butler and Keble on the way, has insisted, probability is a sufficient guide for all our purposes.

Ruth Page claims that ambiguity is the salient characteristic of the created order as we have come to know it post-Marx, post-Darwin and post-Freud. The world is marked by change, uncertainty and plurality. The experience of ambiguity is endemic in the modern and post-modern eras. She sees no reason to fear it. Christianity is at home in the tensions of ambiguity. Christians who attempt to set up barriers against it are untrue to the method that God has chosen in creation, revelation and salvation.[19]

III. FROM *ENFANT TERRIBLE* TO ARCHBISHOP OF CANTERBURY: WILLIAM TEMPLE

We have been here before, of course – many times. The Jenkins episode was a mere hiccough compared to the furore caused by the notorious symposium *Essays and Reviews* in 1860.[20] A generation later Charles Gore, the rising hope of the stern, unbending high churchmen of Pusey's school, set alarm bells ringing when he revealed in the symposium *Lux Mundi* (1889) his acceptance of the principles of biblical criticism, the theory of evolution and the synthesis of these in a developmental doctrine of the Incarnation in which the earthly Jesus lacked omniscience and was at the mercy of the knowledge of his time.[21] Gore was the most consistent of men and never changed his views. But as thought moved on, he who had seemed a dangerous radical became the symbol of conservative reaction.

Against this background, I turn now to the instructive episode of the ordination of William Temple a century ago. Temple had always wanted to be ordained. His father, Frederick Temple, had been Archbishop of Canterbury. But nearly thirty years before that, in 1869, there had been an attempt to prevent Frederick Temple becoming consecrated as Bishop of Exeter because he had contributed to *Essays and Reviews*.[22]

In his chapter, 'The Education of the World', published only a year after Darwin's *The Origin of Species*, he assumed the truth of the theory of evolution and advocated a progressive, developmental understanding of salvation history that involved some relativising of the authority of the Bible and dogma. He set the Old Testament revelation alongside the cultural achievements of ancient Greece and Rome and the wisdom of the East: 'Thus the Hebrews may be said to have disciplined the human conscience, Rome the human will, Greece the reason and taste, Asia the spiritual imagination' (19). The normative significance of the New Testament for Christian beliefs was tacitly undermined: 'We read the New Testament, not to find there forms of devotion, for there are few to be found; nor laws of church government, for there are hardly any; nor creeds, for there are none; nor doctrines logically stated, for there is no attempt at logical precision' (28). The theological value of the New Testament is found in what it reveals of the life of Christ and of the corporate life of the early Church. But humanity's theological perception has progressed since the first centuries and the thought forms of those days cannot be 'elevated into immutable statements of truth' (44). The Bible must be interpreted in the context of its time. Conscience must be supreme in interpreting Scripture. The trust deeds of the Christian faith must be subjected to rigorous investigation – philosophical, scientific and historical. Biblical criticism shows that divine inspiration did not protect the sacred narrative from inaccuracy and the biblical literature contains occasional interpolations and forgeries (47). That was going it rather, thirty years before Charles Gore and *Lux Mundi*!

In 1901, while his father was still Archbishop of Canterbury, William Temple, then not yet twenty, looked back on that episode and commented: 'It is time to go further now, and to wound more deeply: for we have to tell people not only that their views on inspiration are absurd, but that their most cherished beliefs and their brightest hopes have no foundation.' 'The Christ men believe in and worship', he continued, 'is to a great extent a myth and an idol – very different from Him who lived and died "to bear witness to the truth", and Whose Spirit lived and spoke in Socrates and Buddha and Mahomet as it did also in Hosea and Luther and Browning.' At this point William Temple did not believe that it would be right for him to be ordained in the Church of England: 'I may feel (I don't think I shall, but I may) that my own association with her formulae would be so deceptive as to be impossible.'[23]

At this time, the doctrine of the virginal conception was not a barrier, though Temple felt ambivalent about it: 'I am inclined, I think honestly, to assent to the Virgin Birth, though I am pretty clear that it ought not to be in the creed, because it fastens attention on the wrong point.'[24] Temple was a little less tentative about the physical resurrection, but on neither point was he sufficiently assured to satisfy the Bishop of Oxford (Francis Paget), whom he approached about ordination in 1906. Archbishop Randall Davidson described Temple's position on the resurrection to Paget two years later: 'while he declines to be dogmatically certain as to the mode of the mystery, he could explain neither Christianity nor European History if he did not firmly believe that our Lord was in visible tangible personal contact with the Disciples as Teacher and Guide after His Death and Resurrection'. Davidson's verdict was: 'I myself regard him as being, *in all essential particulars*, an orthodox believer both in the Virgin Birth of Our Blessed Lord and in His Resurrection.' Davidson added: 'I see no adequate reason why he shd. not now be ordained.'[25] And he was, by the Archbishop himself in Canterbury Cathedral. But that was not the end of Temple's ambiguous stance on certain articles of the creed.

In 1912 the symposium *Foundations* appeared with Temple as one of the contributors.[26] Its subtitle was *A Statement of Christian Belief in Terms of Modern Thought*. It stood in the tradition of *Essays and Reviews* and of *Lux Mundi*, the latter having been inspired and edited by Gore, who had himself exerted a profound influence on Temple. The editor of *Foundations* was the New Testament scholar B. H. Streeter, whose view of the resurrection as a series of objective or externally generated visions, given to the disciples of Jesus, went beyond what his colleagues felt able to endorse.[27] Streeter set out the rationale of the collection thus:

> Christianity and its traditional theology have come down to us from an age very different from our own, an age when the sun and the stars moved round the earth, when the meaning of natural law and evolution was only dimly apprehended, when the psychology of religion, the historical method and the critical study of ancient documents were yet unborn.[28]

These matters, he insisted, affect the foundations of traditional beliefs.

Temple contributed a couple of inoffensive essays, on the deity of Christ and on the Church. Ronald Knox, then an Anglo-Catholic, who objected as much to the open, critical approach of the collection as to any of its specific conclusions, launched a riposte, a parody of Dryden's *Absalom and Achitophel*, entitled with a stroke of genius *Absolute and Abitofhell*, in which he referred to Temple as

> A man so broad, to some he seem'd to be
> Not one but all Mankind in Effigy:
> Who, brisk in Term, a Whirlwind in the Long,
> Did everything by turns, and nothing wrong,
> Bill'd at each Lecture-hall from Thames to Tyne
> As Thinker, Usher, Statesman, or Divine.
> Born in the Purple, swift he chose the Light,
> And Lambeth mark'd him for a Nazirite[.][29]

Knox followed this magnificent parody with a more serious attack in his book *Some Loose Stones*. In a personal reply Temple clarified his position:

> I have no presupposition against miracles, and I believe Christ walked on the water. I believe in the Virgin Birth, but I cannot in my own mind find any real theological significance in it; still, it wonderfully holds before the imagination the truth of our Lord's Deity and so I am glad that it is in the Creed. Similarly I believe in our Lord's Bodily Resurrection, but if it could (*per impossibile*) be disproved, I don't think it would affect my faith as a whole.[30]

The ambiguity persists.

In his chairman's introduction to the Doctrine Commission report *Doctrine in the Church of England* (1938) Temple, then Archbishop of York, returned to the question of belief in the two articles of the creed that had troubled his early career. His statement[31] is significant in several ways. First, his qualms about the degree of assurance that it was right to entertain about the historicity of these doctrines has gone; he is now not at all 'tentative':

> In view of my own responsibility in the Church I think it right here to affirm that I whole-heartedly accept as historical facts the birth of our Lord from a virgin mother and the resurrection of his physical body from death and the tomb.

Second, he now sees, though not as clearly, the theological significance of the doctrines that previously he had taken on trust:

> I anticipate, though with less assurance, that these events will appear to be intrinsically bound up with his deity when the relations between the physical and spiritual elements in our nature are more completely understood.

Third, far from unchurching those who remain closer to his early doubts than to his later assurance, he goes out of his way to give them their due place in the Church:

> I fully recognise the position of those who sincerely affirm the reality of our Lord's incarnation without accepting one or both of these two events as actual historical occurrences, regarding the records rather as parables than as history, a presentation of spiritual truth in narrative form.

At first glance Temple, as an archbishop, appears to tolerate the sort of views that David Jenkins would defend fifty years later as Bishop of Durham. However, Temple's expression 'in view of my own responsibility in the Church' suggests that he set a higher threshold of 'orthodoxy' for bishops than for other clergy.

IV. ACCEPTABLE EXPLORING

The Durham affair erupted in the General Synod in 1985, and the House of Bishops produced a statement on the nature of Christian belief and the role of the bishop in relation to it.[32] While the report affirmed the literal interpretation of both the virginal conception and the empty tomb as part of the faith of the Church of England, it was careful to allow scope for exploring different approaches:

> The questioning and creative process is a necessary part of Christian discipleship. Provided that it is positive, and undertaken out of concern for truth, with faith in the God who has brought us thus far, and with prayerful dependence on his Spirit, it will never be hurtful. In the past, crucial insights have been won by those who had the courage to question in faith. The Church of England is committed to this process with openness and integrity, and with a confidence, born of experience, that, however exacting it may be, essential truths of the Gospel will emerge from it more clearly understood[.][33]

The report clearly did not exclude bishops from playing their part in these explorations, though it laid down certain safeguards:

> As teachers of the faith themselves, bishops need to be in sympathetic touch with those in the vanguard of knowledge. At the same time they need to distinguish in their own teaching between the well-established fruits of scholarship and those more speculative and controversial hypotheses which have not yet been tested or found acceptance either in the scholarly community as a whole or within the Church.[34]

Furthermore,

> Bishops [. . .] have to work under a discipline of mutual responsibility and accountability, and to be sensitive to traditional beliefs within the Church as well as to fresh insights. A bishop may properly enter into questionings on matters of belief [. . .]. But in all he says he must take care not to present variant beliefs as if they were the faith of the Church[.][35]

This is wise counsel, but the ambiguity remains.

It seems that ambiguity is inescapable when a bishop is also a theologian. Every bishop is called to be a theologian (though not necessarily, of course, an academic one) in so far as a bishop is ordained to teach the faith in a relevant way, to make judgements on the application of Scripture and tradition to topical issues, and to enter into dialogue with those of different beliefs or none. The distinction between theologising in defence of the faith, on the one hand, and engaging in theological exploration, on the other, is artificial and probably impossible to sustain in practice. The openness of the quest for truth and the negotiation that arises from dialogue are inevitably in tension with the bishop's role as the guardian of doctrine and teacher of the faith.

Keith Ward's reminder that 'a truly comprehensive church should permit or even encourage a plurality of interpretative traditions, and especially traditions of dissent', and his warning about Christianity's tendency to assume that there should be a 'correct doctrine' on every topic and an authority that can say what this doctrine is, are both well taken.[36] But Ward's attractive reflections do not address the difficult questions about the responsibilities of office and of oversight, the 'applied' aspects of ecclesiology. Here, as I have suggested, ambiguity is inescapable. How can this ambiguity be handled constructively? There can be no infallible recipe for this, but I offer a few points for reflection, which apply to all pastors and clergy but especially to bishops.[37]

First, a basis of trust needs to be built up between a bishop and his people before he ventures to spring any theological surprises or advance any major challenges in the area of belief. Wise leaders give their people the opportunity to get to know them, to respect them and perhaps to hold them in affection. In this way, they could be said to build up their power base. Jenkins did not give himself the opportunity to do this: he spilt the beans in a television interview before his consecration. Second, there is no need to confront people with all the issues at once. You can try to take them forward in their understanding a step at a time. Wise leaders avoid provoking their hearers. As they teach, they just turn the corner of the page, so to speak, in order that those who are ready may get a glimpse of what lies beyond. 'Those who have ears to hear, let them hear!' Third, there is no call to issue outright challenges to aspects of belief that have already become moribund. Tilting at windmills is a sign of taking oneself too seriously. Let decaying beliefs wither on the vine. The divine right of kings was once a central plank of Anglican faith. It passed away without bishops (with one or two notorious exceptions) feeling called upon to attack it. Affirm what is good and true; let other items perish by neglect. When we are confronted by the unacceptable beliefs that still crop up, such as the inerrancy of the biblical text, the damnation of all non-Christians, hell as eternal torment, the historicity as actual people of Adam and Eve, or notions derogatory to the worth of women, we have to take issue – but not in such a way that those who have never questioned their assumptions on these matters feel stupid and ignorant. When people become confused they feel threatened. When they are confronted by academic discourse they feel intimidated. Then you can count on some getting hold of the wrong end of the stick.

If I were a bishop called upon to give my views, to a general audience, on a controversial theological question, I would try to observe the following rules. Make one point at a time. Use short sentences, avoiding subordinate clauses. Don't lapse into technical terms or in-group jargon. Do not assume that you are under oath to give the whole picture, leaving no aspect unaddressed (there is something to be said for what the Tractarians called reserve in religious knowledge). If in conversation, look at the questioner and do not be evasive. Finally, be positive. If you have to make a negative point, set it in a context of affirmation. Give reassuring signals to your audience by using familiar and traditional terms as far as possible. Explain your motives and so get people on your side. Always finish on a positive note. Build them up where their faith is sound. Even as you try to broaden their horizons, give people something to feed their faith. Then, I believe, they will be grateful to you.[38]

NOTES

1 Cf. Paul Avis, 'Theology in the Dogmatic Mode', in Peter Byrne and Leslie Houlden (eds), *Companion Encyclopedia of Theology* (London and New York: Routledge, 1995), 976–1000.

2 Keith Ward, *Religion and Revelation* (Oxford: Clarendon Press, 1994), 6, 46, 48.

3 On the relationship between the roles of theologian and bishop, cf. W. A. Visser 't Hooft, *Teachers and the Teaching Authorities: The Magistri and the Magisterium* (Geneva: World Council of Churches Publications, 2000).

4 On Hooker see briefly Paul Avis, 'Hooker, Richard', in Adrian Hastings *et al.* (eds), *The Oxford Companion to Christian Thought* (Oxford: Oxford University Press, 2000), 308–9. For Hooker and a galaxy of Church of England scholar-bishops see Paul Avis, *Anglicanism and the Christian Church*, rev. and enlarged edn (Edinburgh: T&T Clark, 2002).

5 See Walter M. Abbott (ed.), *The Documents of Vatican II* (London and Dublin: Geoffrey Chapman, 1966), 42–4 ('Lumen Gentium', art. 22); House of Bishops of the Church of England, *Bishops in Communion* (London: Church House Publishing, 2000); Colin Podmore, 'Primacy in the Anglican Tradition', in Colin Podmore (ed.), *Community, Unity, Communion: Essays in Honour of Mary Tanner* (London: Church House Publishing, 1998), 277–93.

6 Archbishops' Group on the Episcopate, *Episcopal Ministry* (London: Church House Publishing, 1990). A statement on 'The Ministry of Bishops' issued by the House of Bishops of the Episcopal Church of the USA in 1991 emphasises a creatively interpretative teaching role for the bishop: 'to transmit the tradition [. . .] is to interpret it: to grasp new dimensions of its meaning, to envisage it in fresh perspectives': J. Robert Wright (ed.), *On Being a Bishop* (New York: Church Hymnal Corporation, 1993), p. 90, ¶16.

7 Abbott (ed.), *The Documents of Vatican II*, 47 ('Lumen Gentium', art. 25).

8 Ibid., 405 ('Christus Dominus', art. 13).

9 Ibid., 572 ('Presbyterorum Ordinis', art. 19).

10   J. M. R. Tillard, 'How is Christian Truth Taught in the Roman Catholic Church?', *One in Christ*, 34 (1998), 293–306.

11   Ibid., 295.

12   Ibid., 200.

13   William Telfer, *The Office of a Bishop* (London: Darton, Longman and Todd, 1962), ch. 8.

14   David Jenkins, *The Contradiction of Christianity* (London: SCM Press, 1976).

15   David Jenkins and Rebecca Jenkins, *Free to Believe* (London: BBC Books, 1991), 21–2.

16   Ibid., 24.

17   Ibid., 25–6; cf. 67.

18   On the interpretation of the resurrection, see Paul Avis (ed.), *The Resurrection of Jesus Christ* (London: Darton, Longman and Todd, 1993).

19   Ruth Page, *Ambiguity and the Presence of God* (London: SCM Press, 1985), 216.

20   *Essays and Reviews* (London: John W. Parker and Son, 1860).

21   Charles Gore (ed.), *Lux Mundi* (London: John Murray, 1889), ch. 8. On Gore see Paul Avis, *Gore: Construction and Conflict* (Worthing: Churchman, 1988), 'Gore, Charles', in Alister E. McGrath (ed.), *The SPCK Handbook of Anglican Theologians* (London: SPCK, 1998), 126–31, 'Gore, Charles (1853–1932)', in Trevor A. Hart (ed.), *Dictionary of Historical Theology* (Carlisle/Grand Rapids: Paternoster/Eerdmans, 2000), 231–3.

22   Peter Hinchliff, *Frederick Temple, Archbishop of Canterbury: A Life* (Oxford: Clarendon Press, 1998),120–9.

23   F. A. Iremonger, *William Temple, Archbishop of Canterbury: His Life and Letters* (Oxford: Oxford University Press, 1948),102, 103–4. On Temple see also John Kent, *William Temple* (Cambridge: Cambridge University Press, 1992); Paul Avis, 'Temple, William', in McGrath (ed.), *The SPCK Handbook of Anglican Theologians*, 214–21.

24   Iremonger, *William Temple*, 106.

25   Ibid., 116, emphasis in original.

26   B. H. Streeter (ed.), *Foundations* (London: Macmillan, 1912).

27   Ibid., 113f.

28   Ibid., p. vii.

29   Iremonger, *William Temple*, 158–9.

30   Ibid., 163.

31   Church of England Commission on Christian Doctrine, *Doctrine in the Church of England* (London: SPCK, 1938), 12.

32   Church of England House of Bishops, *The Nature of Christian Belief* (London: Church House Publishing, 1986).

33   Ibid., p. 10, ¶12.

34   Ibid., p. 36, ¶70.

35   Ibid.

36   Keith Ward, *Religion and Community* (Oxford: Clarendon Press, 2000), 168, 179.

37   Cf. Paul Avis, *Authority, Leadership and Conflict in the Church* (London/New York: Mowbray/Trinity Press International, 1992), ch. 10.

38   This chapter originated in a presentation at the College for Bishops at General Theological Seminary, New York City.

17

Love Cosmic, Human and Divine: Pierre Teilhard de Chardin's Thoughts on the Phenomenon of Love

URSULA KING

Love is one of the great themes in Teilhard de Chardin's work. But what does love mean? Love appears to be involved in almost every human activity from religion to literature, music, drama, philosophy, psychology and theology. It has been said that 'the idea of love has left a wider and more indelible imprint upon the development of human culture in all its aspects than any other single notion.'[1] A bold statement, but is it true? Have human cultures explored love to its fullest measure, ventured on all its paths, or is there yet more to love than we have hitherto thought possible?

Retracing the lineaments of love in human history and civilisations would be an exciting yet arduous task, impossible for a single individual to achieve. Even a look at love in Christianity alone would require a large collaborative team rather than one writer. Besides traditional metaphysical and theological reflections on love we possess today a large literature in psychoanalysis and psycholinguistics, but also in social philosophy, education and pastoral theology, analysing the many different forms of love, the deep human need for love, and the complex webs of power and pain associated with love. For many people love is primarily allied with desire and means above all erotic and sexual love. But love can also mean affectionate love between friends; it can relate to divine love, as both the love *of* God and love *for* God, that is to say God's love of us and our love for God.

According to Christian belief 'God is love'[2] and creates, sustains and orders all things in love. All finite love flows from God's infinite love, even though human beings may not always be conscious of this ultimate origin of all love. If love is God's very essence, then eternal love subsists at the heart of all things and manifests itself through them. But the principle that love is the ultimate reality of everything is widely contested, so that rejection of this love is part of the spiritual conflict through the ages. Logically, the acceptance or rejection of this principle of love can lead to faith and hope, to optimism and love of life, or to its pessimistic negation. It belongs to the heart of Christian belief that transcendent love is the creator and sustainer of the world, and immanent love is part of all life. Its force pulsates through all of life as ceaseless energy of the divine Spirit operating in nature and humanity. Yet many people regard such faith centred on the powers of love to be a delusion. So the question remains: can we hold such a faith and live by it, or is it simply a mirage? Is love an outworn theme, approachable only with the cynicism of post-modern sceptics?

Many Christian theologians from the early Church until today have reflected on the nature and relationship of faith and love, but the Christian understanding of love is perhaps best exemplified in the writings of the Christian mystics, where the power of love is more vividly expressed than in abstract theological works. I will focus here on the twentieth-century theologian, scientist and great Christian mystic, Pierre Teilhard de Chardin (1881–1955), who wrote extensively on what he called 'the phenomenon of love'. He assigned the greatest significance to love, in the whole universe and in human life, where it is central to personal and social development, an essential source of human subjectivity and personal identity. He also experienced the tension between human and divine love, and reflected on the need for the further growth of love in an evolving universe, on love's potential for a further flowering beyond current practice.

Like all other themes in Teilhard de Chardin's work, his thoughts on love are deeply rooted in the personal experiences of his life. Reflections on love appear in his earliest works, the *Writings in Time of War* (1916–19),[3] recur throughout most of his essays, and are especially important in the autobiographical essays 'The Heart of Matter' (1950) and 'The Christic' (1955).[4] Like a musician Teilhard developed the theme of love in a succession of variations set for different occasions and contexts. To explore fully the depth of this theme one would not only have to trace his thoughts but connect them to the rich web of his personal relationships, which provided the experiential matrix for his creativity. As explained in his best-known, though difficult and controversial, book *The Phenomenon of Man*, now retranslated and more correctly entitled *The Human Phenomenon*,[5] he wanted to study every aspect of human development from a scientific, evolutionary point of view in which the most refined scientific analysis was complemented by a larger synthesis and vision. Such an approach also includes the systematic study of the phenomena of thought and of love, as well as the careful investigation of the phenomena of religion, of spirituality and even of mysticism.[6]

The most comprehensive study of Teilhard de Chardin's all-embracing, dynamic vision of love has been undertaken by the German theologian Mathias Trennert-Hellwig. His book *Die Urkraft des Kosmos: Dimensionen der Liebe im Werk Pierre Teilhard de Chardins*[7] discusses Teilhard's reflections on love in relation to 'physics, metaphysics and mysticism', based on the three parts of Teilhard's 'fundamental vision', explained in an essay of 1948.[8] These three terms are meant to refer to the overall areas of science, philosophical thought and religious practice. In other words, Teilhard de Chardin's world-view, and in particular his approach to love, involves empirical investigations, theoretical conceptualisations and practical applications.

I have chosen another threefold schema, that of 'cosmic, human and divine', which Teilhard used in his later essay 'The Heart of Matter' to explain his vision of the world. Written as a spiritual autobiography, this essay provides the interpretative key for all his thought, including his ideas on love. As with other phenomena, Teilhard wished to trace the evolution of the phenomenon of love. He criticised the traditional concept of love as too static, too 'spiritualised' and too divorced from its cosmic roots, from natural passion in which all love, including the love of God, has its starting point. He spoke of 'the transformation of love' whereby love itself is undergoing a change of state which we have to study as systematically as any other aspect of the human phenomenon, for love not only makes possible and deepens personal growth, but is also necessary for the further development of society.

To begin with, Teilhard saw love as a cosmic energy, a universal form of attraction linked to the inwardness of all things. In a general sense love is the most universal, the most powerful, the most mysterious of cosmic energies working towards the attraction, unification and convergence of divergent elements and forces. We may only think of 'love' in a rudimentary sense when considering the fusion of atoms, molecules and cells into greater units of combination on their way towards the growth of life. The use of the word 'love' in this context might be regarded as most inappropriate and imprecise by those who want to restrict it to something uniquely human, namely close relationships between persons rather than things and elements. But Teilhard was inspired by the epic of evolution, the stream of becoming that is life, and human beings rise within and out of this stream. He wanted to express the continuity as well as the specificity of the human species in relation to other species, all of which are marked in different degrees by processes of association and unification. For him 'The physical structure of the universe is love' and 'the manifestations of this fundamental power' reveal itself 'to our consciousness in three successive stages: in woman (for man), in society, in the All – by the sense of sex, of humanity and of the cosmos'.[9] This quotation expresses in brief how he sees the sense of sexuality, the sense of humanity and the cosmic sense as closely interwoven in the phenomenon of love. All three have a structurally essential place and are interrelated in the full development of love. In his essay 'The Spirit of the Earth' he links the human 'sense of the Earth', or what we today would call the globe or the planet, to love, to a search for greater human unity and the need for more scientific research. To quote from this essay:

> Love is the most universal, the most tremendous and the most mysterious of the cosmic forces. After centuries of tentative effort, social institutions have externally dyked and canalized it. [. . .] the moralists have tried to submit it to rules. [. . .] Socially, in science, business and public affairs, men pretend not to know it, though under the surface it is everywhere. Huge, ubiquitous and always unsubdued – this wild force seems to have defeated all hopes of understanding and governing it. It is therefore allowed to run everywhere beneath our civilization. We are conscious of it, but all we ask of it is to amuse us, or not to harm us. Is it truly possible for humanity to continue to live and grow without asking itself how much truth and energy it is losing by neglecting its incredible power of love?[10]

For Teilhard love is also 'the primal and universal psychic energy', and 'hominized' love is distinct from all other love: 'No longer only a unique and periodic attraction for purposes of material fertility; but an unbounded and continuous possibility of contact between minds rather than bodies; the play of countless subtle antennae seeking one another in the light and darkness of the soul; the pull towards mutual sensibility and completion.'[11] One needs to compare these remarks with similar ones on the connections between cosmos and sexuality in other essays, as when he writes: 'By the love of man and woman a thread is wound that stretches to the heart of the world.'[12] Teilhard's abstract reflections on love were much influenced by his concrete relationships with people, especially his friendship with several professional women he met during the course of his life. His thoughts on love *and* friendship are intimately related to his personal experiences of 'the feminine', as he called it, experienced throughout his life, first in his own family through his close bonds with his mother and sisters, then in his love for his cousin Marguerite Teillard-Chambon and later for other women friends, especially the American sculptress Lucile Swan. Their deep love and mutual collaboration is vividly described in their correspondence of over twenty years.[13] The essay 'The Heart of Matter' concludes with a section on 'The Feminine, or the Unitive', where Teilhard says that the story of his inner vision would leave out an essential element if he did not mention that from the critical moment when he rejected many of the old moulds in which his family life and religion had formed him, and he began to wake up and express himself in terms that were really his own, he had experienced no form of self-development without some feminine eye turned on him, some feminine influence at work. Generalising from his personal experience he writes:

> however primordial in human psychism the plenifying encounter of the sexes may be, and however essential to its structure, there is nothing to prove [. . .] that we yet have an exact idea of the functioning of this fundamental complementarity or of the best forms in which it can be effected. We have a marriage that is always polarized, socially, towards reproduction, and a religious perfection that is always represented, theologically, in terms of separation: and there can be no doubt but that we lack a third road between the two. I do not mean a *middle* road, but a higher, a road that is *demanded* by the revolutionary transformation that has recently been effected in our thought by the transposition of the notion of 'spirit'. For the spirit that comes from dematerialization, we have seen, we have substituted the spirit that comes from synthesis. *Materia matrix*. It is no longer a matter of retreating (by abstinence) from the unfathomable spiritual powers that still lie dormant under the mutual attraction of the sexes, but of conquering them by sublimation. Such, I am ever more convinced, is the hidden essence of Chastity, and such the magnificent task that awaits it.[14]

Love is deeply personal but it is also 'a higher form of human energy',[15] a power both human and divine. The dynamic energy and transforming power of love is summed up in the words: 'Love is the free and imaginative outpouring of the spirit over all unexplored paths.'[16] Perhaps no passage better expresses that love is a gracious gift – an outpouring of the spirit – as well as a task to be learnt and practised. Learning to live must mean learning to love – to give love and to receive love in order to become fully human. Such love involves dependency and vulnerability, it consists of interrelationality, of enfolding, of helping the other, so that human flourishing can happen. For the mystics, love is the burning desire for God which enflames and surrounds all things, but it also translates into active love for others. Yet as George Herbert's well-known poem on love expresses so movingly: 'Love bade me welcome: yet my soul drew back' – we are hesitant, anxious and inexperienced, we do not have enough courage and faith to accept the healing, binding power of love. We need above all *faith* in love and its tremendous, transformative power. Teilhard de Chardin saw this as the truly important 'grand option' facing us, to use the powers of love to shape our human and planetary future into greater fullness and completion.

Today more than ever before, though, we wrestle with the question of how to account for and deal with differences, whether religious, cultural, sexual or political. We can rejoice in and celebrate the great diversity around us and we need significant others for our own development, for enriching relationships, but the *otherness* of *others* can also be deeply disconcerting and lead to rejection and exclusion. There exist some poignant passages on 'the other' in Teilhard's works, as when he writes:

> I find no difficulty in integrating into my inward life everything above and beneath me [. . .] in the universe – whether matter, plants, animals; and then powers, dominions and angels [. . .]. But 'the other man', my God – by which I do not mean 'the poor, the halt, the lame and the sick', but 'the other' quite simply as 'other', the one who seems to exist independently of me because his universe seems closed to mine, and who seems to shatter the unity and the silence of the world for me – would I be sincere if I did not confess that my instinctive reaction is to rebuff him? and that the mere thought of entering into spiritual communication with him disgusts me?[17]

This is an honest acknowledgement of an initial disposition which many perhaps share. It is not always easy to 'love your neighbour', as the Gospel commands. On the contrary, as Teilhard de Chardin also knew, while it required not much effort to love those he was personally attracted to, he experienced an initial hostility to all others. We all know that the experience of the other intruding into our world disrupts our complacency and closure. Teilhard de Chardin expressed his difficulty in the form of a personal prayer:

> I confess, my God, that I have long been, and even now am, recalcitrant to the love of my neighbour. Just as much as I have derived intense joy in

the superhuman delight of dissolving myself and losing myself in the souls for which I was destined by the mysterious affinities of human love, so I have always felt an inborn hostility to, and closed myself to, the common run of those whom You tell me to love. [. . .]

Grant, O God, that the light of Your countenance may shine for me in the life of that 'other'. The irresistible light of Your eyes shining in the depth of things has already guided me towards all the work I must accomplish, and all the difficulties I must pass through. Grant that I may see You, even and above all, in the souls of my brothers, at their most personal, and most true, and most distant.[18]

Otherness breaks the boundaries of our existence through new openings, leading to new questions, new horizons, possibly to infinity, to God. Teilhard de Chardin realised that he was not drawn to the other simply through personal sympathy, but he was motivated to meet with and love the other through his love for God. For the Christian, it is through the sacrament of the eucharist, through communion, where love divine and human touch each other, that the other becomes spiritually especially significant. Teilhard de Chardin wrote a great deal on the love of the world *and* the love of God. The dedication of his famous book *The Divine Milieu* reads 'For those who love the world'. He passionately loved the world, that is first the natural world and the cosmos rather than the social and personal world to which his thought turned much later. As a young man he experienced a great tension between these two different kinds of love, but he came to see that the love of God can only be achieved through a love of the world and of people. He saw it as his particular task to integrate and thereby transform the two loves into a sense of fullness and plenitude, considering it his mission to make other people see the great power and energy of these intertwined loves. He saw God's living presence shining through all things, and through Christ's incarnation at the cosmic and human level 'christic elements' are incarnationally present everywhere, working towards the spiritual transfiguration of all realities. That is why he spoke of the 'divine diaphany' visible to those who have eyes of faith, but more often he compared the extraordinary power of transformative divine love to the blaze of fire, drawing on a well-known image found in the Bible and many Christian mystics.[19] In one of his early essays he expressed the hope that he might find in all created beings 'the divine Fire which plays in them as though in purest crystal'[20] and in 'The Mass on the World'[21] and other mystical writings he calls on the divine fire to come down to Earth and transform it.

Teilhard spoke of the spiritualisation of love, whereby lovers converge on the same divine centre, creating a love which is both universal and personal, a 'super-love'. This idea of 'super-love' is linked to a 'super-centre' of evolutionary development which culminates for him in 'Christ-Omega'. Linked to this is the specific form of Christian love, the love of others expressed through charity or what Pitirim A. Sorokin calls 'altruistic love'.[22] Teilhard describes the phenomenon of Christian love as 'a specifically new state of consciousness', considering it as one of the most distinctive elements of Christianity. At the end of *The Human Phenomenon* he writes:

Christian love is incomprehensible for those who have never tasted it. The fact that the infinite and the intangible can be lovable, that the human heart can beat in true charity for its neighbor seems simply to be impossible to many people I know – almost unnatural. And yet, whether or not it is based on an illusion, how can there be any doubt that such a feeling exists and that it is even abnormally powerful? [. . .] Is it not positively a fact that for twenty centuries thousands of mystics have drawn such burning passion from its flame that their brilliance and purity far outstrips the impulses and devotion of any kind of human love? [. . .] And finally, is it not a fact [. . .] that if the love of God were ever to be extinguished in the souls of the faithful, the enormous edifice of rites, hierarchy and doctrines the church represents would instantly fall back into the dust from which it came?

What is truly a phenomenon of capital importance for the science of the human is that a zone of thought has appeared and grown over an appreciable region of the Earth, one in which a genuine universal love has not only been conceived and preached, but has shown itself to be psychologically possible and operational in practice – and what is more, far from dying out, the movement seems to be bent on gaining speed and intensity.[23]

If Christianity is centred on the mystery of the love of God, and if this love is universal, reaching all people, places and situations, then it must relate to all our experiences, to our 'activities' and 'passivities', as Teilhard would say. Theologians have reflected on the mystery of love, mystics have celebrated and praised it, but are contemporary scientists open to a rigorous, probing analysis of love, as Teilhard suggested?

The traditional Christian teaching about love and a benevolent nature governed by a loving creator, so in evidence in early and medieval Christian thinkers, was abandoned during the modern period, especially under the influence of evolutionary theory from the mid-nineteenth century onwards. Nature, so long interpreted by theologians as another 'book' which revealed something about God, second only to Scripture, came to be seen as governed by the struggle for existence, a realm where the survival of the fittest and self-assertion counted more than self-sacrifice. This disenchantment with nature is summed up in Tennyson's often quoted description of nature as 'red in tooth and claw'. Yet it can never have been so straightforward to move in one's thinking from the natural world to the nature of God. The experience of nature has always been profoundly ambivalent, as giving humans support and nourishment but also expressing brute, savage powers, whether in the animal world or through fire, floods and tempests whose destructive force we still periodically experience today in spite of the immense growth of our scientific knowledge about the natural world and our technological ability to control many parts of it.

Some scientists acknowledge the presence of an infinite, eternal energy in the cosmos, but is this energy identical with what Christians mean by love? Even with all the scientific data available to us the meaning of nature is by no means self-evident. The mystery of the universe is not unequivocally made clear to those who study it; its meaning must always be chosen and interpreted. The evaluation of factual scientific data is open to widely varying interpretations, and nowhere is this more evident than in the acrimonious debates about the meaning of evolution carried out between different evolutionary biologists themselves, and also between scientists and theologians. Is evolution occurring merely at random, or has it a purpose and direction due to a divine creator? Keith Ward has debated these questions many times, especially in *God, Chance and Necessity*,[24] where his detailed arguments refute evolutionary naturalism and reductionism, defending classical theism as a more convincing explanation of the overall pattern of cosmic and human evolution.

For some scientists of a religious bent creative evolution is one of the signatures of God's revelation. What is now sometimes described as 'the great epic of evolution' can be read as a rise of spirit and a way of unfolding God's purpose and ultimate goal, as Teilhard de Chardin so convincingly argued, and Henry Drummond before him. If the divine spirit is not only cosmic mind and intelligence, but love itself, the history of evolution cannot be equated with the evolution of life and consciousness alone, but must also include the evolution of love. It is this extraordinary power of love, the recognition of its intrinsic and ultimate value as well as the necessity for its further animation and growth among human beings, which Teilhard saw as a tremendous task that science has to take up now in a systematic manner.

Is this possible for science, and what would be the aim of such a programme? According to Teilhard de Chardin, the task of the further development of love is necessary for the understanding of ourselves and for the completeness of the human project, for the greater unification or 'planetisation' of humanity. This development of an increasing human convergence, intertwined with the process of what is now called 'globalisation', is closely related to what he described as the 'noosphere', a thinking layer enveloping the Earth similar to the biosphere or the atmosphere.[25] This 'sphere of mind' can be understood as an interactive web of human influence and interthinking and, most importantly, as connecting threads of love which represent a new stage in human development. Collective thinking has been immensely increased through tremendous growth in education, science and research, but what must be equally harnessed are the powers of love and human interaction. Often quoted are Teilhard's words: 'The day will come when, after harnessing the ether, the winds, the tides, gravitation, we shall harness for God the energies of love. And, on that day, for the second time in the history of the world, man will have discovered fire.'[26]

Is this 'rediscovery of fire' – the analysis of the powerful and transformative energies of love and the channelling of 'this wild force' for the good of individuals and communities – possible in our contemporary global situation torn by warring conflicts, competitive individualism and the rationalistic cynicism of many academic minds? Teilhard was convinced that far from being a spent force, love has incredible power for bringing humanity more closely together, but the full extent of this power has not yet been sufficiently tested:

Love has always been carefully eliminated from realist and positivist concepts of the world; but sooner or later we shall have to acknowledge that it is the fundamental impulse of Life [. . .]. With love omitted there is truly nothing ahead of us except the forbidding prospect of standardisation and enslavement – the doom of ants and termites. It is through love and within love that we must look for the deepening of our deepest self, in the life-giving coming together of humankind. Love is the free and imaginative outpouring of the spirit over all unexplored paths. It links those who love in bonds that unite but do not confound, causing them to discover in their mutual contact an exaltation capable, incomparably more than any arrogance of solitude, of arousing in the heart of their being all that they possess of uniqueness and creative power.[27]

   Teilhard's thoughts on love are an invitation to test the strength and lasting value of Christian spirituality centred on love. For him the fire of Christianity burnt most ardently in a mysticism of love and union centred on the love of God in Christ, but expressed in a new way, based on bringing together the insights of Christian faith with those of mysticism and modern science. The emergence of 'noogenesis', the great cosmic event of reflection and the rebound of thought which has led to the progressive growth of the noosphere, has now to be complemented by what he calls 'the break-through in *amorization*', another Teilhardian neologism by which he means the activation of love within the framework of evolution. 'To amorize' means to energize *to a maximum*.

   For Teilhard love, divine, cosmic and human, is an inexhaustible source of energy which creates all worlds, whether cosmic, social or personal. He is not alone in thinking that at our present critical stage in history we cannot create a more united world without greater powers of love. However, just as human thought has been greatly developed and advanced through systematic, critical reflection on the processes and methods of thinking, the art of loving has to be cultivated, learnt and practised in order to develop its full potential. For both individuals and communities, this requires a strong emphasis on learning to love. But Teilhard also envisaged the powers of love to be more systematically explored through empirical investigations, conceptual clarifications and new practical applications. Interestingly, some people now speak about the growing presence of 'noospheric institutions' at a global level,[28] and a recent news item drew attention to the creation of a new Institute for Research on Unlimited Love in the medical school of a university in Ohio, partly inspired by Sorokin's work and devoted 'to progress in the scientific understanding and practice' of such remarkable phenomena as altruism, compassion and service'.[29]

   Teilhard de Chardin would have been delighted with this innovative example of researching the tremendous energy potential of the phenomenon of love. Love was for him the thread to the heart of the universe and to the heart of God, a thread to which he himself contributed through the powers of his intellect, the depth and warmth of his feeling, and the practical orientation of his love-inspired spirituality. By drawing on the resources of science, faith, mysticism and personal relationships in his reflections on love, he combined different, mutually enriching perspectives which are often kept far too separate. He also expressed the idea that humanity is still sleeping as long as it remains 'imprisoned in the narrow joys of its little closed loves. A tremendous spiritual power is slumbering in the depths of our multitude, which will manifest itself only when we have learnt to *break down the barriers* of our egoisms and, by a fundamental recasting of our outlook, raise ourselves up to the habitual and practical vision of universal realities.'[30]

Teilhard de Chardin's thoughts on human, cosmic and divine love can be tremendously inspiring at a personal level, but their main significance consists in his firm belief that love can be systematically cultivated and greatly increased among human beings, and that this further development of the powers of love is an absolute necessity for the future well-being of the human community on earth. An essential, indispensable element in the growth of the noosphere, the transformative powers of love need to be fathomed far more systematically than has happened hitherto, for love, more than anything else, can heal a wounded world, strengthen bonds among human beings, and help to create a more just and peaceful global community.

NOTES

1   J. Bruce Long, 'Love', in Mircea Eliade (ed.), *The Encyclopedia of Religion*, vol. ix (New York: Macmillan, 1987), 31.
2   1 John 4.8.
3   Pierre Teilhard de Chardin, *Writings in Time of War* (London: Collins, 1968).
4   Both essays are found in Teilhard's book *The Heart of Matter* (London: Collins, 1978).
5   Pierre Teilhard de Chardin, *The Human Phenomenon: A New Edition and Translation of 'Le Phénomène humain'*, ed. and tr. Sarah Appleton-Weber (Brighton and Portland: Sussex Academic Press, 1999).
6   For further details see my illustrated biography, *Spirit of Fire: The Life and Vision of Teilhard de Chardin* (Maryknoll, NY: Orbis Books, 1996).
7   Mathias Trennert-Hellwig, *Die Urkraft des Kosmos: Dimensionen der Liebe im Werk Pierre Teilhard de Chardins*, Freiburger theologische Studien 153 (Freiburg, Basle and Vienna: Herder, 1993).
8   See Pierre Teilhard de Chardin, 'My Fundamental Vision', in *Toward the Future* (London: Collins, 1975), 163–208.
9   Pierre Teilhard de Chardin, 'Sketch of a Personalistic Universe', in *Human Energy* (London: Collins, 1969), 72.
10 Pierre Teilhard de Chardin, 'The Spirit of the Earth', ibid., 32f.
11 Ibid., 33.
12 Teilhard de Chardin, 'Sketch of a Personalistic Universe', 78.
13 See Ursula King, *The Letters of Teilhard de Chardin and Lucile Swan: A Personal Interpretation*, Teilhard Studies 32 (Lewisburg, Pa.: The American Teilhard Association, 1995).
14 Teilhard de Chardin, *The Heart of Matter*, 59–60, italics in original.
15 Teilhard de Chardin, *Human Energy*, 145–60.
16 Pierre Teilhard de Chardin, *The Future of Man* (London: Collins, 1959), 55.
17 Pierre Teilhard de Chardin, *Le Milieu divin* (London: Collins, 1960), 138, original in italics throughout.
18 Ibid., original in italics throughout.
19 As Teilhard de Chardin made such abundant use of this image and was so captivated by it, I chose to describe him as a 'spirit of fire' in my biography; see n. 6 above.

20 Pierre Teilhard de Chardin, *Science and Christ* (London: Collins, 1968), 75.

21 Pierre Teilhard de Chardin, 'The Mass on the World', in *The Heart of Matter*, 119–34.

22 See Pitirim A. Sorokin, *Altruistic Love: A Study of American 'Good Neighbors' and Christian Saints* (Boston: Beacon Press, 1950; repr. New York: Kraus Reprint Co., 1969) and *The Ways and Power of Love: Types, Factors and Techniques of Moral Transformation* (Boston: Beacon Press, 1954; repr. Radnor, Pa.: Templeton Foundation Press, 2002).

23 Teilhard de Chardin, *The Human Phenomenon*, 212f.

24 See Keith Ward, *God, Chance and Necessity* (Oxford: Oneworld Publications, 1996). I find entirely convincing its lucid restatement of the main arguments of classical theism, supplemented by some Indian insights into absolute being, consciousness and bliss. But its concept of God, framed as it is in terms of 'cosmic mind' and 'intelligence', remains too formal and rationalistic for me. If science 'shows the mind of God' and religion 'the heart of God' (165), then little of this heart comes across in this book and 'the mystery of divine love' (204), mentioned on its last page, has hardly been explored with the same persistence and power as the idea of God as ultimate intelligence. For Teilhard, however, the extraordinary truth that God is love was of greater importance than anything else. The profound Christian insight that God is love cannot be left to prayer and worship, or the writings of the mystics, but must be fully fathomed by modern theologians too, so that it assumes a place of importance equal to that of reflections on God's mind and intelligence.

25 'Noosphere' is derived from the Greek 'nous', the integral mind or spirit, and covers the Earth as a spheric globe. It is a collective phenomenon created through the interconnections between numerous individuals. The term was first coined in 1925 by Teilhard de Chardin and the French philosopher Édouard Le Roy. From the 1930s 'noosphere' was also used by the Russian scientist Vladimir I. Vernadsky. The concept has parallels with contemporary Gaia theory. For the interesting history, usage and future significance of the noosphere see Paul R. Samson and David Pitt (eds), *The Biosphere and Noosphere Reader: Global Environment, Society and Change* (London and New York: Routledge, 1999). The World Wide Web is sometimes considered a special manifestation of the noosphere as a kind of 'global brain' forming around the earth.

26 Teilhard de Chardin, *Toward the Future*, 86f.

27 Teilhard de Chardin, *The Future of Man*, 54f.

28 See Samson and Pitt (eds), *The Biosphere and Noosphere Reader*, 184f.

29 Stephen Post, 'Unlimited Vision: The Institute for Research on Unlimited Love', *Research News and Opportunities in Science and Theology*, 7:2 (Mar. 2002), 10. The same number also contains an article by Keith Ward, 'Nature, Red in Tooth and Claw: Can There Be a Theology of Nature?' (20–1).

30 Teilhard de Chardin, *Le Milieu divin*, 139f., original in opposite font throughout.

Part V
KEITH WARD: A GUIDE FOR THE PERPLEXED

18

Keith Ward:
A Guide for the Perplexed

KEITH WARD

I was born in a rural area of northern England at the beginning of the Second World War. My earliest experience of religion was a mixture of Anglican and Methodist worship, though my parents did not strongly participate in either. I also encountered a number of esoteric schools, like that of Rudolf Steiner and the Rosicrucians. So I had a very clear sense from an early age that there was a wide variety of religious opinions, and that religion as such was a minority interest. Very important in my early life were gaining knowledge about the natural world in the sciences, the pursuit of culture in music and the arts, the friendship I found in the world of rural Methodism, and the love of nature.

I think that I was always naturally religious, in the sense that I seemed to apprehend a spiritual presence (or presences) both in the natural world and in music. The particular doctrines of Christianity that I came across were presented in such a way that critical questioning and exploration were encouraged. They were also varied enough that such questioning was virtually bound to arise. There was always a sort of tension (though not an uncomfortable one) between the natural feelings of my heart and the critical questions of my mind. I had powerful experiences which seemed to be of God, but was also keenly aware of critical and sceptical arguments about all religious beliefs, or even about all beliefs. Although I did not discover it for some time, this was quite a good preparation for being a philosopher, and at university I took to the subject immediately.

Something that may seem like an ambiguity in my published work between orthodox Christian belief and a more or less radical scepticism is in fact a continuation of this tension. At its extreme, it suggests that, like many people, I am not one but two selves. There is the self which is a simple pious believer, strongly aware of the presence of Christ as an inward spiritual power. But there is also a self which stands back and, hearing the many voices of atheism and unbelief, sees the weakness of all human arguments, and the absurdity of any human claiming to have certain knowledge of a supernatural realm.

My pious self was never strongly orientated towards doctrine. Indeed, I was unaware of the classical formulation of the major Christian doctrines of the Trinity, Incarnation and Atonement for quite a number of years. I was always encouraged to be eclectic and wide-ranging in my reading, so I read Radhakrishnan before I read any Christian theologian, and I probably knew more about Indian religions and esoteric traditions like Anthroposophy (from books) than I did about the Christian faith, theoretically speaking. But I had no doubt that I experienced a spiritual presence which had become known to me through various very different Christian communities I encountered.

I would say, looking back, that in early life I had a real, vivid, experiential but doctrinally vague religious faith. At a later stage (between school and university, when I served in the Royal Air Force) I did encounter Evangelical Christians, and was vastly impressed by their commitment and their deep experience of Christ, which in fact renewed my own faith in quite a dramatic way. I also encountered Catholicism, and was again impressed by the beauty of the liturgy and the appealingly 'mystical' approach I found there. But I was never convinced of the intellectual plausibility of many of the beliefs I encountered in these traditions, which often struck me immediately as both rather myopic and unduly restrictive. People just seemed to be remarkably ill informed about what the various religious traditions of the world said, though that did not seem to stop them knowing such traditions were wrong! They also seemed to be unjustifiably confident about the truth of doctrines which were widely disputed and denied by intelligent people.

So part of the context of my development was the growing awareness of the many world-views, religious and non-religious, which during my early life were becoming much better known in Britain, and the consequential awareness that Christian beliefs were not at all obviously true or even rational to many people. At that time, many hitherto inaccessible works in Indian and Chinese philosophy were being translated, and scholars from eastern traditions were coming to Britain to expound their faiths in their own way. So there was a vast increase in the possibilities of reading the primary texts of the world religions in translation, and of discussing their contents with scholars in those religions. There was no longer any excuse for confining one's religious knowledge to just one western version of Christianity.

At university, where I first of all studied philosophy, the dominant school of philosophical thought was what is often called 'linguistic analysis'. It concentrated on analysing the meaning of words, especially difficult words like 'beauty', 'goodness' and 'God'. And it was usually pretty insistent that all words which claimed factual content had to be rooted in realities which were observable by means of the senses. Two of the most influential philosophers when I was a student were A. J. Ayer and Gilbert Ryle. Ayer was particularly vehement in his rejection of religion as based on meaningless terms or empty hypotheses. Ryle was more sympathetic, but seemed to assume that religious beliefs were little more than expressions of emotional needs. Even philosophers who were religious were very muted in the claims they made. Ian Ramsey, the Nolloth Professor of the Philosophy of the Christian Religion at Oxford, had a great influence on me. He sometimes described himself as a 'religious empiricist'. His view was that the term 'God' was used to mark moments of disclosure, when one discerned the empirical facts and 'more', but a more which could only be expressed in symbol and metaphor. Religion was not about belief in mighty acts of God which broke the laws of nature. It was not about abstract metaphysical dogmas, which could establish truths about a creator of the world by reason. It was basically about total life-commitments which arose from discernments of a transcendent dimension in experience.

When I decided to follow up my philosophy degree by studying theology, it was with this academic background. So it was not surprising that the language of Karl Barth seemed to come from some alien universe, where people were not concerned with clarity or with the precise analysis of the meanings of the terms they used. The language of Paul Tillich was redolent of the grand metaphysical systems of Hegel and the idealists, whose pretensions were supposed to have been deflated simply by asking precisely what they meant. And many theologians, when they were interested in doctrines, were still involved in fourth- and fifth-century debates about ancient Greek philosophical terms (or, if Catholic, about thirteenth-century neo-Aristotelian terms) which again belonged to a past philosophical landscape. My problem was to avoid the solvent acids of philosophical atheism, while preserving the positive goods of definitional clarity, analytical precision, logical rigour, and insistence on reasoned justification which linguistic philosophy had established, at least in the academic world of philosophy.

Although I appreciated the theology I studied, the main immediate effect it had on me was to weaken my Christian faith. The impression it made on me (and I do not seek to justify this now) was that, where it was scholarly and precise, it was obsolete (for example, commentary on the Church Fathers), and where it was dealing with contemporary intellectual problems of belief, it was fuzzy and imprecise. I left with the feeling that we knew too little about Jesus to make him an object of worship, that the Church was committed to archaic philosophical beliefs which it seemed afraid to revise, and that its attitudes to sexuality and gender, in particular, were based on principles of biblical interpretation that it had itself thoroughly undermined.

I got a job teaching philosophy – the last refuge of lost belief – and for a number of years I had the freedom to pretend that I had no beliefs at all, though I could criticise everyone else's beliefs as ruthlessly as possible. During this time I wrote two books, *Ethics and Christianity* and *The Development of Kant's View of Ethics*, both of which are rigorously agnostic about the truth of the texts under analysis, but aim to give sympathetic as well as critical accounts of them. These studies were important to me in emphasising the rationality of at least certain sorts of religious beliefs, and in causing me to be as critical of the generally atheistic fashions of modern philosophy as I was of eighteenth- or nineteenth-century works. After seven years, I decided that philosophical agnosticism was a retreat from commitment. Systems of atheistic philosophy, like logical positivism or materialism, were just as shakily founded and ideological as most religious systems were, and a great deal more dogmatic – and, frankly, one-sided – than contemporary British Christianity. Although many philosophers mocked religion as based on irrational postulates of faith, they themselves did not hesitate to accept ultimate axioms (like 'Everything is material' or 'Everything is composed of sense-data') on faith, and to hold extremely controversial views as though they were perfectly obvious. I began to suspect that belief in God was more, not less, rational than atheism, and this enabled me to take my Christian experiences seriously again.

One contributory factor to this return to faith was the amazing fact of a new convergence that was becoming apparent between many sciences, particularly mathematical physics, and religion. The sciences have developed enormously during my lifetime. I have always been fascinated by science, especially by physics. The discovery of nuclear fission, the development of quantum mechanics, the unravelling of the structure of DNA, and the development of computing are just four of the world-changing scientific breakthroughs which have happened within my lifetime. New physics, biology and information technology provide new knowledge about at least the ultimate nature of physical reality. Of course, to some religious believers, all these things are deeply disturbing. They see monumental problems in relating traditional beliefs, formulated entirely in pre-scientific cultures, to these amazing new discoveries about the nature and history of the physical universe. But there are many scientists for whom these new visions approach the religious. The sheer awesomeness, elegance and integrated complexity of the universe have always seemed to me to suggest the existence of a cosmic intelligence or mind, and so, I found, they seem to do to many scientists whom I got to know.

It is wise for people like me to tread delicately in these areas, which grow more complex and refined by the day. But it seems to me an abrogation of responsibility for anyone interested in the truth of basic religious doctrines to ignore this new information, and it seems equally irresponsible to fail to realise that the intelligibility of the universe points to a possible convergence with religious insights, when those insights are understood to be largely framed in symbolic or metaphorical ways.

As I tried to face up to the problems raised by philosophical criticism of religion and by new scientific advances, I was encouraged enormously by meeting a number of theologians who were well aware of the problems and were engaged in developing responses to them. John Hick, Geoffrey Lampe, John Macquarrie, Arthur Peacocke, John Polkinghorne, Ian Ramsey, John Robinson and Maurice Wiles are perhaps the best known of those who influenced my thought. To some people, this may seem for the most part like a litany of sceptics, and I have tried from time to time to defend a more robustly traditional faith than they seem to have. But I increasingly came to feel that they embodied both the virtues of critical enquiry and width of vision, and commitment to the God they discerned in and through the person of Jesus, which I found it hard to discover anywhere else. This might only be one strand of Christian faith, but it did exist as an important part of twentieth-century British religious thought, and it was one I could affirm.

It was slightly surprising to me that many of these thinkers did not seriously consider religions in general, though of course one cannot do everything in one lifetime. It seemed to me, though, that the sort of interpretation they gave to Christian faith was equally applicable to many elements of religious life throughout the world. As I read the works of A. C. Bouquet, John Hick, Ninian Smart and Wilfred Cantwell Smith, I began to gain some idea of the way in which the diverse religious traditions of humanity might fit into a broad pattern which was coherent and intelligible. Henceforth, I came to feel, Christianity could only be properly understood in its global context, as one element of a broad pattern of faiths, rooted in the diverse but interlinked histories of human cultures.

I also began to think that I should unequivocally commit myself to the Christian faith which had nurtured my spiritual experience. To counter my own vacillations in matters of intellectual belief, I needed to do something drastic, something unusual, at that time and place, for a philosopher. I was ordained in 1972, in the chapel of King's College London, as an Anglican minister. I continued to teach in universities as a philosopher, but began to work in local parishes as a non-stipendiary priest, first in various parishes in London and then in a rural parish in a small Hampshire village. Since my ordination I have always worked for a good part of my time as a parish priest, and from 1991 as a cathedral canon. These pastoral and liturgical activities have no doubt affected the sorts of things I have written. One effect was my constant efforts to make academic theology accessible to non-academic members of my congregations. I wrote a number of small books which arose from Lent talks that I gave in the parishes I worked in, and sometimes they tackled the sorts of anti-religious arguments that tend to dominate the world of popular publishing. The aim was to present philosophically competent arguments in a generally accessible form, and to show that theological thinking should be as sophisticated and self-critical as scientific thinking. Their intended audience was the people who came to the churches I worked in, and also the large number of people who lived in the parishes and took an intelligent interest in questions about human nature and destiny, but thought that the Christian faith had somehow become obsolete and intellectually untenable.

I continued to write more academic books, the specific nature of which tended to depend on my academic context at the time. I wrote *The Concept of God* as a lecturer in the philosophy of religion at King's College London, as a sort of Wittgensteinian reaction to the heavily dualist metaphysics of H. D. Lewis, who then held the Chair of the History and Philosophy of Religion at King's. When I became Dean and Chaplain of Trinity Hall, Cambridge, with a direct but low-key evangelical role in a secular college, I wrote *Rational Theology and the Creativity of God*. This was meant to be a philosophical formulation and defence of a Christian idea of God. Back in King's College London, and now teaching a number of more or less religiously radical students in a religious studies course, I wrote *Images of Eternity* (later reissued as *Concepts of God*) and *A Vision to Pursue*, trying to place Christian ideas in a wider global religious context, and to commend Christian faith as an undogmatic and exciting intellectual challenge.

At that point, completely to my surprise, I was offered the Regius Chair of Divinity and a canonry of Christ Church at Oxford University. This reoriented my work in a more overtly theological direction, and in this context I produced, over a period of eight years, my 'Comparative Theology', which appeared in four separate volumes, and brings together the three main themes which have dominated my intellectual life – an interest in global religions, in a philosophical approach to religious beliefs, and in the sciences. It seeks to present a systematic Christian theology in the context of the development of religion globally, and to bring out both its distinctive insights and its peculiar limitations. It also seeks to explore a number of main pathways that religious commitment has taken throughout the world, in as sensitive and yet critical a way as possible. It is comparative, because it compares and contrasts, in a broadly descriptive way, various religious beliefs about revelation, God, human nature, and the right way to live. It is theological, because it is concerned with issues of rationality and truth. Thus it is normative, providing constructive suggestions about how to understand one particular faith tradition in a rationally justifiable way.

I have discovered that there have been two major misunderstandings of what that work was doing. One is that I was from the first a Christian apologist, using or misusing ideas from other faiths, taken out of context, to demonstrate the superiority of my own. The other is that I was claiming to stand outside religions and judge them all from some better standpoint, or advocate some new global religion which would supersede all present faiths. I am comforted by the fact that these criticisms accuse me of opposite tendencies, which makes me think that at least they cannot both be fair. In fact I did write from a particular Christian viewpoint, looking for insights from other faiths and trying to present my own views persuasively, though in full awareness that believers in other faiths would be expected to do just the same thing from their own different viewpoints. And though my approach to Christianity may be regarded as revisionist, it is certainly not one that tries to supersede Christianity or any other faith, and propose some superior form of religion. My aim was, in short, to be descriptively fair to all faiths, and prescriptively reasonable in showing how one form of Christian faith could be justifiably maintained in face of so many competing world-views.

Some of the main results of my enquiry were these. First, all faiths are subject to the same sorts of internal diversities, tensions and ambiguities that are familiar in Christianity. Second, in the last two hundred years Christianity has, rather painfully, come to accept critical attitudes to Scripture and to authority as part of its complex being in the world. All traditions will, I think, have to face such criticism sooner or later. Third, I was confirmed in my suspicion that Christianity itself has changed fairly radically, and more than once, from its first beginnings in Galilee, and that it is actually part of its inner nature to encourage new self-transformations in response to new moral and factual insights. Fourth, I concluded that some central beliefs about God and the spiritual life were held in common by the major religious traditions, but were expressed in different cultural and historical symbols, deriving from different histories and background views of the world. Fifth, I turned out (and this surprised me in some ways) to belong pretty squarely in a theological tradition that probably begins with Schleiermacher early in the nineteenth century, and that, while still controversial, has continued as an important strand of Christian theology ever since.

This is sometimes called 'liberal Christianity', and I would ally myself with that tradition, while not at all wishing to denigrate what I suppose are the other major Christian traditions of Catholicism, Orthodoxy and Evangelicalism. I have discovered that the word 'liberal' can mean many different things to different people. For me, the distinctive characteristic of religious liberalism lies in its attitude to revelation and authority in religion. For some forms of Catholicism, the magis-terium of the Church, located finally in the person of the Pope, has the authority to define what is essential to Christian faith, and such defined teaching must be accepted by all Catholic Christians. For Eastern Orthodoxy, the general ecumenical councils of the Church are protected from error by the Holy Spirit, and their teach-ings are irreformable – but there have only been seven such councils, and the subsequent councils of the Roman church do not count. The Protestant Reformers denied that any human institution, however exalted, has the authority to define irreformably and infallibly what the content of the Christian faith is. That is the view of my own church, the Church of England, which asserts in Article 21 of the Thirty-Nine Articles that 'General Councils [. . .] may err, and sometimes have erred, even in things pertaining unto God.'

Many Evangelicals, however, hold that the Bible itself is inerrant and changelessly definitive, so there is still a source of inerrant beliefs for Christians. Liberals deny that even the Bible can be properly treated as inerrant and irreformable in all its teach-ings. On this understanding, what is definitive of liberalism is its rejection of any inerrant authority in matters of religion.

This should be carefully distinguished from a rejection of all authority or revela-tion. Liberals have not usually said that individuals should be encouraged to make up all their beliefs for themselves, without appeal to revelation, to Scripture or to Church tradition. It is the kind of revelation and authority which is in question, not its existence. If revelation is a disclosure by God of the nature and purpose of God, such disclosures can be real and vital, without being framed in inerrant propositions. That was, in my opinion, Schleiermacher's major contribution to theology – a view of revelation as a genuine disclosure of the presence and nature of God which is not embodied in inerrant propositions, and which is not understood with complete clarity.

The Apostles, for example, acknowledged a disclosure of God in the person of Jesus, but misunderstood (according to the Gospels) most of what he said and stood for. Is there good reason to think that the writers of the Gospels managed to achieve an inerrant understanding of what the God revealed in Jesus was like after Jesus was dead, even though those who knew him best had only partly understood this during his life? Some Christians think so, but I do not, and I do not think it is essential to faith in Jesus as a genuine revelation of God to think so.

For such a liberal, the record of the words and acts of Jesus, and the many letters to early Christian churches which are found in the New Testament, have genuine authority. They give us the only information we have about Jesus, the revelation of God, and about how his earliest followers understood him. They are indeed, we may reasonably think, inspired by the Spirit of God. But the very fact that there are four different Gospels, with rather different points of view, and letters reflecting differing interpretations of the role of Jesus in the story of human salvation, may suggest that the human reception and recording of revelation is always partial, incomplete, and sometimes downright inadequate.

Liberal Christians stand for authority without inerrancy, and more generally for the provisionality of all human understandings of truth. There can be a total commitment to the fact that God is manifested authentically in Jesus, together with an acceptance that what is shown needs to be reflected on, continually reinterpreted in wider contexts of knowledge, and internalised in different ways in each new generation. In most areas of human knowledge, there can be claims to truth along with acknowledgement of revisability and fallibility. Why not in religion?

I say this because there exists a particular understanding of my development, that I swung from a radical view in *A Vision to Pursue* to a much more orthodox view in my Comparative Theology. I do not think this is correct (though I admit an author is not always the best judge of what he or she thinks). In all my published work, I have been exploring the limits of a liberal approach to Christianity. Sometimes those limits push towards more radical views – a call for a complete reinterpretation of all past formulations of doctrine. As I have suggested, this has been prompted by my contacts with students who have had a deep distrust of ancient and apparently over-dogmatic traditions. Then the question is how far such a reinterpretation can go without losing touch with the primal revelation in Jesus. Sometimes the limits push towards orthodoxy, and as great an acceptance as possible of defined dogmas or biblical utterances. This in my case has been prompted by encounters with virulently anti-religious academics, whose claimed rejection of any intellectual authority has just been too implausible to accept. Then the question is why one should distance oneself from a strictly orthodox view at all, and not just submit to the Church (but which one?).

My conclusions to that exploration are that I draw back from radicalism by insisting on the objectivity of a creator God, who discloses the divine nature as unlimited love in the person of Jesus. I draw back from orthodoxy by insisting on the right and duty to come to conscientious beliefs, especially about ethical matters concerned with sexuality, genetics and animal welfare, which may be at odds with the consensus or defined doctrines of some churches. At the same time, I give a high status both to biblical teachings and official Church teachings, and do not simply disregard them. I think it important, if one has a view which challenges current understandings, to find some intelligible basis in the tradition itself from which that view can be developed, and some good reason, drawn from better understandings of the universe or of human nature, why the traditional views should be revised. Thus in matters of sexuality one should look for understandings of equality and compassion in the tradition which may be held to lie deeper than, and which suggest very different positions to, some explicit statements of female subordination or condemnations of homosexual practice. New insights must be intelligible developments of the revealed tradition, though they may subvert long-held and even officially formulated beliefs. I understand and appreciate the beliefs and arguments of both radicals and the orthodox, and share many of them. But I want to see an assured place in the range of Christian traditions for a liberal view which is wholly committed to the fact of God's self-revelation in and through the person of Jesus, and also to the fallibility and incompleteness of all human understandings of that revelation. Revelation, on this view, is a past fact which demands and motivates a continued effort at a future understanding, hopefully greater but never completed, under the guidance of the Holy Spirit.

The upshot of all this has been to confirm me in what I fully recognise to be just one strand of Christian believing, but to make me feel that it is vitally important to learn to understand and respect all that is good in other conscientiously formulated traditions, both Christian and non-Christian. I believe that the most basic and fundamental religious belief is, in a rather vague but still important sense, the same in most of the religious traditions of which I am aware. This is that there is a spiritual realm which is in some sense more real than, and probably the basis of, the material world. There are many ways of construing and representing this realm, but there develops in most traditions the idea of one being or state of supreme value, which it is possible to apprehend in some form. Furthermore, the way to that apprehension is a way of overcoming egoism, pride and hatred, so as to let that spiritual reality be expressed in one's own life. The religious life is one of seeking to apprehend the supreme value and let it be manifest in human life, in face of a constant human tendency to egoism and hatred. This belief and commitment has been worked out in various ways in human history, and part of a broader spiritual understanding is to appreciate the history of humanity's religious search in all its incompleteness and ambiguity.

As I see it, the distinctiveness of Christian faith is that it sees its paradigm revelation as given in the life, death and resurrection of Jesus, seen as the historical and personal form of God on this planet. It sees God as a being of limitless and universal love. It sees human lives as trapped in bondage to desire, pride and hatred, but also as able to be liberated and united to God through the inner action of the Spirit of God. It sees the Church, the many communities of the disciples of Christ, as called to the vocation of proclaiming the good news of liberation and eternal life, and of serving the world in love. It sees the ultimate destiny of human life, and in some sense of the whole cosmos, as being taken up into the life of God, where all evil is redeemed and all good is conserved for ever.

My approach in theology has been to try to work out how this form of contemporary Christianity can formulate its own distinctive approach in the light of the many intellectual and moral criticisms of religion in post-eighteenth-century Europe, of the increased possibility of understanding religious traditions in a global way, and of the new world-view which the sciences are opening up to us.

The theology that results is perhaps more tentative, questioning and consciously provisional than some would like. But I think it is compatible with a commitment to that passionate love of God, as discerned in Jesus Christ, which is central to Christian faith. Living in faith, and living with uncertainty, are, after all, not so very far removed from one another.

Bibliography of
Keith Ward's Publications

To the best of my knowledge, the following is a complete list of Keith Ward's published works up to 30 April 2003, apart from a handful of occasional pieces in non-academic publications, and is arranged in chronological order within each category. Entries for further works will be added to the Internet version of this bibliography, available at Keith Ward's website (http://users.ox.ac.uk/~theo0015).

T. W. B.

I. Books and monographs

Fifty Key Words in Philosophy (London: Lutterworth Press, 1968).

Ethics and Christianity (London: Allen and Unwin, 1970).

The Development of Kant's View of Ethics (Oxford: Basil Blackwell, 1972).

The Concept of God (Oxford: Basil Blackwell, 1974; repr. London: Fount, 1977).

The Christian Way (London: SPCK, 1976).

The Divine Image: The Foundations of Christian Morality (London: SPCK, 1976).

The Promise (London: SPCK, 1980).

The Law of Christ, the John Coffin Memorial Lecture (London: University of London Publications Department, 1981).

Holding Fast to God: A Reply to Don Cupitt (London: SPCK, 1982).

Rational Theology and the Creativity of God (Oxford: Blackwell, 1982; repr. Oxford: Blackwell, 1985).

The Living God (London: SPCK, 1984).

The Battle for the Soul: An Affirmation of Human Dignity and Value (London: Hodder and Stoughton, 1985); repr. as *Defending the Soul* (Oxford: Oneworld Publications, 1992).

The Turn of the Tide: Christian Belief in Britain Today (London: BBC Books,1986).

Evidence for the Virgin Birth (Oxford: publ. by Mowbray for the Christian Evidence Society, 1987).

Images of Eternity: Concepts of God in Five Religious Traditions (London: Darton, Longman and Todd, 1987); repr. as *Concepts of God: Images of the Divine in Five Religious Traditions* (Oxford: Oneworld Publications, 1998).

The Rule of Love: Reflections on the Sermon on the Mount (London: Daybreak, 1989).

Divine Action (London: Collins, 1990).

A Vision to Pursue: Beyond the Crisis in Christianity (London: SCM Press, 1991).

Is Christianity a Historical Religion?, Friends of Dr Williams's Library Lecture 46 (London: Dr Williams's Trust, 1992).

Religion and Revelation: A Theology of Revelation in the World's Religions (Oxford: Clarendon Press, 1994); vol. 1 of the tetralogy in comparative theology.

God, Chance and Necessity (Oxford: Oneworld Publications, 1996).

Religion and Creation (Oxford: Clarendon Press, 1996); vol. 2 of the tetralogy in comparative theology.

God, Faith and the New Millennium: Christian Belief in an Age of Science (Oxford: Oneworld Publications, 1998).

Religion and Human Nature (Oxford: Clarendon Press, 1998); vol. 3 of the tetralogy in comparative theology.

Christianity: A Short Introduction (Oxford: Oneworld Publications, 2000).

Religion and Community (Oxford: Clarendon Press, 2000); vol. 4 of the tetralogy in comparative theology.

God: A Guide for the Perplexed (Oxford: Oneworld Publications, 2002).

II. Articles

'Myth and Fact in Christianity', *Scottish Journal of Theology*, 20 (1967), 385–96.

'The Unity of Space and Time', *Philosophy*, 42 (1967), 68–74.

'Existence, Transcendence and God', *Religious Studies*, 3 (1968), 461–76.

'The Headless Woman', *Analysis*, 29 (1968/9), 196.

'Christian Ethics and the Being of God', *Scottish Journal of Theology*, 22 (1969), 78–89.

'Freedom and the Irenaean Theodicy', *Journal of Theological Studies*, n.s., 20 (1969), 249–54.

'Incarnation and Atonement', *Theology*, 72 (1969), 386–92.

'The Ascription of Experiences', *Mind*, n.s., 79 (1970), 415–20.

'Moral Seriousness', *Philosophy*, 45 (1970), 114–27.

'Kant's Teleological Ethics', *Philosophical Quarterly* (Scotland), 21 (1971), 337–51.

'Theology in a University Context', *Scottish Journal of Theology*, 24 (1971), 290–304.

'A Comment' [on Laurence Bright, OP, 'Humanist and Christian in Action', *Theology*, 75 (1972), 525–33], *Theology*, 75 (1972), 533–5.

'Language and Understanding in Morality', *Philosophy*, 47 (1972), 249–62.

'Explanation and Mystery in Religion', *Religious Studies*, 9 (1973), 23–37.

'Recent Thinking on Christian Beliefs. II: The Concept of God', *Expository Times*, 88 (1976/7), 68–71.

'Changing Ethical Values: A Christian Assessment', in John Howe (ed.), *Today's Church and Today's World, with a Special Focus on the Ministry of Bishops*, The Lambeth Conference 1978: Preparatory Articles (London: CIO Publishing, 1977), 73–8.

'Incarnation or Inspiration – A False Dichotomy?', *Theology*, 80 (1977), 251–5.

'Gegenwärtige Strömungen in der Ethik in Großbritannien', tr. C. Frey, *Zeitschrift für evangelische Ethik*, 25 (1981), 244–57.

'The Just War and Nuclear Arms', in Francis Bridger (ed.), *The Cross and the Bomb: Christian Ethics and the Nuclear Debate* (London: A. R. Mowbray, 1983), 47–66.

'Miracles and Testimony', *Religious Studies*, 21(1985), 131–45.

Untitled review article on Oliver O'Donovan, *Begotten or Made?* (Oxford: Oxford University Press, 1984), *Theology*, 88 (1985), 37–42.

'Persons, Kinds and Capacities', in Peter Byrne (ed.), *Rights and Wrongs in Medicine: King's College Studies 1985–6* (London: King Edward's Hospital Fund for London, 1986), 53–79.

'Reinhold Niebuhr and the Christian Hope', in Richard Harries (ed.), *Reinhold Niebuhr and the Issues of Our Time* (Oxford: A. R. Mowbray, 1986), 61–87.

'The Step of Faith', in Tony Moss (ed.), *In Search of Christianity* (London: Firethorn, 1986), 66–79.

'The God of the Doctrine Commission: A Critique of *We Believe in God*', *King's Theological Review*, 11 (1988), 1–3.

'Miracles', in Andrew Walker (ed.), *Different Gospels: Christian Orthodoxy and Modern Theologies* (London: Hodder and Stoughton, 1988), 97–111; repr. in Andrew Walker (ed.), *Different Gospels: The New Edition* (London: SPCK, 1993), 54–66.

'Philosophy and the Philosophy of Religion in the *Encyclopedia of Religion*', *Religious Studies*, 24 (1988), 39–46.

'Christian Ethics', in Geoffrey Wainwright (ed.), *Keeping the Faith: Essays to Mark the Centenary of 'Lux Mundi'* (London: SPCK, 1989), 66–79.

'God as Creator', in Godfrey A. Vesey (ed.), *The Philosophy in Christianity*, Royal Institute of Philosophy Lectures 25 (Cambridge: Cambridge University Press, 1989), 99–118.

'Imperialism and Co-existence in Religious Ideology', in Ian Hamnett (ed.), *Religious Pluralism and Unbelief: Studies Critical and Comparative* (London: Routledge, 1990), 13–28.

'An Irresolvable Dispute?', in Anthony Dyson and John Harris (eds), *Experiments on Embryos*, Social Ethics and Policy Series (London and New York: Routledge, 1990), 106–19.

'The Study of Truth and Dialogue in Religion', in Ursula King (ed.), *Turning Points in Religious Studies: Essays in Honour of Geoffrey Parrinder* (Edinburgh: T&T Clark, 1990; repr. Edinburgh: T&T Clark, 1996), 221–31.

'Truth and the Diversity of Religions', *Religious Studies*, 26 (1990), 1–18; repr. in Robin Gill (ed.), *Readings in Modern Theology: Britain and America*, SPCK Essential Readings (London: SPCK, 1995), 163–72.

'Evidence for the Virgin Birth', in Gillian Ryeland (ed.), *Beyond Reasonable Doubt* (Norwich: publ. by the Canterbury Press Norwich for the Christian Evidence Society, 1991), 53–70.

'Expanding Vision: Pursuing Global Religious Awareness', *World Faiths Encounter*, no. 1 (Mar. 1992), 3–9.

'Is a Christian State a Contradiction?', in Dan Cohn-Sherbok and David McLellan (eds), *Religion in Public Life* (Basingstoke and London: Macmillan, 1992), 5–16.

'Is God a Person?', in Gisjbert van den Brink, Luco J. van den Brom and Marcel Sarot (eds), *Christian Faith and Philosophical Theology: Essays in Honour of Vincent Brümmer* (Kampen, Netherlands: Kok Pharos Publishing House, 1992), 258–66.

'Religion after the Enlightenment', in Dan Cohn-Sherbok (ed.), *Many Mansions: Interfaith and Religious Intolerance* (London: Bellew, 1992), 137–48.

Untitled review response [to an untitled review article by J. Begbie on *A Vision to Pursue*, *Anvil*, 9 (1992), 67–9], *Anvil*, 9 (1992), 159–60.

'Divine Ineffability', in Arvind Sharma (ed.), *God, Truth and Reality: Essays in Honour of John Hick* (Basingstoke and London: Macmillan, 1993), 210–20.

'God as a Principle of Cosmological Explanation', in Robert John Russell, Nancey C. Murphy and Chris J. Isham (eds), *Quantum Cosmology and the Laws of Nature: Scientific Perspectives on Divine Action* (Vatican City: Vatican Observatory Publications, 1993), 247–62.

'God, Time and the Creation of the Universe', *Explorations in Science and Theology* (London: RSA, 1993), 61–7.

'The Question of Truth in Religion', *Journal of Dharma*, 19 (1994), 209–23.

'The Concept of God', in Peter Byrne and Leslie Houlden (eds), *Companion Encyclopedia of Theology* (London: Routledge, 1995), 342–66.

'Reply' [to Stephen Williams, 'Keith Ward on *Religion and Revelation*', *Scottish Journal of Theology*, 48 (1995), 251–8], *Scottish Journal of Theology*, 48 (1995), 258–62.

'A Classical Portrait of God', in N. T. Wright, Brian Hebblethwaite and Keith Ward, *The Changing Face of God*, Lincoln Studies in Theology 2 (Lincoln: Lincoln Cathedral Publications, 1996), 30–41.

'The Decline and Fall of Reason: From Modernity to Postmodernity', in Ursula King (ed.), *Faith and Praxis in a Postmodern Age* (London: Cassell, 1998), 15–27.

'Christianity and Evolution: A Case Study', in Marcel Sarot and Gisjbert van den Brink (eds), *Identity and Change in the Christian Tradition* (Frankfurt am Main: Peter Lang, 1999), 91–104.

'God, Time and Eternity', in C. W. du Toit (ed.), *Reading the Universe through Science, Religion and Ethics: The Evolving Science and Religion Debate* (Pretoria: Research Institute for Theology and Religion, University of South Africa, 1999), 124–39.

'Why God Must Exist', *Science and Christian Belief*, 11 (1999), 5–13; text of the Gore Lecture, Westminster Abbey, 26 Nov. 1997; also publ., with minor changes, as pp. 52–65 of *God, Faith and the New Millennium*.

'Christian Vedanta: An Absurdity or an Opportunity?', in Terrence Merrigan and Jacques Haers (eds), *The Myriad Christ: Plurality and the Quest for Unity in Contemporary Christology*, Bibliotheca Ephemeridum Theologicarum Lovaniensum 152 (Leuven: Leuven University Press, 2000), 235–47.

'Comparative Theology: The Heritage of Schleiermacher', in J'annine Jobling and Ian Markham (eds), *Theological Liberalism* (London: SPCK, 2000), 60–74.

'Convergent Spirituality', in Deborah A. Brown (ed.), *Christianity in the 21st Century* (New York: Crossroad Publishing Co., 2000), 47–71.

'Divine Action in the World of Physics: Response to Nicholas Saunders', *Zygon*, 35 (2000), 901–6.

'Gene Wars', in Russell Stannard (ed.), *God for the 21st Century* (London: SPCK, 2000), 77–9.

'Religion and the Question of Meaning', in Joseph Runzo and Nancy M. Martin (eds), *The Meaning of Life in the World Religions* (Oxford: Oneworld Publications, 2000), 11–30.

'Cosmos and Kenosis', in John Polkinghorne (ed.), *The Work of Love: Creation as Kenosis* (Grand Rapids/London: Eerdmans/SPCK, 2001), 152–66.

'Religion and the Possibility of a Global Ethics', in Joseph Runzo and Nancy M. Martin (eds), *Ethics in the World Religions* (Oxford: Oneworld Publications, 2001), 39–62.

'The Temporality of God', *International Journal for Philosophy of Religion*, 50 (2001), 153–69; repr. in Eugene Thomas Long (ed.), *Issues in Contemporary Philosophy of Religion* (Dordrecht: Kluwer, 2001), 153–69.

'Believing in Miracles', *Zygon*, 37 (2002), 741–50.

'Cosmology and Religious Ideas about the End of the World', in George F. R. Ellis (ed.), *The Far-Future Universe: Eschatology from a Cosmic Perspective* (Radnor, Pa./Vatican City: Templeton Foundation Press/Pontifical Academy of Sciences, 2002), 235–48.

'The Importance of Liberal Theology', in Mark D. Chapman (ed.), *The Future of Liberal Theology* (Aldershot: Ashgate Publishing, 2002), 39–53.

'Nature, Red in Tooth and Claw: Can There Be a Theology of Nature?', *Research News and Opportunities in Science and Theology*, 7:2 (Mar. 2002), 20–1.

'Two Forms of Explanation', in Willem B. Drees (ed.), *Is Nature Ever Evil? Religion, Science and Value* (London: Routledge, 2003), 247–64.

III. Book reviews

F. H. Cleobury, *A Return to Natural Theology* (London: James Clarke, 1967), in *Scottish Journal of Theology*, 21 (1968), 347–9.

Austin Farrer, *Faith and Speculation* (London: A. and C. Black, 1967), in *Scottish Journal of Theology*, 21 (1968), 224–5.

Walter Moberly, *The Ethics of Punishment* (London: Faber and Faber, 1968), in *Scottish Journal of Theology*, 22 (1969), 220–1.

Helmut Thielecke, *Theological Ethics*, vol. 1 (London: A. and C. Black, 1968), in *Scottish Journal of Theology*, 22 (1969), 99–101.

H. P. Owen, *The Christian Knowledge of God* (London: Athlone Press, 1970), in *Scottish Journal of Theology*, 23 (1970), 469–70.

H. R. Schette, *Epiphany as History* (London: Sheed and Ward, 1969), in *Scottish Journal of Theology*, 23 (1970), 352.

W. Taylor Stevenson, *History as Myth* (New York: Seabury Press, 1969), in *Scottish Journal of Theology*, 23 (1970), 352–3.

Raeburne S. Heimbeck, *Theology and Meaning* (London: Allen and Unwin, 1969), in *Religious Studies*, 7 (1971), 279–80.

James Richmond, *Theology and Metaphysics* (London: SCM Press, 1970), in *Theology*, 74 (1971), 274–5.

Helmut Thielecke, *Theological Ethics*, vol. 2: *Politics* (London: A. and C. Black, 1969), in *Scottish Journal of Theology*, 24 (1971), 353–4.

Dom Illtyd Trethowan, *Absolute Value: A Study in Christian Theism* (London: Allen and Unwin, 1970), in *Theology*, 74 (1971), 274.

R. W. Beardsmore, *Moral Reasoning* (London: Routledge and Kegan Paul, 1969), in *Religious Studies*, 8 (1972), 83–5.

Paul Roubiczek, *Ethical Values in the Age of Science* (Cambridge: Cambridge University Press, 1969), in *Scottish Journal of Theology*, 25 (1972), 237–8.

J. L. Stocks, *Morality and Purpose* (London: Routledge and Kegan Paul, 1969), in *Religious Studies*, 8 (1972), 82–3.

N. H. G. Robinson, *The Groundwork of Christian Ethics* (London: Collins, 1971), in *Religious Studies*, 9 (1973), 108–10.

Brand Blanshard, *Reason and Belief* (London: Allen and Unwin, 1974), in *Theology*, 79 (1976), 45–6.

James Barr, *Fundamentalism* (London: SCM Press, 1977), in *Theology*, 81 (1978), 145–7.

E. L. Mascall, *Theology and the Gospel of Christ* (London: SPCK, 1977), in *Theology*, 81 (1978), 214–16.

John J. Shepherd, *Experience, Inference and God* (London: Macmillan, 1975), in *Modern Churchman*, n.s., 21:4 (Autumn 1978), 45–6.

Robert Young, *Freedom, Responsibility and God* (London: Macmillan, 1975), in *Modern Churchman*, n.s., 21:4 (Autumn 1978), 46–7.

Michael Goulder (ed.), *Incarnation and Myth: The Debate Continued* (London: SCM Press, 1979), in *Theology*, 82 (1979), 450–2.

Paul Abrecht and Ninan Kosky (eds.), *Before It's Too Late: The Challenge of Nuclear Disarmament* (Geneva: World Council of Churches Publications, 1983), in *Expository Times*, 94 (1983), 381.

Donald B. Kraybill, *Facing Nuclear War* (Scottdale, Pa.: Herald Press, 1982), in *Expository Times*, 94 (1983), 381.

Anthony Kenny, *Faith and Reason* (New York: Columbia University Press, 1983), in *Theology*, 87 (1984), 373–4.

Helen Oppenheimer, *The Hope of Happiness* (London: SCM Press, 1983), in *Religious Studies*, 21 (1985), 110–11.

Hugh Montefiore, *The Probability of God* (London: SCM Press, 1985), in *King's Theological Review*, 9 (1986), 29–30.

Thomas W. Ogletree, *The Use of the Bible in Christian Ethics* (Oxford: Blackwell, 1983), in *Journal of Theological Studies*, n.s., 37 (1986), 295–6.

Frederick Copleston, *Religion and the One: Philosophies East and West* (London: Search Press, 1982), in *Journal of Theological Studies*, n.s., 38 (1987), 280–1.

Janet Martin Soskice, *Metaphor and Religious Language* (Oxford: Clarendon Press, 1985), in *King's Theological Review*, 10 (1987), 34–5.

Brian Hebblethwaite, *The Ocean of Truth* (Cambridge: Cambridge University Press, 1988), in *New Blackfriars*, 69 (1988), 506.

Fergus Kerr, *Theology after Wittgenstein* (Oxford: Blackwell, 1986), in *Religious Studies*, 24 (1988), 267–9.

Linda Tessier (ed.), *Concepts of the Ultimate* (London: Macmillan, 1990), in *Religious Studies*, 27 (1991), 136–7.

Simon Tugwell, *Human Immortality and the Redemption of Death* (London: Darton, Longman and Todd, 1990), in *New Blackfriars*, 72 (1991), 297–8.

Brian Davies, *An Introduction to the Philosophy of Religion* (Oxford: Oxford University Press, 1993), in *New Blackfriars*, 74 (1993), 430.

Richard Swinburne, *Revelation: From Metaphor to Analogy* (Oxford: Clarendon Press, 1991), in *New Blackfriars*, 74 (1993), 47–9.

William P. Alston, *Perceiving God* (Ithaca, NY: Cornell University Press, 1991), in *Philosophy*, 69 (1994), 110–12.

Stephen Bevans, *John Oman and his Doctrine of God* (Cambridge: Cambridge University Press, 1992), in *Journal of Theological Studies*, n.s., 45 (1994), 424–5.

Peter Clarke and Peter Byrne, *Religion Defined and Explained* (London and Basingstoke: Macmillan, 1993), in *Religious Studies*, 30 (1994), 121–2.

Gordon D. Kaufman, *In Face of Mystery: A Constructive Theology* (Cambridge, Mass.: Harvard University Press, 1993), in *Journal of Theological Studies*, n.s., 45 (1994), 428–9.

Wolfhart Pannenberg, *Toward a Theology of Nature: Essays in Science and Faith* (Louisville, Ky.: Westminster/John Knox Press, 1993), in *Zygon*, 30 (1995), 343–5.

Richard Swinburne, *The Christian God* (Oxford: Clarendon Press, 1994), in *New Blackfriars*, 76 (1995), 159–60.

Stephen Ross White, *Don Cupitt and the Future of Christian Doctrine* (London: SCM Press, 1994), in *Epworth Review*, 22:2 (May 1995), 167–8.

Nicholas Lash, *The Beginning and the End of 'Religion'* (Cambridge: Cambridge University Press, 1996), in *Journal of Theological Studies*, n.s., 48 (1997), 753–4.

Christoph Schwöbel (ed.), *Trinitarian Theology Today* (Edinburgh: T&T Clark, 1995), in *Epworth Review*, 24:2 (Apr. 1997), 101–2.

James C. Crabbe (ed.), *From Soul to Self* (London: Routledge, 1999), in *Journal of Theological Studies*, n.s., 51 (2000), 423.

Index